# FINAL DISCLOSURE

ALSO BY DAVID W. BELIN

NOVEMBER 22, 1963: YOU ARE THE JURY

# FINAL DISCLOSURE

## The Full Truth About the Assassination of President Kennedy

## DAVID W. BELIN

Counsel to the Warren Commission

CHARLES SCRIBNER'S SONS • NEW YORK

Charles Scribner's Sons
Macmillan Publishing Company
866 Third Avenue, New York, NY 10022
Collier Macmillan Canada, Inc.

Library of Congress Cataloging-in-Publication Data
Belin, David W.
Final disclosure : the full truth about the assassination of
President Kennedy / by David W. Belin.
p.   cm.
Includes index.
ISBN 0-684-18976-3
1. Kennedy, John F. (John Fitzgerald), 1917–1963—Assassination.
I. Title.
E842.9.B43   1988
973.922′092′4—dc19                      88-16988
CIP

Macmillan books are available at special discounts for bulk pur-
chases for sales promotions, premiums, fund-raising, or educa-
tional use. For details, contact:

Special Sales Director
Macmillan Publishing Company
866 Third Avenue
New York, NY 10022

10   9   8   7   6   5   4   3   2

Printed in the United States of America

To Jon, Jim, Joy, Tom, and Laurie, my wonderful children who have given so much in so many
ways to me

# Contents

# Illustrations

# Preface

In the course of history there are events of such cataclysmic nature that ten or twenty years later most people remember exactly where they were and what they were doing when they first heard the news.

In the past half century there have been two such times: December 7, 1941, when the Japanese bombed Pearl Harbor, and November 22, 1963, when President John F. Kennedy was assassinated.

The lives of all Americans were dramatically affected by both. My own life was especially affected by the Kennedy killing. I was selected by Chief Justice Earl Warren as counsel to the Warren Commission investigating the assassination. This led to my appointment in 1975 by President Gerald Ford as executive director of the Commission on CIA Activities Within the United States, known as the Rockefeller Commission.

These appointments—investigating a presidential assassination and investigating the Central Intelligence Agency (CIA)—led to my writing this book. I want principally to counter the continuing deception of the American people about what took place on that tragic Friday afternoon in Dallas between 12:25 P.M. and 1:25 P.M., when two Americans of widely different backgrounds were killed: President John F. Kennedy and Dallas police officer J. D. Tippit. Most Americans and even former Speaker of the House Tip O'Neill have fallen victim to what I call the assassination scam.

This book also addresses the deceit, obstructionism, and cover-up by the CIA and the National Security Council (NSC) in a manner all too similar to the 1987 obfuscation by these same agencies of the sale of arms to Iran and the transfer of those funds to the Contras in Nicaragua. It deals, too, with questionable acts by the dead president's brother, Robert Kennedy, as well as other high officials in both Democratic and Republican administrations. There are parallels between activities of the Kennedy administration and the CIA in the 1960s, the actions of Henry Kissinger as President Nixon's security adviser and the CIA in the 1970s, and activities of CIA Director William Casey, Adm. John Poindexter, and Col. Oliver North in the 1980s.

It seems to me especially important to understand just how the American public can be deceived by the CIA when it abuses its charter. For only when the public understands will it be in a position to prevent a recurrence of such abuses.

And abuses were not invented in the 1980s by Adm. John Poindexter and Col. Oliver North. I witnessed cutoffs of Secretary of State Dean Rusk by the CIA and high officials in the Kennedy administration and cutoffs of Secretary of State William Rogers through the machinations of Henry Kissinger and CIA Director Richard Helms in the Nixon administration. And I watched Dr. Kissinger ignore a presidential directive and stonewall the Rockefeller Commission after we discovered CIA attempts to assassinate foreign leaders.

So this book is intended to show how the American public has been misled about the death of their president—by a relatively small combination of assassination sensationalists and assassination cultists—and deceived about what happened inside the CIA by former CIA officers and former high government officials. The truth is incontrovertible.

# Acknowledgments

**M**any people directly and indirectly helped contribute to this book.

Michael Gartner, a wonderful friend whose multifaceted background includes the past presidency of the American Society of Newspaper Editors, was not only a source of enthusiastic encouragement, but he also participated in the final editing of the manuscript (despite the old legal maxim that equity never aids a volunteer). His suggestions were invaluable. I greatly benefited from the basic editing of the manuscript by Edward T. Chase, senior editor at Scribners, to whom I also owe a debt of gratitude for having confidence that a book about the truth of the assassination would be commercially viable. Charles Flowers of Scribners has also ably given much technical assistance in the coordination of the book.

Catherine Sheridan, who has worked as my secretary and assistant for more than twenty-five years, patiently and capably typed and retyped again and again and enabled me to meet all deadlines.

I also owe a great deal to my law partners at Belin Harris Helmick Tesdell Lamson McCormick, who have given me the flexibility to undertake many outside endeavors, ranging from the writing of this book to my activities in support of education and the arts.

My father, Louis Belin (now deceased), and my mother, Esther Belin, indirectly contributed to this book because they inculcated in their children, among many qualities, the highest standards of integrity and justice. My uncle, Marvin Klass, a superb attorney in Sioux City, Iowa, also deserves mention because it was he who helped direct me toward the practice of law.

Other indirect contributors include my brother, Daniel, and many friends who over the years have been so supportive, particularly after the death of my wife, Connie.

Finally, I want to acknowledge the indirect contribution made by my teachers in the public schools of Washington, D.C., and Sioux City, Iowa. These dedicated people gave me lots of encouragement and together with my parents helped develop my interest in reading, writing, and public service. I firmly believe that those of us who have benefited so much from public education have an obligation to help ensure that our nation continues to recognize the critical importance of our public schools in the growth and prosperity of America and the maintenance of our freedom. Accordingly, I am setting aside all royalties from this book for the support of education.

# FINAL DISCLOSURE

# 1

## The Trip to Texas

John F. Kennedy was in political trouble in November 1963 as he faced the 1964 reelection campaign. He had problems both in the South and the Southwest, including Texas, where matters were made worse by the factionalism within the Texas Democratic party.

On June 5, 1963, Kennedy spoke at the Air Force Academy in Colorado Springs. He stopped in El Paso, Texas, to meet with Texas governor John Connally and Vice-President Lyndon Johnson. They agreed that the president should make a one-day whirlwind trip to Dallas and three other Texas cities in late November. Initially, the proposed trip involved short visits to San Antonio, Fort Worth, Dallas, and Houston. There were no motorcades planned because there was not time.

But inside the White House there were discussions about the political benefits of extending the visit. In September it was decided that the trip would be extended to nearly two days, from the afternoon of November 21 through the evening of November 22.

Connally came to Washington and was at the White House on October 4, 1963. Kenneth O'Donnell, special assistant to the presi-

1

dent and close friend, acted as coordinator of the trip, but the details in Texas were left to Connally. O'Donnell, though, urged a motorcade through Dallas. His reasons were strictly political: The Kennedy team wanted the president to be seen by as many people as possible.

The Secret Service was told to arrange a route through downtown Dallas. From a political standpoint, this would take the president, in the words of O'Donnell, "through an area which exposes him to the greatest number of people."

One of those people was Lee Harvey Oswald, a former marine with, as it turned out, a self-styled Marxist political philosophy who had defected to Russia and returned to the United States with a Russian wife, Marina. Oswald owned a rifle and a pistol. He worked in a seven-story building overlooking the parade route selected by the Secret Service.

The trip started with tremendous success. On November 21, there was a motorcade through Houston. The president spoke at Rice University Stadium and attended a dinner in honor of a key Democratic congressman from Texas, Albert Thomas. That night, the president and his wife flew to Fort Worth, where they spent the night at the Texas Hotel.

Kennedy was in a jovial mood. In assessing the activities of November 21 with David Powers of his staff, the president commented that the crowd that came to see him in Houston "was about the same as the one which came before but there were one hundred thousand people on hand to see Mrs. Kennedy."

The November 22 motorcade route for Dallas was selected by Secret Service agents Forrest V. Sorrels and Winston G. Lawson to traverse the distance between the Dallas airport and the site of the luncheon where the president was to speak to business and civic leaders.

There were three potential sites for the luncheon. One building, known as Market Hall, was unavailable for November 22. The second building, located at the state fairgrounds and known as the Women's Building, had the practical advantage that it was a one-story building with few entrances and it was easy to make secure. However, it lacked necessary facilities for food handling and was relatively unattractive. This left as a third possibility a relatively new building known as the Trade Mart. It had the necessary food-handling facilities, but it presented major security problems: There were many entrances and several tiers of balconies overlooking the area where the luncheon would be served.

The Secret Service was most concerned about the security at the Trade Mart. No special concern was given beyond the normal precautions for the parade route itself.

President Kennedy was well aware of the risks in any motorcade. On the morning he was killed, he was in his hotel with Mrs. Kennedy and O'Donnell. They talked about the risks involved in public appearances. Kennedy said that "if anybody really wanted to shoot the president of the United States, it was not a very difficult job—all one had to do was get in a high building someday with a telescopic rifle, and there was nothing anybody could do to defend against such an attempt," O'Donnell recalled.

Once the Trade Mart had been selected for the lunch, the motorcade route was easy to determine. It went from Love Field Airport southwest through suburban Dallas toward downtown, moving westerly along Main Street through the downtown area. From downtown, the motorcade would then have to head north on the Stemmons Freeway to get to the Trade Mart. But there was a problem: Main Street did not have a direct exit onto the freeway. Instead, at the western edge of the downtown area, in a parklike setting known as Dealey Plaza, the motorcade would have to turn right from Main Street onto Houston Street, go one block north, and then make a sharp reflex-angle 300-degree turn to head to the southwest along a street known as Elm Street, which would lead into the Stemmons Freeway.

Between Houston Street and the freeway there was only one building to pass: the Texas School Book Depository, at the northwest corner of Houston and Elm. It was a commercial seven-story brick structure from which school textbooks were sold and distributed to Texas schools. On the afternoon of November 22, 1963, it stood as a silent sentinel overlooking the broad expanse of Dealey Plaza and what was known as the triple underpass.

It was a warm and sunny late-fall day in Dallas. The motorcade was headed by police motorcycles. Next came a pilot car from the Dallas Police Department. The motorcycles and the pilot car were preceding the main portion of the motorcade by about one-quarter mile to alert other police along the route that the president was coming—and to check for signs of trouble.

The heart of the motorcade was led by motorcycle policemen whose primary purpose was to keep the crowd back. They were followed by a car carrying Secret Service agents and police officials who scanned the crowd in the buildings to try to anticipate trouble.

The presidential limousine followed the lead car, about 100– 150 feet behind. It was a specially designed convertible with a Secret Service driver, William Greer, and another Secret Service agent, Roy Kellerman, in the front seat. The president and Mrs. Kennedy were in the back seat, the president on the right. In between were two "jump seats" in which Governor Connally, on the right, and his wife, Nellie, were sitting. Because it was such a lovely day, the clear plastic bubble top (which at that time was neither bulletproof nor bullet resistant) was not used. Kenneth O'Donnell had ruled that if the weather was clear the bubble would be off.

Flanking the rear of the presidential car were two motorcycle policemen, whose purpose was to keep the crowd back. Immediately behind the limousine was a follow-up car specially outfitted for the Secret Service. It was a convertible carrying eight agents— two in the front seat, two in the rear seat, two on the right running board, and two on the left running board. Also inside, sitting in jump seats, were O'Donnell and Powers. The agents were to watch the route for signs of trouble, including not only the crowds on the street but also windows, roofs of buildings, crossings, and overpasses. They were particularly concerned about possible sudden actions in the crowd, any movements toward the presidential car, and any possible thrown objects.

Fifty to a hundred feet behind the follow-up car was the vice-president's car, which had a follow-up car behind it. The remainder of the motorcade included cars for other dignitaries, including the mayor of Dallas and Texas congressmen, a White House com-

munications car, three cars for press photographers, and several
buses for White House staff members and other members of the
press. At the rear of the motorcade was another police car and
several motorcycle policemen, whose job was to prevent unauthorized vehicles from joining the motorcade.

The Dallas police radio had two channels, and one was specifically designated for use in communications with the motorcade.

Shortly after 11:50 A.M., the motorcade left Love Field Airport
at speeds of twenty-five to thirty miles an hour. The crowds at
first were not large, and the president directed two brief stops, one
in response to a sign asking him to shake hands and the other to
speak to a nun and a group of children.

As the motorcade approached downtown, the crowds became
much larger—hundreds of thousands of people. The motorcade
slowed to eleven miles an hour as it entered Main Street.

It was a fabulous success for the president and for the Democratic party in Texas. Nellie Connally was particularly elated. As
the motorcade left Main Street and headed to Houston and Elm,
she turned to the president and said, "Mr. President, you can't say
Dallas doesn't love you."

The president replied, "That is very obvious."

It was 12:30 P.M. as the open limousine started to make the
sharp left turn from Houston onto Elm, passing by the last building
in the downtown area—the depository—and heading toward the
freeway entrance.

# 2

# The Assassination

**H**oward Leslie Brennan, a forty-five-year-old steamfitter, was sitting at the corner of Houston and Elm on a retaining wall across the street from the Texas School Book Depository and was looking around while he waited for the motorcade to arrive. Brennan "observed quite a few people in different windows. In particular, I saw this one man on the sixth floor which left the window to my knowledge a couple of times." Brennan thought the people in the building were standing. (Actually, because the bottoms of the windows were relatively close to the floor, most people in the windows were kneeling or crouching.)

Brennan then turned his attention to the approaching presidential limousine. He watched it turn left at the corner in front of him and then go southwest along Elm and down an incline toward the freeway entrance and a railroad underpass.

"And after the president had passed my position, I really couldn't say how many feet or how far, a short distance I would say, I heard this crack that I positively thought was a backfire."

I was questioning Brennan under oath.

BELIN: "You thought it was a backfire?"

BRENNAN: "Of a motorcycle."

BELIN: "Then what did you observe or hear?"

BRENNAN: "Well, then something, just right after this explosion, made me think that it was a firecracker being thrown from the Texas Book Store. And I glanced up. And this man that I saw previous was aiming for his last shot. . . . As I calculate a couple of seconds. He drew the gun back from the window as though he was drawing it back to his side and maybe paused for another second as though to assure hisself that he hit his mark, and then he disappeared. And, at the same moment, I was diving off of that firewall and to the right for bullet protection of this stone wall that is a little higher on the Houston side."

BELIN: "Well, let me ask you. What kind of a gun did you see in that window?"

BRENNAN: "I am not an expert on guns. It was, as I could observe, some type of a high-powered rifle."

I then asked Brennan how far he was from the assassination window. When I first interrogated him in Dallas, I found that it was a relatively easy measurement to make. Visualize a right triangle with the short leg being the distance between where Brennan was sitting and the front door of the depository, the other leg of the right angle being six stories up, and the hypotenuse being the line of sight from the assassination window to where Brennan was sitting. That line was only 110 feet.

Brennan described the gunman to police officers as being white, slender, possibly five feet ten, weighing 160–170 pounds, in his early thirties. Actually, Lee Harvey Oswald, the assassin, was white, relatively slender, in his mid-twenties rather than early thirties, and only an inch or so shorter than Brennan had described, and just a few pounds lighter. Brennan's description was certainly very close.

After the assassination, Brennan would not positively identify Oswald as the gunman. Later, Brennan said he did identify Oswald as the gunman but was afraid to say so because he feared for his own safety.

Although Brennan was the single most important witness, there were others who also saw the gunman with the rifle in the window or the rifle being withdrawn. These included Robert Hill Jackson, a *Dallas Times-Herald* photographer in a press car toward the rear of the motorcade, and Amos Lee Euins, a fifteen-year-old. Jackson was facing the depository and saw the rifle being withdrawn. He yelled to other newsmen in the convertible in which they were riding: "There is the gun!"

Euins was standing on the corner of Houston and Elm and waved at the president as the limousine made its turn. "I was waving. He looked that way and he waved back at me. And then I had seen a pipe, you know, up there in the window [of the depository]. I thought it was a pipe, some kind of pipe." Euins was facing the building and marked on a picture a window where he said he saw that "pipe."

"Then I was standing here, and as the motorcade turned the corner, I was facing, looking dead at the building. And so I seen this pipe thing sticking out the window. I wasn't paying too much attention to it. Then when the first shot was fired, I started looking around, thinking it was a backfire. Everybody else started looking around. Then I looked up at the window, and he shot again. . . . So—you know this fountain bench here. Well, right around here, well, anyway, there is a little fountain right here. I got behind this little fountain, and then he shot again . . . and then after he shot again, he pulled the gun back in the window. . . ." Euins thought he heard four shots. Most witnesses thought they heard three.

Indeed, the only place where witnesses conclusively saw a gunman and a rifle at the time of the assassination was in the southeast corner of the sixth-floor window of the depository. And there was not just one witness but at least three.

After the shots, there was mass confusion, in part because there were tall buildings on three sides of Dealey Plaza that caused reverberations of the sound. Although many people thought that they heard the shots coming from behind the limousine, there were also many who thought they heard the shots coming from the front.

The presidential limousine sped off to Parkland Memorial Hospital. Within a few minutes Brennan and Euins contacted the police and told them what they had seen. Brennan described the gunman, and a description was broadcast at 12:43 P.M. for a "slender white male about thirty, five feet ten." Police had started to seal off the depository at 12:36 P.M., according to the transcripts of the police radio broadcasts. They started a floor-by-floor search. When police came to the southeast-corner sixth-floor window, they found stacked boxes that had been used as a rifle perch, a large paper bag that had been used to carry the rifle into the building, and the most crucial evidence of all—three cartridge cases.

The search on the sixth floor continued, and at the northwest corner near the back stairway, Eugene Boone, a deputy sheriff from the Dallas Police Department, found a rifle that had been pushed between cartons of books as the gunman fled down the stairs.

Boone testified: "I did not touch the weapon at all." Rather, he called Capt. Will Fritz of the Dallas Police Department, who came to the area with Lt. J. C. Day of the Crime Scene Search Section Identification Bureau. Day photographed the rifle, noted its serial number—C-2766—and then scratched his name, "J. C. Day," on the stock.

Before the rifle was picked up by Day, Boone said that "we were just discussing it back and forth." And he said, "It looks like a 7.65 Mauzer." Assassination sensationalists have seized upon this comment to put forward their claims that there might have been another rifle involved. But the truth is that when the rifle was picked up, after being photographed by Day, it was not a 7.65 Mauzer but rather an Italian-surplus Mannlicher-Carcano 6.5 mm. military rifle, serial number C-2766.

With remarkable speed, the FBI traced the ownership of the rifle. The distributor of surplus Italian 6.5 mm. military rifles was Crescent Fire Arms. According to their records, serial number C-2766 was shipped to Klein's Sporting Goods Co. in Chicago.

A vice-president of Klein's, William J. Walden, testified that his records showed the rifle was shipped to "A. Hidell," P.O. Box

2915, Dallas. Accompanying the mail-order coupon was a postal money order purchased on March 12, 1963. On the money order, opposite the printed word "from," were written the words "A. Hidell, P.O. Box 2915, Dallas, Texas." "A. Hidell" was an alias Oswald used. According to Marina Oswald, "Hidell" came from the first name of Fidel Castro, the Cuban leader whom Lee Harvey Oswald most admired. When Oswald was arrested, he was carrying in his billfold a forged Selective Service card with his picture and the name "Alek J. Hidell." "Alek" was Oswald's nickname when he lived in Russia.

The writing on both the mail-order coupon and the postal money order was determined by handwriting experts to have been the handwriting of Lee Harvey Oswald.

Who rented P.O. Box 2915? Lee Harvey Oswald. We were also able to obtain the money order that was used to pay for the rifle. The postal money order, No. 2,202,130,462, had Klein's endorsement on the back side.

When J. C. Day of the Dallas Police Department examined the rifle, he tried to find fingerprints. There were none. However, when he took the rifle apart, he found a latent palm print, which he "lifted" and which was sent to the FBI Laboratories in Washington. That print was the palm print of Lee Harvey Oswald—and palm prints are just as unique a means of identification as are fingerprints.

By the window near the place where the cartridge cases were discovered was a large brown homemade paper sack. After Day photographed the scene, he wrote on the sack, "Found next to the sixth floor window gun fired from. May have been used to carry gun. Lieutenant J. C. Day." The bag, too, was sent to the FBI Labs. The FBI compared the paper bag with other wrapping paper used in the depository. Scientifically, it was determined that the paper bag was made from a large roll of paper used in the depository. Using an iodine fuming process and a silver-nitrate process, the FBI developed a fingerprint on that paper bag and also a palm print. Both were those of Lee Harvey Oswald.

Immediately below the sixth-floor window where Brennan saw

the gunman, there were three depository employees who were watching the motorcade: Harold Norman, Bonnie Ray Williams, and James Jarman, Jr. Harold Norman said that he could hear cartridge cases hitting the floor above them, and James Jarman, Jr., noticed that Bonnie Ray Williams had some debris on his head that had fallen from the ceiling above them as the shots had been fired. After the assassination, Harold Norman and James Jarman, Jr., went outside and saw Brennan. He was able to identify these people as two of the three employees watching the motorcade from the fifth floor.

After his arrest, Oswald claimed that at the time of the assassination, he was having lunch with "Junior," but the only depository employee by the name of Junior was James Jarman, Jr., who was watching the motorcade from the fifth floor.

No one knew where Oswald was at the exact time of the assassination. However, he was seen on the sixth floor of the depository minutes before the assassination. And he was seen shortly after the assassination on the second floor, heading toward the front door.

He was the only depository employee who was inside the building and who fled it after the assassination.

# 3

# Appointment to the Warren Commission

Two days after the assassination, while all of America—indeed, all of the world—was still in shock, the alleged assassin was murdered.

Both the House of Representatives and the U.S. Senate began to consider congressional hearings to try and determine the facts of the assassination. There were proposals in Texas for a Dallas County grand jury investigation and the possible initiation of a special court of inquiry before a state magistrate. Since the assassination occurred in Texas, the Texas authorities started to claim primary jurisdiction.

Rumors and counterrumors began circulating throughout the world that greatly concerned the State Department. President Johnson was urged to appoint an independent, nonpartisan "blue ribbon" fact-finding body with "the broadest national mandate" to preempt the investigation, and he prevailed upon Chief Justice Earl Warren to be the chairman. The commission was established on November 29, 1963.

At first, Chief Justice Warren wanted to turn down the appointment. He felt it was not proper for a Supreme Court justice to engage in any "extracurricular activities" of this kind. But Johnson called him to the White House and persuaded him that he was the best person in the country, and in the world, to help quell rumors and speculations, some to the effect that either the Russians or the Cubans under Fidel Castro were involved in the assassination.

The clincher, according to Warren, was when Johnson said that issues of war and peace were involved and talked about the horrors of a nuclear war if speculation and rumor began to run out of control. "When he talked about nuclear war, I could not turn him down," Warren said.

For the commission, the president chose Sen. Richard B. Russell, a Georgia Democrat who was chairman of the Armed Services Committee of the Senate; John Sherman Cooper, a Republican senator from Kentucky who was a former U.S. ambassador to India; Hale Boggs, Democratic congressman from Louisiana and majority party whip; Gerald R. Ford, Republican congressman from Michigan and chairman of the House Republican Conference; John J. McCloy, former president of the World Bank and former assistant secretary of defense as well as former U.S. high commissioner for Germany; and Allen W. Dulles, former director of Central Intelligence.

J. Lee Rankin, former solicitor general of the United States, was selected as general counsel for the commission. Earl Warren then chose fourteen lawyers from across the country to complete a staff to undertake the actual investigation. For purposes of dividing the work load, the staff was broken down into various areas of concentration.

For instance, two lawyers concentrated on whether there was a foreign conspiratorial involvement. Two concentrated on possible domestic conspiracy, except for the question of whether a Dallas nightclub operator named Jack Ruby was conspiratorially involved. It was Jack Ruby who killed Lee Harvey Oswald on November 24, 1963. The separate issue of possible conspiratorial involvement by Ruby was explored by two other lawyers.

I was one of the two lawyers concentrating on all of the evidence pertaining to the determination of who actually killed President Kennedy and who actually killed Dallas police officer J. D. Tippit. My colleague, in what was designated as Area II, was Joseph A. Ball, one of the outstanding trial lawyers on the West Coast. By the time we had completed our investigation, we had more first-hand knowledge of the key witnesses and physical evidence of these two murders than any other people in the world.

As experienced trial lawyers, we knew that when there are two or more witnesses to a sudden event, you generally get two or more different stories about what happened.

Often the stories are conflicting. After all, our eyes are not perfect cameras that can recall exactly what took place in a matter of seconds. If you get two conflicting stories with two witnesses, you can imagine how many arise when there are hundreds of witnesses to a sudden event, as there were in Dealey Plaza on November 22, 1963. Almost anyone who wants to concoct a theory can find one or two witnesses who might support his theory.

How many seconds of elapsed time existed between the first shot and the last shot? At the time of the original FBI conclusions that the first shot struck President Kennedy in the neck, the second shot struck Governor Connally, and the third shot struck President Kennedy in the head, it was thought that only six seconds elapsed. On the other hand, the Warren Commission concluded that the first shot that struck President Kennedy in the back of his neck exited from the front and struck Governor Connally, who was sitting directly in front of the president. Since most witnesses thought they heard three shots fired and since three cartridge cases were found at the southeast corner window of the sixth floor of the Texas School Book Depository, this meant that if only two shots struck the occupants of the limousine, the third shot missed, and it could very well be that the two shots that struck were six seconds apart and the shot that missed was a third shot fired several seconds later (although it also could have been fired before the shot that first struck Kennedy).

In any event, whether there were six seconds of elapsed time or ten or twelve, it was a very sudden event that gave rise to many, many different stories from witnesses.

Even when matters do not involve sudden events, the honest recollections of witnesses differ. James Jarman, Jr., who worked every day with Lee Harvey Oswald, swore under oath that Oswald "never hardly worked in a shirt. He worked in a T-shirt." Troy Eugene West, who also worked with Oswald every day, swore under oath, "I don't believe I ever seen him [Oswald] working in just a T-shirt. He worked in a shirt all right, but I never did see him work in a T-shirt."

Conflicts like these give assassination sensationalists a field day. They can pick and choose a few strands here, a few strands there, and make a seemingly convincing story—particularly since their audience is ignorant of the mass of evidence involved in the assassination of President Kennedy and the murder of Police Officer J. D. Tippit.

Because Joe Ball and I were the two lawyers on the Warren Commission charged with the responsibility of determining who killed both President Kenendy and Officer Tippit, if we wanted to pick and choose facts here and there but ignore the overall record, we could write a book about conspiracy that would be more convincing and less vulnerable to refutation than any other conspiratorial book written about the Kennedy assassination. But it would not be true.

Unfortunately, that has not stopped others.

One of the early, better-selling books claiming there was more than one gunman was based on the theory that President Kennedy said after the first shot, "My God, I am hit." Certainly there was evidence to support that claim, for this is exactly what Secret Service Agent Kellerman testified. He was riding in the front seat of the limousine, and he had been in President Kennedy's company numerous times. How could it be argued that Kellerman was wrong?

The author never told his readers what the other four passengers in the limousine said concerning whether Kennedy uttered any words after he was shot.

Sitting next to Kellerman was the driver, Secret Service Agent

William Greer. When asked whether the president said anything after he was hit, Greer testified:

"I never heard him say anything; never at any time did I hear him say anything."

Whom do you believe? Greer or Kellerman? Obviously, you go to other witnesses. In the limousine there were three: John Connally, Nellie Connally, and Jacqueline Kennedy.

GOVERNOR CONNALLY: "He [President Kennedy] never uttered a sound at all that I heard."

MRS. CONNALLY: "He [President Kennedy] made no utterance, no cry."

JACQUELINE KENNEDY: "I was looking this way, to the left, and I heard those terrible noises. You know. And my husband never made any sound."

The key to understanding the facts about the assassination—the key to finding the truth about the assassination—is to recognize that there were hundreds of witnesses interviewed and that recollections do differ. And if one wants to pick and choose one witness here and one witness there and deliberately (and dishonestly) ignore witnesses with a differing view, you can pick and choose and come up with a remarkably logical conclusion, albeit a false one.

But the evidence is otherwise. Lee Harvey Oswald was the gunman, and the only gunman, who fired at President Kennedy and at Dallas police officer J. D. Tippit on that tragic day in Dallas. It was the murder of Officer Tippit that triggered the arrest of Oswald. I call the Tippit murder the "Rosetta Stone" to the determination of who was the assassin of President Kennedy.

# 4

## Tippit's Murder – The Rosetta Stone

A Chevrolet pickup truck was heading west on a suburban street in the Oak Cliff section of Dallas, not too far from downtown Dallas. The driver, Domingo Benavides, was a young automobile mechanic. Heading west on Tenth Street, approaching the corner of Patton, at approximately 1:15 P.M., he saw a police car parked on the south side of Tenth Street, facing east. The policeman had gotten out of the car. There was a man standing on the other side of the car by the curb. Benavides heard a shot, ducked down and slowed the pickup, and pulled to the curb. He heard additional shots.

BELIN: "Then what happened?"

BENAVIDES: "And I looked up and the policeman was in, he seemed like he kind of stumbled and fell. . . . Then I seen the man turn and walk back to the sidewalk and go on the sidewalk, and he walked maybe five foot and then kind of stalled. He didn't exactly stop. And he threw one shell and must have took five or six more steps and threw the other shell up and then he kind of stepped up to a pretty good trot going around the corner."

After the gunman left, Benavides went to the police car and called on the police radio to headquarters to tell them an officer had been shot.

Later that afternoon, Benavides turned over to the police two empty cartridge shells that he had seen the gunman throw in the bushes as he fled the scene. Because Benavides didn't think he was very good at identifying people, the Dallas Police Department did not take him to see a police lineup of their suspect. This was a gross error.

But Benavides was not the only person who saw the Tippit murder. Around the corner, on the east side of Patton Street, cabdriver William W. Scoggins was sitting in his taxi, eating his lunch. He saw the police car driving east on Tenth Street, saw the police car stop just after it crossed Patton Street, saw the policeman get out, heard the shots, and saw the policeman "falling, grab his stomach and fall." Scoggins got out of his cab to make certain it was not commandeered by the gunman, for the gunman had started heading back toward Patton Street, where Scoggins's cab was parked. The gunman passed as close as twelve feet.

"I saw him coming kind of toward me. . . . I could see his face, his features, and everything plain . . . kind of loping, trotting. . . . He had a pistol in his left hand."

BELIN: "Did you hear the man say anything?"

SCOGGINS: "I heard him mutter something like, 'poor damn cop,' or 'poor dumb cop.' He said that over twice."

Although the Dallas police never took Benavides to a police lineup, they did take Scoggins, and he identified the gunman. The gunman's name: Lee Harvey Oswald.

Scoggins was not the only one who identified the gunman. As Oswald was trotting toward Scoggins's cab, he was seen by two sisters-in-law who were in the house at the southeast corner of Tenth and Patton streets. After hearing gunshots, they rushed to the door and saw the gunman coming across their front yard with the gun in his hand. "It was open, and he had his hands cocked like he was emptying it," said Barbara Jeanette Davis.

She said that as the gunman cut across her front yard, he was seven or eight steps from her—about twenty or twenty-five feet. She then testified about the police lineup. At first, the police had four men stand facing Mrs. Davis, and then they had the four men turn sideways. "When they made them turn sideways, I was positive that was the one I seen." She identified Lee Harvey Oswald.

Her sister-in-law, Virginia Davis, also saw the gunman cutting across their front yard, holding his gun in his right hand and "emptying the shells in his left hand." She, too, identified Oswald.

BELIN: "Did you see what he did with the shells when he emptied them into his left hand?"

DAVIS: "After we, well, he was dropping them on the ground because we found two."

They did not actually see the gunman toss the shells into the bushes, but after the gunman left, they went into their yard and found two cartridge cases that they turned over to the police.

As Oswald continued trotting south down Patton Street with gun in hand past Scoggins's taxicab, he was seen by two more people: Ted Callaway and Sam Guinyard. Both had heard the gunshots. They ran out on the sidewalk and saw the man holding the gun. In the words of Callaway, the gun was being held "in a raised pistol position. . . . I hollered, 'Hey, man, what the hell is going on?' . . . He slowed his pace, almost halted for a minute. Then he said something to me, which I could not understand. And then kind of shrugged his shoulders and kept on going."

Callaway went to the scene of the shooting, saw the squad car, saw the police officer lying in the street, opened the car door, picked up the police microphone inside, and called to inform headquarters of the murder—they had already been informed by Benavides. Callaway then took the police officer's gun and went over to Scoggins's cab. He told Scoggins to drive around the area as he unsuccessfully tried to find the gunman. Both Callaway and Guinyard identified Oswald in a police lineup as the man with the gun.

Another witness was Helen Markham, a waitress who was walking across the street to catch a bus to go to work. She saw the gunman fire at Officer Tippit and then head south on Patton with his pistol in his hand. Although William Scoggins, Helen Markham, Barbara Davis, Virginia Davis, Ted Callaway, and Sam Guinyard differed in the details of what they saw in the vicinity of the murder, they all agreed on one thing: When they were taken to the police station to try to identify the gunman in a lineup, every single one of these witnesses identified the gunman as Lee Harvey Oswald.

If you read the books of the assassination sensationalists about the Dallas tragedy, you will find this common denominator: Most of the books fail to mention that there were six witnesses who were at the scene of the Tippit murder or saw the gunman running from the scene, gun in hand—six witnesses who individually identified the gunman as Lee Harvey Oswald.

This pattern of half-truths on the part of assassination sensationalists started with the biggest money-maker of all, Mark Lane, whose best-selling book, *Rush to Judgment*, was published shortly after the assassination by Holt, Rinehart & Winston. Between royalties from the book, profits from a film that Lane made in which he compounded the misrepresentations of his book, and lecture fees, Lane reportedly has grossed between $500,000 and $2 million.

Not content with Lane's book, Holt, Rinehart in 1986 published *Reasonable Doubt*, subtitled "An Investigation into the Assassination of John F. Kennedy," written by Henry Hurt.

Hurt's only reference to Scoggins was that Scoggins thought that the gunman was walking "west toward Tippit's car prior to the shooting" rather than what most other witnesses thought—east —which was the same direction in which Tippit's car was heading. Nowhere does Hurt tell his readers that Scoggins saw the gunman come as close as twelve feet and unequivocally identified the gunman as Lee Harvey Oswald. Nowhere does Hurt tell his readers about Barbara Davis, Virginia Davis, Ted Callaway, or Sam Guinyard. The only reference by Hurt to an eyewitness to the Tippit murder is to Helen Markham, whom Hurt calls (as did Mark Lane) "the Commission's star witness," when, in fact, Scoggins was a much more crucial witness.

What about the cartridge cases? Hurt would have the reader

believe that the cartridge cases turned over by Benavides to the Dallas police might have been planted by someone else. Hurt ignores the cartridge cases turned over by Barbara Davis and Virginia Davis.

The best that Hurt can suggest is that there was one witness who said he was able to pick Oswald out of a police lineup because Oswald was complaining loudly at that particular lineup "that he was being framed by the procedure" and "was the only one in the lineup with a bruised and a swollen face," and then Hurt goes on to write that "five of the witnesses who identified Oswald as the man fleeing the scene picked him out of the lineup under the dubious conditions described." Nowhere is there any evidence that Scoggins, Barbara Davis, Virginia Davis, Callaway, and Guinyard picked out Oswald because of something that Oswald said or because his face was swollen. When someone passes as close as twelve feet (in the case of Scoggins) or as close as twenty or twenty-five feet (as in the case of Barbara Davis and Virginia Davis), you don't need a swollen lip to be able to pick someone out of a police lineup.

Hurt fails to disclose these facts to his readers, as did his predecessor, Mark Lane. Again, like Mark Lane, Hurt does not mention witnesses Barbara Davis, Virginia Davis, Ted Callaway, and Sam Guinyard. Hurt's omission of any references to these crucial witnesses typifies his book's weaknesses. Omission of available evidence is the besetting sin of all the assassination sensationalists' books.

# 5

# The Real Cover-up About Oswald's Arrest

**A**ccording to British professor Hugh Trevor-Roper, who himself fell victim to the ploys of assassination profiteer Mark Lane:

> The plain fact is that there is no evidence at all to explain how or why the Dallas Police instantly pounced on Oswald, and until some adequate explanation is given, no one can be blamed for entertaining the most likely hypothesis, viz: that the Dallas Police had undisclosed reasons for arresting Oswald even before they had avowable evidence pointing towards him. Once that hypothesis is admitted, almost all the evidence accepted by the Commission can be reinterpreted in a different way.

Trevor-Roper's comments appeared in the introduction of Lane's book *Rush to Judgment*.

A more recent purveyor of distorted information is Robert Sam Anson, an executive producer for public television station WNET in New York. In 1975 he wrote what became one of the all-time best-selling paperback books about the Kennedy assassination:

22

*They've Killed the President.* Its initial press run was 250,000 copies. Undoubtedly with a view toward increasing sales, the publisher emblazoned in red letters across the cover "Twelve years is a long time to have buried the truth. . . ." Like most of his fellow assassination sensationalists in the 1960s and 1970s, Robert Sam Anson has claimed that the Warren Commission was nothing more than a "Blue-Ribbon Coverup."

Anson's thesis is that there was a conspiracy in the assassination of President Kennedy, most probably involving the CIA and also probably involving organized crime, the FBI, and anti-Castro elements, Jimmy Hoffa or his supporters, and/or "right-wing" elements. The inaccuracies underlying Anson's theories can be so readily discovered that one wonders why the media did not take the time to expose them, particularly in light of the continued national interest in the murder of Kennedy.

The most vivid demonstration of how Anson and, as we have seen, his fellow sensationalists attempt to rewrite history involves the murder of Tippit. Anson declares:

"Tippit's murder was a crucial occurrence. It was the event which brought the Dallas police, sirens screaming, into the neighborhood where Oswald was soon discovered. But if Oswald did not kill Tippit, who did and why?"

Anson is right on one point: Tippit's murder is the crucial occurrence.

But consider how Anson handled this: Johnny Calvin Brewer testified that on the afternoon of November 22 he heard a radio news flash that a police officer had been shot approximately eight blocks away from the Hardy's shoe store that Brewer managed. Shortly thereafter, Brewer said he heard a police siren coming down Jefferson Street, and "before I looked up and saw the man enter the lobby [of the shoe store] . . . he stood there with his back to the street."

The police car made a U-turn and went back down the street away from Brewer's shoe store.

"And when they turned and left, Oswald [he didn't know it was Oswald at the time] looked over his shoulder and turned around and walked up West Jefferson toward the [Texas] Theatre," a few doors away.

Brewer became suspicious and decided to trail the man into the Texas Theatre. He asked the cashier if she had sold a ticket to the man "and she said no, she hadn't. She was listening to the radio herself." So Brewer went into the theater, which had only fifteen or twenty patrons at the time. It was dark, and he couldn't see the man either downstairs or in the upstairs balcony. He then went to the cashier and asked her to call the police.

BELIN: "Then what happened?"

BREWER: "Well, just before they came, they turned the house lights on, and I looked out from the curtains and saw the man. . . ."

BELIN: "Then what happened?"

BREWER: "I heard a noise outside, and I opened the door, and the alley, I guess it was filled with police cars and policemen were on the fire exits and stacked around the alley, and they grabbed me, a couple of them and held and searched me and asked me what I was doing there, and I told them that there was a guy in the theater that I was suspicious of, and he asked me if he was still there.

"And I said yes, I just seen him. And he asked me if I would point him out. And I and two or three other officers walked out on the stage and I pointed him out, and there were officers coming in from the front of the show, I guess, coming toward that way, and officers going from the back."

BELIN: "Then what did you see?"

BREWER: "Well, I saw this policeman approach Oswald, and Oswald stood up and I heard some hollering, I don't know exactly what he said, and this man hit Patrolman [M. N.] McDonald. . . ."

BELIN: "Did you say this man was the same man?"

BREWER: "The same man that had stood in my lobby that I followed to the show."

BELIN: "Who hit who first?"

BREWER: "Oswald hit McDonald first, and he knocked him to the seat."

Oswald pulled out a gun. He was finally subdued by Patrolman McDonald and several other police officers and taken down to the

Dallas Police Station, where he was held and then charged with the murder of Officer J. D. Tippit.

Now examine how Anson treats Brewer's testimony:

> A dozen, perhaps two dozen people were in the theater. In the dark, Brewer could not pick out the man he had seen by his store. By now it didn't matter. The police were arriving. . . . M. N. McDonald, one of the officers, looked out over the rows of seats. There were twelve or fifteen people sitting on the lower level. McDonald couldn't be sure who he was supposed to be looking for. As McDonald scanned the theater, a man sitting near the front spoke up quietly. The man the police were looking for, he said, was sitting on the ground floor, in the center, about three rows from the back. . . .
>
> The police had their man. As they led him away the man in the front row who had fingered him rose from his seat, walked outside, and quietly disappeared.

Thus we see the web of deceit woven by Anson and his implications of conspiracy. According to Anson, there was a man in the front row who "fingered" Oswald and who then "walked outside and quietly disappeared."

Anson picked up the thread by quoting a book written by a fellow assassination sensationalist, George O'Toole, suggesting that movie theaters were a "favored rendezvous for agents." Anson incorporates a paragraph from O'Toole's book purporting to quote statements from a Soviet intelligence manual:

> Intelligence Officers can make extensive use of movie theaters when organizing agent communications by spending a certain amount of time in them before a meeting. The fact is that there are few people in most movie theaters, especially on weekdays during working hours. Movie theaters located away from the center of the city are often practically empty. Thus, by arriving at a designated time at a previously predetermined movie theater and taking advantage of many empty seats, the intelligence officer and the agent can hold a meeting right in the theater.

Anson then continues:

> The Texas Theatre was, just as the Soviet manual predicted, virtually empty when Oswald entered it, and there was at least one other man

in the theater who knew him—the person who fingered him for the police and then disappeared during the ensuing melee.

And then, in the concluding chapter of his book, Anson asks the reader, Why did the Dallas police "concentrate on the Texas Theatre, where a man matching Oswald's description was said to have run in without buying a ticket?" According to Anson:

> [The only reasonable] "explanation is that Oswald did buy a ticket, and that someone else ran into the theater to draw the police to the scene. This other person could either have run out the back or remained, becoming the mysterious man in the front row who informed the police where the man they were looking for was sitting. As M. N. McDonald, the officer who arrested Oswald, remembered him: "A man sitting near the front, and I still don't know who it was, tipped me the man I wanted was sitting in the third row from the rear, not in the balcony."

When Anson writes that "in the dark, Brewer could not pick out the man he had seen by his store," Anson does not go on to say that when the house lights were turned on, Brewer "looked out from the curtains and saw the man. . . ." Anson fails to disclose these crucial facts. Why?

What about Anson's allegation about the unknown man who was sitting in the front row and then quietly disappeared? There is no footnote to corroborate the statement that the man "who had fingered him [Oswald] rose from his seat, walked outside, and quietly disappeared." However, Anson does give a footnote for Patrolman McDonald's alleged statement: "A man sitting near the front, and I still don't know who it was, tipped me the man I wanted was sitting in the third row from the rear, not in the balcony." If you read that footnote, number 26 in chapter 12, you will find that it states, "First-person story by N. M. McDonald, *Dallas Morning News*, Nov. 24, 1963." This same source was first quoted by Sylvia Meagher in 1967 in her book *Accessories After the Fact*. What neither Anson nor Meagher tells the reader is that McDonald later learned the name of the person who had pointed out the gunman and that McDonald testified under oath that that person was Johnny Calvin Brewer.

SENATOR COOPER: "Who was it that pointed out to you the suspect when you entered the theater?"

McDONALD: "I learned his name later."

COOPER: "Did some person there point out to you, though, this man sitting in the row whom you later arrested?"

McDONALD: "Yes, sir. He was a shoe store salesman. His name was Brewer. He was the one that met us at the rear exit door and said that he saw this person run into the Texas Theatre."

Anson leaves out other major parts of the record. For instance, he adopts the thesis of Edward Epstein's book, *Inquest*, that, according to Secret Service Agent Kellerman, President Kennedy supposedly said after the first shot, "My God, I am hit." Like Epstein, Anson never tells his readers about the contrary testimony of Secret Service Agent William Greer, Nellie Connally, Governor John Connally, and Jacqueline Kennedy.

Similarly, Anson leaves out major parts of the record concerning the witnesses to the Tippit murder. For instance, on pages 35–36, Anson refers to cabdriver William Scoggins, who witnessed the murder of Officer Tippit, in one brief paragraph where he tells the reader that Scoggins saw the gunman shoot Officer Tippit and then run back toward Scoggins muttering, "Poor dumb cop."

Anson doesn't tell the reader that the gunman passed as close as twelve feet to where Scoggins was crouching behind his cab and that the next day, before Scoggins had seen any television, he was taken to the Dallas police station, where he identified Oswald as the man he had seen at the Tippit murder scene.

BELIN: "Would it have been on the afternoon of November 23, to the best of your recollection?"

SCOGGINS: "When they took me down there it was along about dinner time."

REP. GERALD FORD: "What do you mean by dinner time? In various parts of the country dinner and supper get confused a little bit. Was it the noon meal or the evening meal?"

SCOGGINS: "Yes."

FORD: "Yes what? It was the noon meal?"

SCOGGINS: "Yes."

BELIN: "They took you down about the time of the noon meal, is that correct; they took you to the police station?"

SCOGGINS: "I would think that would be about the time . . ."

BELIN: "How many people were in the lineup, if you can remember?"

SCOGGINS: "Four."

BELIN: ". . . did you identify anyone in the lineup?"

SCOGGINS: "I identified the one we are talking about, Oswald. I identified him. . . ."

BELIN: ". . . did all of these men look different to you? Were most of them fat, or were most of them thin, or some fat, some thin, some tall, some short?"

SCOGGINS: "There were two of them—the one that I identified as the one I saw over at Oak Cliff, and there was one I saw similar to him, and the other two was a little bit shorter."

Anson's book doesn't mention Barbara Davis or her sister-in-law Virginia Davis, nor does he mention Ted Callaway or Sam Guinyard. The same omissions occur in the more recent books, such as Anthony Summers's *Conspiracy*, which was published in 1980. Summers, however, mentioned that William Scoggins saw the gunman. But Summers fails to tell the reader that Scoggins conclusively identified the gunman as Lee Harvey Oswald. Instead, Summers argues that Oswald was not physically able to get to the Tippit murder scene by 1:15 P.M. Not only Scoggins but Helen Markham, Barbara Davis, Sam Guinyard, and Ted Callaway would urge otherwise, and there was the physical evidence of the cartridge cases that independently proves that Oswald killed Officer Tippit. Summers is so successful that he fooled Robert MacNeil, executive editor of the "MacNeil-Lehrer News Hour."

A 1981 best-seller called *Best Evidence*, by David Lifton, goes one step further than Summers's book. Lifton not only omits mentioning Callaway, Guinyard, and the Davis sisters-in-law, but he also fails to disclose the existence of Scoggins, Markham, and Brewer. The most significant contribution of Lifton is that after fifteen years of allegedly meticulous study, he is forced to admit that the conclusions of the Warren Commission were basically right based on the evidence it had before it. But Lifton seeks to weave a fictitious web of conspiracy, claiming that between the time President Kennedy's body left Dallas and its arrival in the autopsy room in Washington, there were a group of conspirators who removed the body from the casket and performed some sort of surgical operation that made the wounds appear to have come from the back instead of the front and that there were other conspirators who planted bullets from Oswald's rifle in Parkland Memorial Hospital near Governor Connally's stretcher. These preposterous claims were prominently featured on national television programs as well as in news magazines such as *Time*. Lifton's thesis is destroyed both by the eyewitnesses to the Tippit murder and the physical evidence such as the cartridge cases that Benavides, Barbara Davis, and Virginia Davis found at the Tippit murder scene and turned over to the police.

The bullets in Tippit's body were too mutilated to be ballistically identifiable, according to FBI experts, although one expert retained by the Warren Commission believed that he could identify one of those bullets as having been fired from Oswald's revolver. However, cartridge cases can also be identified as having been fired from a particular weapon, to the exclusion of all other weapons in the world. Irrefutable ballistic evidence proved that the cartridge cases found at the Tippit murder scene by Benavides, Barbara Davis, and Virginia Davis came from the revolver that Oswald pulled out in the Texas Theatre. Robert Sam Anson and others simply ignored this available and conclusive ballistic evidence.

Another instance of the suppression of ballistic evidence occurs in *Assassination Tapes*, a book commissioned by *Penthouse* magazine. The author was George O'Toole, whom Anson used as his source for the statement that movie theaters are a favorite rendezvous for agents.

O'Toole's thesis is that Oswald was telling the truth at a press conference at the Dallas Police Station when he said that he didn't shoot anybody on November 22. O'Toole claims that he has an instrument called a psychological stress evaluator and that if you hear a tape recording of a person's voice, you can determine whether that person is telling the truth. He had listened to the tape recording of Oswald's voice at the Dallas press conference, held after Oswald's arrest. According to O'Toole, his instrument shows Oswald was telling the truth when he denied killing anyone. Of course, no such instrument exists. The CIA would be the first agency to use one, for it would then have a scientific instrument to determine whether a person was a double agent.

More to the point, the basic problem Mr. O'Toole faces, and the basic problem faced by all other authors proclaiming Oswald's innocence, is the Tippit murder. Like Anson, O'Toole ignores crucial witnesses who identified Oswald as the gunman. When it comes to the cartridge cases, O'Toole writes, "the spent shells seemed to have been put deliberately where they would be found after a brief search." Thus, O'Toole implies that there was an attempt to frame Oswald, just as Anson implied such an attempt when he came up with the man in the front row of the Texas Theatre who purportedly pointed out Oswald to the police. Of course, O'Toole doesn't tell his readers that Benavides saw the gunman toss the cartridge cases into the bushes and that Benavides took the cases out of the bushes and turned them over to the police. Nor does O'Toole say that Barbara Davis and Virginia Davis, who saw Oswald and identified him in a police lineup, each took a cartridge case out of the bushes and turned it over to the police and that, as I have noted, they were proven to have come from Oswald's gun.

Mark Lane manages to have no problems with Brewer's testimony, simply refusing to acknowledge Brewer's existence either in his book or film. He baldly asserts that there was no reason for the Dallas police to arrest Oswald.

In turn, Lane's tactics have been adopted by a whole raft of authors who have followed in his footsteps, most recently by David Scheim in a 1988 book entitled *Contract on America* and subtitled "The Mafia Murder of President John F. Kennedy" (Shapolsky Publishers). Not only does Scheim ignore Brewer, but he also ignores William Scoggins, Ted Callaway, Sam Guinyard, Barbara Davis, Virginia Davis, and the irrefutable ballistic evidence of the cartridge cases found by Benavides and Virginia and Barbara Davis. He also omits Brennan, Euins, and Robert Jackson.

Scheim cites the books of Mark Lane and Robert Sam Anson as a part of a category of "Principal Sources" for his book. He also uses Lane's spurious claims as a foundation for his own theories. For instance, Scheim says (p. 36):

> Another eyewitness to the Tippit slaying, Acquilla Clemons, was questioned by independent investigators. She reported that the gunman was "kind of a short guy" and "kind of heavy," a description incompatible with Oswald's appearance. Clemons also related that just two days after the Kennedy and Tippit killings, a man who appeared to be a policeman came to her house. His message: "He just told me it'd be best if I didn't say anything because I might get hurt."

The paragraph is footnoted to a filmed and tape-recorded interview made by Lane in Dallas on March 23, 1966.

As a matter of fact, Mark Lane filmed a number of collateral witnesses and together with Emile d'Antonio produced a film, which was also entitled *Rush to Judgment*. In August 1966, I received from Lane and d'Antonio a letter stating that they had completed a film on the assassination of President Kennedy and offered me "the opportunity to rebut the film on camera—with the understanding that anything you say on camera will be used intact without any cuts, additions, or deletions on our part." This put me in a quandary. I knew that Mark Lane's claims were a sham—a shrewd concoction of specious arguments based on misrepresentations of the overall record. I also knew that Mark Lane, when he sent the letter, undoubtedly anticipated that I would refuse the request, because he knew of my contempt for his lack of conscience and his making the assassination of President Kennedy his lifetime "meal ticket."

I also reasoned that if I turned down the invitation, at the end of the film they would read the invitation and state that I turned it down. Undoubtedly, the film would reach hundreds of thousands and perhaps millions of viewers, and I thought that I just could not let Lane get away with this. Therefore, I decided to accept the invitation. There was only one problem: As soon as I accepted the invitation, Lane tried to run away. I wrote eight letters, none of which was answered except for one brief postcard from Mr. d'Antonio to write to Mark Lane at a specific address in New York. I wrote Lane at that address—but no reply. Finally, I wrote to Lane in care of his publisher, where he was collecting his book royalties, and following my ninth letter, Mark Lane withdrew the offer. I won the battle, but I lost the war, because the film has been seen by millions throughout the world; however, there is no rebuttal to the deception and misrepresentation that permeates the film production.

Even if there had been no witnesses to the Tippit shooting, the apprehension of Oswald less than forty-five minutes after the murder, with the murder weapon in his possession, was certainly strong evidence that Oswald was the killer. And when you add to this evidence the action of Oswald in the theater in taking out his gun and resisting arrest and the actions of Oswald before he went into the theater that aroused the suspicion of Johnny Calvin Brewer, the case against Oswald becomes incontrovertible. And when you add to this the positive identification by the six witnesses who were taken to the Dallas Police Department—William Scoggins, who saw Oswald pass within twelve feet of his cab; Ted Callaway and Sam Guinyard, who saw Oswald running from the scene with gun in hand; Helen Markham, who saw the murder from across the street; and Barbara J. Davis and Virginia Davis, who saw Oswald cut across the front yard of their house—there can be no reasonable doubt that the murderer of Dallas police officer J. D. Tippit was Lee Harvey Oswald.

My Warren Commission colleague Joe Ball, who has lectured on criminal law at the University of Southern California, put it succinctly: "In all of my courtroom experience, I have never seen a more 'open and shut case.' "

The impact of the Tippit murder—the reason it is "the Rosetta Stone" to the question of who killed President Kennedy—can be summed up:

1. The Tippit murder weapon, like the Kennedy murder weapon, was purchased by Lee Harvey Oswald through the mail and was shipped to Lee Harvey Oswald under his alias, A. Hidell, to his post-office box in Dallas.

2. That Oswald was carrying a concealed weapon at the time of his arrest, that he pulled it out as policemen approached him, and that this turned out to be the Tippit murder weapon constitute demonstrative evidence of Oswald's guilt.

3. The FBI experts and an independent expert agreed that all of the cartridge cases unequivocally were fired by Oswald's revolver. This alone, in light of Oswald's acts of pulling out the gun as policemen approached him, would have been enough to identify him as a gunman. And once it is shown that Oswald murdered someone within an hour of the assassination of President Kennedy, then the additional evidence of Oswald's direct involvement in the assassination becomes fortified. Oswald was the owner of the assassination weapon and closely fits the description of the assassin by Howard Brennan, who saw the gunman fire the last shot.

4. There were many other incriminating factors, such as Oswald's palm print on the gun and his fingerprint on the paper bag found at the assassination window as well as the fact that he was the only Texas School Book Depository employee having access to the assassination window who was inside the depository at the time of the assassination and had fled the building after the assassination.

There is other evidence, as well. Had Oswald not been killed, the evidence would have come to trial, and there is no doubt that Oswald would have been convicted.

Oswald did not come to trial, of course, because he was murdered by Jack Ruby.

Why?

# 6

## Jack Ruby and the Murder of Oswald

The date was Monday, November 25, 1963. The place was the Dallas County jail, a relatively unfamiliar location for Rabbi Hillel Silverman to be calling on a member of his Conservative congregation. The bronzed, handsome rabbi of Congregation Shearith Israel in Dallas did not relish the task. Nevertheless, he felt an obligation to call upon Jack Ruby, who the day before had committed a murder witnessed by millions of Americans on their television screens.

Jack Ruby's victim was Lee Harvey Oswald, who, on the previous Friday, November 22, had murdered President John F. Kennedy and Dallas police officer J. D. Tippit.

For the entire country it had been a weekend of bereavement. On Friday night, after the assassination, Ruby—a nightclub owner who knew policemen in Dallas—had gone to the Dallas police station and walked into a press conference at which Oswald was being interviewed. According to Rabbi Silverman, at his first meeting with Ruby on the following Monday, Ruby told him that "had I intended to kill him, I could have pulled my trigger on the spot, because the gun was in my pocket."

This is a crucial statement! It bears directly on the claims of conspiracy made by assassination buffs who assert that Ruby was conspiratorially involved in the assassination. It was pure happenstance that Ruby had an opportunity to kill Oswald on November 24. If Ruby were actually conspiratorially involved, the time to have killed Oswald was when he knew he had a chance to do it—on the evening of November 22.

What took place between Friday evening, November 22, and Sunday morning, November 24, to cause Ruby to kill Oswald? The two best people to answer that question are Jack Ruby, in his testimony, and Rabbi Silverman. Assassination sensationalists and buffs who attack Ruby's answers to the questions close their eyes to the compelling testimony of Rabbi Silverman. Yet there is little doubt that Rabbi Silverman was in the best position to judge whether Ruby was telling the truth in the intimate conversations they had in the Dallas County jail after Ruby shot Oswald.

According to Silverman, Jack Ruby told him that on Saturday morning, November 23, he had viewed a telecast from New York City in which a Rabbi Seligson was talking about President Kennedy and the assassination. Ruby found Seligson's words extremely moving—so much so that he dressed, went to his car, and drove to the site of the assassination, where he walked by the wreaths that had already been placed there.

Ruby then told Silverman that on the next morning, November 24, he read in the newspaper that Jacqueline Kennedy might have to return to Dallas for the trial of Lee Harvey Oswald. He said that this greatly upset him.

Shortly before 11:00 A.M. on that Sunday morning, Jack Ruby left his apartment building to go to the downtown Western Union office to wire money to an employee, "Little Lynn," who lived in Fort Worth. According to Rabbi Silverman, Ruby believed Oswald had already been transferred from the city jail to the county jail, but when he saw people and policemen standing around the police station, he decided to return after he wired the money.

The time stamp at the Western Union office was 11:17 A.M. The

ramp from the street leading to the basement where Oswald was
to board a vehicle for transfer was barely a half block away.

Ruby left the Western Union office, gained access to the ramp
when a policeman's back was turned, and walked down the ramp
into the basement area where members of the press were waiting
for Oswald to appear. Within a minute or two—at 11:21 A.M.—
Oswald, flanked by police officers, stepped out of the basement
elevator and walked through the dark corridor toward the area
where Ruby and members of the press were standing.

It all happened very quickly. Flashbulbs and strobe lights tem-
porarily blinded the police escort. Ruby generally carried a gun
(as he did on Friday evening after the assassination), and when he
saw Oswald, he took out his gun and pulled the trigger. The police
wrestled Ruby to the floor, and he cried out, "I am Jack Ruby."

Before Ruby was able to reach a lawyer, the police started to
interrogate him. Ruby told Rabbi Silverman that he remembered
telling a policeman on that Sunday right after shooting Oswald:
"I was afraid that Mrs. Kennedy would be asked to return to
Dallas for the trial."

From that first visit on November 25, Rabbi Silverman generally
saw Ruby once or twice a week, until Silverman left Dallas to
accept a pulpit in Los Angeles in July 1964. Whenever Silverman
discussed with Ruby why he had shot Oswald, the answer was
the same: to save Mrs. Kennedy the ordeal of having to come back
for the trial of Lee Harvey Oswald and testify about her husband's
death.

There were many in Dallas—undoubtedly a majority—who believed that the murder of Oswald was part of an overall conspiracy
to assassinate Kennedy. It was not farfetched to assume that Ruby
had killed Oswald to silence him, particularly since Ruby had
contacts with organized crime. The possibility was enhanced because Robert Kennedy, as attorney general, had declared war on
the underworld.

Therefore, on one of my first trips to Dallas, I visited Rabbi
Silverman. We had become friends the previous summer on a study
mission to Israel. I told him that I recognized that what was said
between rabbi and congregant was privileged, but I wondered

whether he had any question about the existence of a conspiracy. Silverman was unequivocal: "Jack Ruby is absolutely innocent of any conspiracy."

I asked Silverman if he was certain. "Without a doubt," he replied. Although the tone of his voice was most convincing and although I realized that Rabbi Silverman had probably become closer to Ruby than any other person in the world, I wanted some corroboration. The most obvious possibility was a polygraph, or lie-detector, examination.

Inside the Warren Commission, we had already had a major debate about the use of polygraphs. I wanted both Jack Ruby and Marina Oswald to undergo polygraph tests. In a memorandum to the staff, I pointed out some inconsistencies in interviews of Marina Oswald with the FBI, and I noted that much of her testimony was not subject to ordinary tests of credibility because it concerned the Oswalds' life together in Russia. I also said that if under a polygraph examination it were to be shown that "Marina had not been truthful in her testimony, it could throw an entirely new light on aspects of the investigation." I also thought that if she would refuse our request, it might indicate she had something to hide.

Most of the staff lined up against me. One member undertook research to prove the limitations of the test and to prove that one could not rely on test results. I admitted that the polygraph had limitations, but I argued that in large part those depended on the qualifications and competency of the polygraph examiner. Although a lie-detector test may not be admissible in court, we were not in a legal proceeding. I urged that we use the polygraph as an investigative aid. (Congressman Ford agreed with me.) Chief Justice Warren sided with the majority of the staff, and my request was denied.

Once the commission had decided against using a polygraph for Marina Oswald, I knew there was no possibility that the commission would consider asking that Jack Ruby undergo a lie-detector test.

I approached Rabbi Silverman directly. I told him that even though he was convinced that Ruby was not involved in an assassination conspiracy, the world would never be convinced unless

Ruby took a polygraph examination. I also told him that the Warren Commission would never ask Ruby to submit to one but that Ruby himself could request one.

Silverman had a dilemma. Ruby was represented by legal counsel, and it was up to the lawyers to decide whether Ruby would submit to the test. The test could undermine the legal defense of temporary insanity. On the other hand, Silverman was convinced Ruby was innocent of any conspiracy, and he recognized that if Ruby would agree to a polygraph examination, it would be a major step in convincing the people of Dallas of his innocence.

My position was simple: Ruby had already been convicted of murder. The situation could not be much worse. Surely, if he were innocent of any conspiracy, he should volunteer to take the test.

Silverman agreed to try to persuade Ruby to ask for the test when he testified before the Warren Commission. Ruby told his rabbi that he would ask for the test.

On June 7, 1964, Earl Warren and Gerald Ford went to the Dallas County jail to interrogate Ruby. At the beginning of Ruby's testimony, he said, "Without a lie detector test on my testimony, my verbal statements to you, how do you know if I am telling the truth?"

His attorney interrupted and said, "Don't worry about that, Jack."

But Ruby continued: "I would like to be able to get a lie detector test or truth serum of what motivated me to do what I did at that particular time. . . . Now Mr. Warren, I don't know if you got any confidence in the lie detector test and the truth serum, and so on."

Chief Justice Warren replied, "I can't tell you just how much confidence I have in it, because it depends so much on who is taking it, and so forth. But I will say this to you, that if you and your counsel want any kind of test, I will arrange it for you. I would be glad to do that, if you want it. I wouldn't suggest a lie detector test to testify the truth. We will treat you just the same as we do any other witness, but if you want such a test, I will arrange for it."

And Ruby replied, "I do want it."

Ruby then described to Chief Justice Warren his actions during the weekend of the assassination, which culminated in his killing Lee Harvey Oswald. Just as he had told Rabbi Silverman about watching the eulogy by a rabbi on television on Saturday morning, November 23, Ruby testified:

"He went ahead and eulogized that here is a man [President Kennedy] that fought in every battle, went to every country, and had to come back to his own country to be shot in the back," and Ruby started crying. After regaining his composure, he continued and told about reading a letter to Caroline Kennedy, the daughter of the president, on Sunday morning in the newspaper. "And alongside that letter on the same sheet of paper was a small comment in the newspaper that, I don't know how it was stated, that Mrs. Kennedy may have to come back for the trial of Lee Harvey Oswald. That caused me to go like I did. . . . I don't know, Chief Justice, but I got so carried away. And I remember prior to that thought, there has never been another thought in my mind; I was never malicious toward this person. No one else requested me to do anything. I never spoke to anyone about attempting to do anything. No subversive organization gave me any idea. No underworld person made any effort to contact me. . . . Suddenly the feeling, the emotional feeling came within me that someone owed this debt to our beloved President to save her the ordeal of coming back."

Although Jack Ruby was not particularly religious, in 1980 Rabbi Silverman told me that when he first asked Ruby to tell him what happened, Ruby replied, "I did it for the Jews of America."

In testimony before Warren and Ford, Ruby added one more facet: "A fellow whom I sort of idolized is of the Catholic faith, and a gambler. Naturally in my business you meet people of various backgrounds.

"And the thought came, we were very close, and I always thought a lot of him, and I knew that Kennedy, being Catholic, I knew how heartbroken he was, and even his picture—of this Mr. McWillie—flashed across me, because I have a great fondness for him.

"All that blended into the thing that, like a screwball, the way it turned out, that I thought that I would sacrifice myself for the few moments of saving Mrs. Kennedy the discomfiture of coming back to trial."

Warren asked Ruby whether he knew Oswald. Ruby replied, "No."

Ruby was asked whether he knew Officer Tippit. Ruby said there were three Tippits on the force, but the one he knew was not the one murdered on November 22. Ruby maintained, "I am as innocent regarding any conspiracy as any of you gentlemen in the room, and I don't want anything to be run over lightly."

Six weeks later, on July 18, 1964, the Warren Commission arranged to have Ruby's testimony taken before a court reporter while Ruby was undergoing a lie-detector test. The man administering the test was one of the ablest in the field, FBI polygraph operator Bill P. Herndon.

At the last minute, Ruby's chief counsel, Clayton Fowler, tried to stop the test. He told Arlen Specter of the Warren Commission that Ruby had changed his mind. But Specter was not to be denied and had the Court reporter start transcribing what was taking place. Reluctantly, Fowler admitted, "He says he's going to take this test regardless of his lawyers, and he says, 'By God, I'm going to take the test.' "

According to the test results, Ruby's testimony before the Warren Commission was the truth. Also, according to the test results, Ruby answered the following questions truthfully:

Q. "Did you know Oswald before November 22, 1963?"
A. "No."
Q. "Did you assist Oswald in the assassination?"
A. "No."
Q. "Between the assassination and the shooting, did anybody you know tell you they knew Oswald?"
A. "No."
Q. "Did you shoot Oswald in order to silence him?"
A. "No."
Q. "Is everything you told the Warren Commission the entire truth?"

A. "Yes."

Q. "Did any foreign influence cause you to shoot Oswald?"

A. "No."

Q. "Did you shoot Oswald because of any influence of the underworld?"

A. "No."

Q. "Did you shoot Oswald in order to save Mrs. Kennedy the ordeal of a trial?"

A. "Yes."

Q. "Did you know the Tippit that was killed?"

A. "No."

There is one final significant fact. Some people have argued, correctly, that the results of a polygraph examination are not 100 percent accurate, particularly if there is a question of the mental state of the person taking the exam. However, not only did FBI polygraph operator Bill Herndon believe that Ruby was telling the truth, but also there is a common-sense factor: If Ruby had been guilty of a conspiracy, he would not have insisted that he take the test—against the advice of his own attorneys.

However, if anyone still has any doubt about Ruby's acting alone, there is one other independent factor—a happenstance that corroborates the conclusion that Ruby was innocent of any conspiracy.

Oswald was scheduled to be transferred from the city jail in the police station to the county jail several blocks down the street at 10:00 A.M. on Sunday, November 24. Before the scheduled transfer, he was to undergo the third of a series of interrogations by Capt. Will Fritz, the head of the homicide section of the Dallas Police Department, and representatives of the Secret Service and the FBI.

If no one else had joined the group, Oswald would have been transferred on schedule, long before Jack Ruby ever got downtown. However, another person entered the interrogation room Sunday morning. He was Postal Inspector Harry D. Holmes, who had helped the FBI trace the money order that Oswald used to purchase the rifle with which he killed Kennedy. Holmes had also helped the FBI trace the ownership of the post-office box to which Oswald's rifle and pistol were shipped.

BELIN: "Just what was the occasion of your joining this interrogation? How did you happen to be there?"

HOLMES: "I had been in and out of Captain Fritz's office on numerous occasions during this 2½ day period.

"On this morning I had no appointment. I actually started to church with my wife. I got to church and I said, 'You get out, I am going down and see if I can do something for Captain Fritz. I imagine he is as sleepy as I am.'

"So I drove directly on down to the police station and walked in, and as I did, Captain Fritz motioned to me and said, 'We are getting ready to have a last interrogation with Oswald before we transfer him to the county jail. Would you like to join us?'

"I said, 'I would.' "

After Fritz, the representative of the Secret Service, and an FBI agent finished their interrogation of Oswald, Fritz turned to Holmes and asked whether he wanted to interrogate Oswald. While the invitation was unexpected, Holmes jumped at the opportunity, and the interrogation continued for another half hour or more.

Ruby shot Oswald approximately five minutes after Ruby left the Western Union office. Had Holmes continued on to church with his wife that morning, the length of interrogation would have been shortened by more than half an hour. Jack Ruby would never have had the opportunity to kill Oswald.

Assassination sensationalists and conspiracy buffs raise all kinds of spurious questions about Jack Ruby, trying to prove conspiratorial involvement. Virtually everyone, from Mark Lane to David Scheim, fails to disclose the testimony of Rabbi Silverman. Moreover, there are five questions that the assassination sensationalists never satisfactorily answer:

1. How do they deal with the fact that Ruby had an opportunity to kill Oswald on Sunday morning only because Postal Inspector Holmes did not go to church that morning and, because of this, the interrogation of Oswald was lengthened and his transfer was postponed? Do the sensationalists assert that Postal Inspector Holmes was part of an alleged conspiracy?

2. If Ruby wanted to silence Oswald, why didn't he kill Oswald on Friday evening, November 22, when he had a perfect opportunity? There is nothing to show that Ruby knew on Friday evening that he would be back downtown at the police station on Sunday morning, just as there is nothing to show that he knew that the transfer of Oswald from the police station to the county jail would be delayed because of Postal Inspector Holmes. Given these facts, if Ruby were conspiratorially involved and wanted to kill Oswald, would he not have done this on November 22?

3. If Ruby were conspiratorially involved, why did he volunteer to take a polygraph examination?

4. If Ruby were conspiratorially involved, why did he agree to go ahead with the polygraph examination against the direct advice of his own attorneys?

5. If Ruby were conspiratorially involved, isn't it reasonable to assume that there would have been some evidence of conspiracy that Rabbi Silverman would have found in their many conversations?

To all of these questions can be added the answers of Jack Ruby in the polygraph examination. Ruby did not know Oswald before the assassination, he did not assist Oswald, he did not shoot Oswald in order to silence him. He shot Oswald to save Mrs. Kennedy the ordeal of a trial. And Ruby did not know Officer J. D. Tippit.

There is also the common-sense fact that so-called Mafia hit men do not kill their victim when the area is surrounded by police officers so that the gunman can be immediately captured and put in jail and subject himself to life imprisonment or capital punishment for murder. The conspiracy buffs ignore practical considerations as well as facts.

# 7

## Mistakes Inside the Warren Commission

Initially, Earl Warren approached our investigation with three concerns:

1. He wanted to find the truth about the assassination.

2. Although he wanted to find the truth, he was desperately concerned about what might happen if the truth were to uncover a conspiracy. Suppose Cuba was involved. Would the United States invade Cuba? Would Russia come to Cuba's defense? Would this lead to nuclear war?

3. He wanted everything wrapped up by the end of May, before the summer presidential nominating conventions.

Warren achieved his goal for the truth. His second concern—about a conspiracy—was put to rest. He missed his third goal. We were able to extend the timetable to September to complete our work.

But Earl Warren and the commission made mistakes. Perhaps the biggest blunder was to yield to the desires of the Kennedy family and not include the autopsy photographs or the X rays of President Kennedy as exhibits in the material and physical evidence examined by the commission staff. In any trial, the attorneys and the judges are entitled to see the key exhibits. Certainly Officer Tippit's widow could not have denied us an opportunity to see any autopsy X rays of Officer Tippit had they been taken. Why should the Kennedy family have been treated any differently?

Instead of submitting the physical evidence to us, Warren directed that the physicians furnish us their own drawings, which depicted what the photographs and X rays showed. From an evidentiary point of view, this was wrong; one is entitled to the "best evidence." Moreover, this shortsighted decision helped breed the various false theories of assassination sensationalists—claims that could have been demolished if the autopsy photographs and X rays had been shown.

(I finally saw them myself when I served as executive director of the Rockefeller Commission. Charges were made in 1975 that the CIA was conspiratorially involved in the assassination and that shots had come from the front as well as from behind. Thus, it became necessary to examine the photographs and X rays as a part of our investigation. An independent panel of physicians helped reevaluate all the evidence and determine whether there was any evidence of shots coming from the front. The photographs were horrifying, but the evidence showed beyond a reasonable doubt that all of the shots that stuck Kennedy came from the rear. Governor Connally also was struck from the rear, and there has never been any doubt about this—even by assassination sensationalists.)

Although the conclusions of the autopsy physicians who testified before the Warren Commission were supported by every panel of physicians that has examined the materials since then—an independent panel appointed by Atty. Gen. Ramsey Clark in 1968, the independent panel appointed by the Rockefeller Commission in 1975, and the panel appointed by the House Select Committee on Assassinations in 1978—much of the disbelief in the Warren Commission's conclusions could have been avoided if Earl Warren had exercised better judgment and allowed the autopsy photographs and X rays to be included as a part of the physical evidence.

There were also other errors of judgment by Warren. For instance, when we obtained the testimony of Jack Ruby, the chief justice did not permit participation in the interrogation by the two lawyers on the commission staff who were charged with investigating Ruby's life and activities to see if there was any conspiratorial aspect to his shooting of Oswald. These two attorneys were the late Leon D. Hubert, Jr., and Bert W. Griffin. A Dallas police officer had complained that Griffin had been excessively harsh, attacking the police officer's credibility during an interrogation, and Warren and General Counsel J. Lee Rankin were sensitive to criticism of staff conduct. Both Hubert and Griffin, brilliant lawyers, were crushed that they were not allowed to be present at the interrogation of the man they had been investigating for so many months. No matter how capable other lawyers on the staff were, they could not have done as good a job as Hubert and Griffin because they did not have as much background about Ruby's life. Ultimately, it made no difference, but the decision was nevertheless wrong.

A similar error occurred in the case of taking the testimony of Marina Oswald. She had undergone many interviews with the FBI, and several of us lacked confidence in her credibility because of inconsistencies in some of her answers to questions.

Marina Oswald's testimony was taken by Rankin. She should have been interrogated by the two lawyers who were concentrating on the entire background of Oswald's life in the United States as well as the two lawyers concentrating on the foreign-conspiracy area. These four attorneys had far more background in knowing which questions to ask and how to ask them and were therefore better equipped to interrogate her. For instance, Albert E. Jenner, Jr.—Bert Jenner—one of the outstanding trial lawyers in the United States and a past president of the American College of Trial Lawyers, and Wesley J. Liebler, cum laude graduate from the University of Chicago Law School and now professor of law at UCLA Law School in Los Angeles, spent months combing every aspect of Oswald's life in this country. W. David Slawson, Phi Beta Kappa graduate from Amherst College, magna cum laude graduate from Harvard University, and now professor of law at the University of Southern California Law School; and William T. Coleman, Jr., summa cum laude graduate from the University of Pennsylvania and magna cum laude graduate from the Harvard Law School and now a partner in the Washington office of the Los Angeles law firm of O'Melveny and Myers, spent months concentrating on every aspect of possible foreign conspiracy. Lee Rankin, a former solicitor general of the United States, was very capable, but he just did not have the background of these other attorneys.

So Marina Oswald was not questioned as thoroughly as she should have been. In part, this was because Earl Warren was a compassionate person and I believe somewhat naive when it came to Marina Oswald. Virtually all of the Warren Commission counsel saw Marina Oswald as a person who had lied during the course of her interrogation by the FBI and Secret Service and who was capable of lying before the Warren Commission. Earl Warren, in contrast, saw her as a young widow with two small children living in a strange country who was very scared and needed comfort and support. He was convinced from the beginning that there was no Russian conspiratorial involvement, he was convinced of Oswald's guilt, and accordingly he did not believe there was any need for intensive interrogation of Marina.

Although I do not believe Marina Oswald or any Soviet agent was conspiratorially involved in the assassination, I believe that she did not make full disclosure to the Warren Commission. This, in turn, encouraged the theories of the assassination sensationalists. If one wants to find out about Marina Oswald, one has to supplement her Warren Commission testimony, which is not the way it should have been. The best supplement is a book called *Marina and Lee* written by Priscilla McMillan Johnson.

There was another mistake made inside the Warren Commission, and that concerned the nature of the report itself. Some urged that the report include substantial portions of the transcript testimony of the key witnesses so that the readers of the report in general, and particularly the members of the press, would have direct familiarity with the strong foundation of testimony on which the conclusions of the commission were based.

Warren, Rankin, and others wanted everything put together in a one-volume report because it would be read by the greatest number of people. Some—including me—argued for a two-volume report and asserted that it would be more important to have 100,000 people read a two-volume report that included the bedrock of testimony and evidence on which our conclusions were based than it would be to have 200,000 or 300,000 people read a one-volume report and have it more susceptible to question.

A one-volume report was issued.

The staff and the commissioner shared goals and ideas but faced different pressures. The staff had no government position to protect, no political ax to grind. The commissioners were politically oriented and were either serving in government or had recently held government positions; thus, they were not devoid of government influence. Moreover, all were busy men with many outside responsibilities; none could devote full time to the work of the commission. Sen. Richard B. Russell was almost always absent, and even when the most important witnesses were brought to Washington to testify before the seven commissioners, several commissioners were usually absent. Often only one or two were present, and when we took the testimony of witnesses outside Washington, generally no commissioner was present.

To be sure, transcripts of the testimony of all witnesses were promptly prepared. Each commissioner would receive a set of the transcripts, if he had the time to read and study them. Even here, however, the procedure left much to be desired. The testimony of a witness is not just his actual words. His demeanor, the way in which he answers questions—all the observations of a witness that can be made by a judge and jury in the course of his testimony— are important. These impressions are lost in the transcript. No commissioner not present, no reader, no historian, no scholar, will ever be fully able to recapture them. That is why it was so critical to have an independent staff with the highest standards of objectivity and professionalism in the conduct of the investigation.

# 8

## Trying to Prove Conspiracy

**B**efore I went to Washington in the middle of January 1964, the FBI had already reached its conclusions:

1. Three shots were fired at the presidential limousine from the southeast-corner window of the sixth floor of the Texas School Book Depository. The first shot struck the president from behind, entering the back of his neck and exiting from the front. The second shot struck Governor Connally from behind. The third shot struck the president's head from behind and was the fatal bullet.

2. The assassination weapon was a Mannlicher-Carcano rifle, serial number C-2766.

3. The person who owned the assassination weapon was Lee Harvey Oswald, an employee of the depository who had regular access to the southeast-corner window on the sixth floor from which Howard Brennan and Amos Euins had seen the gunman fire at the presidential limousine.

4. Lee Harvey Oswald was also the gunman who killed Dallas police officer J. D. Tippit.

5. Lee Harvey Oswald was the lone assassin who killed President Kennedy. There was no evidence of any conspiracy.

Like most Americans, I had assumed there may have been a conspiracy. I knew that Lee Harvey Oswald was reputed to be a great admirer of Fidel Castro. On the other hand, President Kennedy and his brother, Robert Kennedy, who was then attorney general of the United States, were outspoken enemies of Castro. It was John F. Kennedy who gave the final go-ahead orders for the ill-fated invasion of the Bay of Pigs in Cuba, and there were many rumors that the killing of the president might be some sort of retaliatory act on the part of the Castro regime. Accordingly, I was concerned with all kinds of possibilities of conspiracy.

There was a time when I thought I had indeed proved there was more than one gunman, which therefore meant a conspiracy. Here is how I came to this position.

At the time of the assassination, there was an amateur photographer, Abraham Zapruder, who photographed the assassination on a movie camera. We had 35 mm. slides made from each frame, numbered each slide consecutively, and tried to determine every possible bit of information from this film. We determined that the camera ran at 18.3 frames per second. From that camera and other scientific data we determined that the presidential limousine was moving at 11.2 miles an hour.

On Zapruder's film you could vividly see the fatal shot hitting Kennedy's head. Evidence of the gunshot appears in a frame that we numbered 313. Two ballistically identifiable bullet fragments from the fatal shot were found in the presidential limousine, and a nearly whole bullet was found at Parkland Memorial Hospital. It had rolled off Connally's stretcher.

In examining the film, it was not possible to see precisely when Connally was hit, nor was it possible to see precisely when the president was *first* struck, because the view from Zapruder's camera to the limousine was obstructed between frames 205 and 224 by a large freeway sign. As the presidential car moved past the freeway sign from frame 225 onward, President Kennedy's hand is seen moving toward his throat, and it is obvious he has been struck. How long it took between the instant he was hit and the instant his hand moved toward his throat was impossible to determine.

As I studied the film, I hit upon an idea that might demonstrate that there was a second gunman and that therefore there must have been a conspiracy. My idea was simple: Prove that the same rifle had not fired all the shots. According to FBI tests, the rifle, number C-2766, could be fired no faster than 2.25 seconds of elapsed time between shots. (Subsequent tests after the completion of the work of the Warren Commission showed that the FBI was wrong and that the rifle could be fired even faster.)

I reasoned that if the movie camera ran at 18.3 frames a second and if the rifle could be fired no faster than every 2.25 seconds, you would have to have more than 40 frames of elapsed time between rifle shots. If I could show that Governor Connally was hit closer than 40 movie frames from either the fatal shot or the time when President Kennedy was first hit, then I thought it would prove that there was a second gunman involved.

Governor Connally's physicians all agreed he was hit by a single bullet fired from behind. Although the photography experts could not tell us exactly where Connally was when he was hit, I thought we might be able to have his physicians reconstruct the position that Connally had to be in in order to sustain his wounds and then compare it with his position in the Zapruder film and slides. At the very least, we could determine where Governor Connally could *not* have been hit on the film.

To appreciate the full impact of what happened next, the reader should have the following frame of reference: Almost everyone had assumed up to this point that the first shot struck Kennedy, the second shot struck Governor Connally, the third shot struck President Kennedy, and all three shots had been fired from one weapon. The FBI had reached this conclusion, as had the Secret Service. No physical evidence had been found that would prove otherwise.

I was trying to prove—in the face of the FBI and the Secret Service—that this conclusion was wrong. And I succeeded. Governor Connally was not in the position to be hit as reconstructed by his doctors at any time after frame 240.

If Connally could not have been hit after frame 240 and if Kennedy was hit between frames 210 and 225, then there would be a maximum of 30 frames between the time Kennedy was first hit and the time Connally was hit. If the film speed was 18.3 frames per second, which meant that the elapsed time from Kennedy's first wound to Connally's wounds was less than two seconds, then there must have been another rifle involved in addition to the one that was found on the sixth floor of the depository that fired the bullet fragments found in the presidential limousine and the nearly whole bullet found at Parkland Memorial Hospital. In turn, this would mean there must have been at least two different riflemen, and therefore there must have been a conspiracy—except for only one possibility: that the first shot that struck Kennedy in the back of his neck and exited from the front of his neck also struck Connally.

Ultimately, we concluded that the same bullet that struck Kennedy did indeed strike Connally. The evidence supporting that conclusion was overwhelming, and this evidence, which became known as the "single-bullet theory," was developed by a brilliant commission lawyer, Arlen Specter, now a U.S. senator from Pennsylvania.

The single-bullet theory was corroborated by scientific evidence. Wound ballistic tests showed that the bullet that entered Kennedy's neck entered at a velocity of approximately 1,900 feet per second and exited at a velocity of approximately 1,800 feet per second. The bullet had to either hit the inside of the limousine as it was continuing in its downward trajectory, causing great damage, or hit someone in the limousine.

There was no serious damage to the car, although there were some marks on the inside of the windshield, no doubt caused by fragments from the shot that hit the president's head. Connally was sitting directly in front of the president. It became increasingly clear that the bullet that exited Kennedy's neck hit Governor Connally.

We then reconstructed the motorcade, using the slides from the Zapruder film and other photographs taken at the assassination. We pinpointed the location of the car on the street for each frame of the Zapruder film and correlated this with photographs taken with a single-lens reflex camera through the telescopic sight of Oswald's rifle perched in the window of the depository. Except for a split instant at frame 186, the reconstruction revealed that because of the foliage of a large oak tree, the rifleman did not have a clear view from frame 166 to frame 210 and that at all times after frame 210 there was no obstruction from the sixth-floor window.

We also found in the reconstruction that Governor Connally was in a position from frame 207 to frame 225 to receive a bullet that would have caused the wounds he suffered. Marks were placed on "stand-ins" for the President and Connally to show the locus of their wounds. The reconstruction showed the marks to be on a straight line with the rifle barrel. In the words of FBI expert Robert Frazier, "They both are in direct alignment with the telescopic sight at the window. The Governor is immediately behind the President in the field of view."

There was corroborating evidence; the fibers in the back of President Kennedy's shirt were pointed inward, and the fibers on the front of his shirt were pointed outward. The ballistic tests also showed that the bullet that was found on Connally's stretcher was capable of causing the wounds to both the president (which would have had little effect on the bullet itself) and Connally.

At the time the first shot struck President Kennedy, the limousine was approximately 180 feet from the window of the depository. Oswald's rifle had a four-power scope, which made the actual distance appear to be only 45 feet—15 yards.

The limousine was moving directly away from the line of fire. In other words, it was what is known as a "line shot" rather than a cross-shot, with the target moving across the horizon. A "cross-shot" requires far more movement on the part of the rifleman and the rifle from the first shot to the next shot than a line shot, where the rifle is pointed directly at an object that is moving either toward or away from the rifle. You can simulate this yourself by holding an imaginary rifle and aiming at a target moving across from your left to right or right to left and comparing this with an imaginary target moving on a straight line away from you.

The second and fatal shot struck Kennedy when the limousine was only 265 feet from the window of the depository—about 88 yards. Through a four-power scope, this made the president appear only 22 yards away. In fact, from the viewpoint of the rifleman, the shots were relatively easy.

Since 1963, several panels of medical experts have examined the evidence to determine whether the "single-bullet theory" was correct and whether there was any evidence of any shots striking Kennedy from any direction other than the rear. All these panels have concluded that indeed there was a bullet that entered the back of Kennedy's neck, exited from the front, and then struck Connally.

Moreover, since 1963, a new test known as "neutron-activation analysis" has been performed on the bullet fragments from Connally's wrist and the nearly whole bullet that fell off his stretcher. This test takes two samples of material and bombards them with neutrons and compares their radioactive characteristics. The comparison reveals the minute composition of these two samples, including any minor impurities, and if there are virtually none, the results will mean that the material is identical and came from the same source.

There were minute bullet fragments that had been removed from Connally's wrist. The physician who operated on that wrist said these fragments weighed less than a postage stamp. The Warren Commission critics have asserted that the single bullet, Exhibit 399, could not cause all of the damage it did because there was too much weight of bullet fragments that still remained in Connally and that since Exhibit 399 was nearly whole, it must have been a different bullet that struck his wrist.

But the wrist wounds could not have been caused by a pristine bullet. Otherwise, the wrist would have been shattered. The neutron-analysis test corroborated that, indeed, all of Connally's wounds had been caused by the single bullet.

That bullet, according to ballistic tests, lost little of its velocity as it passed through Kennedy's neck. It struck no bones. The arguments of the Warren Commission critics that Exhibit 399 could not be the single bullet did not depend on whether the bullet had passed through Kennedy's neck but really on the argument that two different bullets struck Connally. His physicians disputed this, the wound ballistics' tests on the wrists of cadavers disputed this, and all of the neutron-analysis tests refuted these claims. The overall record is clear: One shot did indeed strike the back of President Kennedy's neck, exited in the front, and hit Connally, causing all of his wounds. And the fatal shot did strike President Kennedy from behind.

# 9

---

# Leaving the Scene of the Crime

At the time of the assassination, most Texas School Book Depository employees were watching the motorcade with friends either inside the building or outside. Lee Harvey Oswald was inside the depository—but he wasn't with any other employee. He was the only employee who had access to the sixth floor and who was inside the building at the time of the assassination and who left the scene shortly after the assassination and did not return.

The last person to see Oswald before the assassination was Charles Douglas Givens—on the sixth floor with a clipboard. Oswald was a warehouse employee who filled book orders. He and other warehouse workers would use a clipboard to carry the order forms for books. After seeing Oswald on the sixth floor, Givens left the building to watch the motorcade. He came back to the building later that afternoon.

Oswald's clipboard was not found until ten days after the assassination. Frankie Kaiser, another depository employee, was searching for a teacher's edition of *Catholic Handbooks*, copies of which were stored in the northwest corner of the sixth floor near the stairway. While looking for these books, Kaiser found Oswald's clipboard. It was hidden by book cartons a few feet from where Oswald's rifle had been found: "right next to the stairway—right in the corner." The FBI was notified, and the clipboard was turned over. On the clipboard were unfilled orders for books. The date of the unfilled orders: "November 22, 1963."

After the rifle was found, police started checking all depository employees who had access to the sixth floor. The employees themselves noticed that Oswald was missing. In the words of James Jarman, Jr.:

"When we started to line up to show our identification, quite a few of us asked where was Lee. That is what we called him, and he wasn't anywhere around. We started asking each other, have you seen Lee Oswald, and they said no."

The first employee to see Oswald after the assassination was Superintendent Roy S. Truly, who encountered Oswald on the second floor of the building. Oswald was next seen by Mrs. Robert A. Reid. She saw him on the second floor, headed toward the front stairway leading to the front door.

At the time of his arrest Oswald had a bus transfer in his possession showing that he tried to take a bus from downtown Dallas to his rooming house in the Oak Cliff section of Dallas—not too far from the Tippit murder scene. Every bus driver in Dallas had a distinctive punch mark he put on every transfer he issued. Oswald could have caught the bus in front of the depository. Instead, he walked several blocks east and boarded a westbound bus. By happenstance, Mary E. Bledsoe, a former landlady of Oswald's, was on the bus and recognized him. The buses were backed up in traffic. For some reason, Oswald was in a hurry. He asked the driver for a transfer, left the bus, walked two blocks, and entered a taxicab.

Instead of having the cab drop him off in front of his rooming house, he had it drop him off a few blocks away. Oswald was next seen at the rooming house around one o'clock. He came in, and a minute or two later, he left. Then at around 1:15 P.M., he was at the scene of the Tippit murder, where he was identified by the six witnesses.

Assassination sensationalists have tried to assert that Oswald could not have gotten there so quickly.

I personally reconstructed the time sequences. It was clearly feasible for Oswald to have gone from the depository to his rooming house, where he picked up his revolver, and then to the Tippit murder scene. (I don't believe he would have taken his revolver into the depository, because if he had been searched after the assassination, the concealed weapon would have been found. That would have cast great suspicion on him and resulted in his immediate detention. Carrying a concealed weapon is a crime.)

At the rooming house, Oswald was registered under the name of "O. H. Lee" rather than Lee Harvey Oswald. He lived in a small room that was furnished, including curtains and curtain rods. Those particular furnishings were of special import.

During the week, Oswald stayed at his rooming house. On the weekends, he rode to the Dallas suburb of Irving, where Marina and their children were staying with the family of Ruth Paine. Next door to Ruth Paine lived Linnie Mae Randle, her husband, and her brother, Buell Frazier, an employee at the depository. Frazier gave Oswald rides on the weekends to and from Irving.

The assassination of President Kennedy occurred on a Friday. Ordinarily, Oswald would not have gone to Irving to visit his wife until Friday night. However, on Thursday, November 21, on the day before the assassination, Oswald asked Frazier for a ride home to Irving. The next morning, November 22, Oswald got into Frazier's car to ride back to the depository. There was a major difference—apart from the fact that Oswald was riding back on a Friday instead of on the Monday after the weekend. For the first time, Oswald did not bring his lunch that day. In the words of Frazier:

"When he rode with me, I say he always brought lunch except that one day on Nov. 22. He didn't bring his lunch that day."

On the Thursday when Oswald asked to ride home with Frazier, in the words of Frazier:

"And he says, 'I am going home to get some curtain rods.' He said, 'You know, put in an apartment.' "

The next morning Frazier arose at about six-thirty in the morning and started eating breakfast at about seven. While Frazier was eating in the kitchen, his mother "just happened to glance up and saw this man, you know, who was Lee looking in the window for me and she said, 'Who is that?' "

"And I said, 'That is Lee,'. . . He just looked through the kitchen window."

Interrogator Ball then asked Frazier: "When your mother mentioned, 'Who is that,' you looked up and saw Lee Oswald in the kitchen window?"

FRAZIER: "I just saw him for a split second and when he saw I saw him, I guess he heard me say, 'Well, it is time to go,' and he walked down by the back door there."

REP. GERALD FORD: "When he would go with you on Monday, on any Monday, was this the same procedure for . . . getting in contact with you?"

FRAZIER: "You mean coming in there and looking through the window?"

FORD: "Yes."

FRAZIER: "No, sir; it wasn't. I say, that is the first time he had ever done that. I say, most times I would usually call him, you know, I was already out in the car fixing to go out the driveway there, and, you know, around to pick him up if he hadn't come down but most times, once in a while I picked him up at the house and another time he was already coming down the sidewalk to the house when I was fixing to pick him up and I usually picked him up around the corner there."

Frazier testified that both entered the car at about the same time.

BALL: "When you got in the car did you say anything to him or did he say anything to you?"

FRAZIER: "Let's see, when I got in the car I have a kind of habit of glancing over my shoulder and so at that time I noticed there was a package laying on the back seat. I didn't pay too much attention and I said, 'What's the package, Lee?'

"And he said, 'Curtain rods,' and I said, 'Oh, yes, you told me you was going to bring some today.' "

As Frazier walked to the depository that morning, Oswald walked ahead of him, carrying the paper bag into the building. (Frazier said he thought he saw the package being carried by Oswald under Oswald's armpit, but the rifle was actually too long to be carried that way.)

There is corroborating evidence for the curtain-rod story. Frazier's sister, Mrs. Randle, testified that on Thursday evening (November 21) she saw Oswald get out of her brother's car. Her brother told her that Oswald had come home to get some curtain rods. The next morning, she saw Oswald walking toward the house and her brother's car, carrying a long package wrapped in brown paper.

There were additional factors pointing toward Oswald's guilt. In Oswald's belongings was a picture of him holding a rifle and wearing his pistol. Oswald, in his interrogation, claimed he never owned a rifle. When confronted with the picture, he claimed it was a composite made by superimposing his head on someone else's body holding a rifle. However, what Oswald did not know was that if someone has a negative of a picture, and a camera, there are individualistic markings by which it is possible to determine whether that negative came from the particular camera to the exclusion of all other cameras in the world. The negative of the picture was found as was Oswald's camera. It was determined that the picture was taken by Oswald's camera. Marina Oswald later admitted she took the picture.

Why did Oswald lie about the picture? Why did he lie about the rifle? He claimed he purchased his pistol in Fort Worth, whereas, in fact, it had been acquired by mail and shipped to the same post-office box as the rifle. Why did he lie about this? Oswald refused to answer questions about the alias "A. J. Hidell," which was used to acquire the pistol and rifle. Why? Why did he lie when he claimed that he was having lunch with "Junior" (Junior Jarman) at the time of the assassination when Junior Jarman was on the fifth floor with two other depository employees, Harold Norman and Bonnie Ray Williams.

There were other lies by Oswald during his interrogation. He claimed he didn't carry a long brown package into the building with "curtain rods" on the morning of the assassination. Rather, he claimed that it was his lunch. He claimed he didn't purchase the rifle from Klein's Sporting Goods Co. in Chicago. He claimed he didn't shoot Connally. He claimed he didn't shoot Kennedy. He claimed he didn't shoot Tippit.

There was a pattern in Oswald's lies. He only lied when there were major factors involved in the overall investigation of the two murders. He didn't lie about unimportant matters. I have elaborated on this for reasons that will soon be apparent.

There was one other lie that Oswald repeatedly told in the course of his interrogation. He said he had not been to Mexico City in September when in fact he had. Why would he have lied about this? It was a question that has remained unanswered but that forms the foundation of my personal theory about the motive for the assassination—a theory that did not fully develop until I served with the Rockefeller Commission and learned about CIA assassination plots directed against Fidel Castro. I shall return to this point shortly.

# 10

## What Might Have Been

The last-minute decision of Postal Inspector Holmes to see Captain Fritz on November 24 was just one of a whole series of "what might have beens." There were other examples that could have prevented the murder of Oswald by Ruby. On Sunday morning, November 24, two members of the Dallas Police Department suggested to Captain Fritz that Oswald should be taken from the building by another exit, leaving the press "waiting in the basement . . . and we could be to the county jail before anyone knew what was taking place." But Dallas police chief Jesse E. Curry had yielded to the pressures of the media and promised that Oswald would be transferred when newsmen could take pictures.

One vivid description of how the media inundated the police department occurred in the testimony of Detective James R. Leavelle. He was being interrogated by Joe Ball and Samuel Stern. According to Leavelle, the hallway inside the police station was crowded with reporters, newsmen, and television cameramen. ". . . in fact, I was plumb up to my chin with those people. . . . If you ever slopped hogs and throw down a pail of slop and saw them rush after it you would understand what that was like up there—about the same situation. . . . One time when I was trying to escort some witness out of there . . . I stopped and I looked down and there was a joker had a camera stuck between my legs taking pictures so that's just some indication of how they acted."

In fact, when Oswald was being transferred, the press was supposed to remain behind an iron railing in the basement. If they had done this, the railing would have prevented Ruby from rushing forward to shoot Oswald.

There is one "what might have been" that could have prevented the murder of Tippit. When news photographer Robert Hill Jackson, who was riding in the presidential motorcade, saw a gun barrel being withdrawn in the assassination window and yelled out to his colleagues, "There is the gun!" he and his colleagues had two choices. One was to immediately contact a policeman, who was stationed on the street, tell him what they had seen, and ask him to seal off the building. The other was to continue in the motorcade and chase the presidential limousine. There were four photographers in Jackson's car. Not one contacted a policeman. If this had been done and if the building had been sealed immediately instead of several minutes after the assassination, Oswald would not have had an opportunity to leave, and Tippit would not have been killed.

There was incident after incident of happenstance involving the assassination of Kennedy, tending to prove again and again the absence of any conspiracy. In early October 1963, a day or two after he returned to Dallas from Mexico City, Oswald applied for a position with the Padgett Printing Corp., located a number of blocks from the parade route ultimately selected for the motorcade. Oswald impressed the plant superintendent, who checked out Oswald's prior job references, one of which was from a firm for which Oswald had done photography work from October 1962 to April 1963. When that reference was checked, Oswald was not recommended, and on the reverse side of Oswald's application to the Padgett Printing Corp. the plant superintendent noted: "Bob Stovall does not recommend this man. He was released because of his record as a troublemaker—has Communistic tendencies." If only the reference had not been checked out, or if only the comment about Communist tendencies had not been made, Oswald might have been hired by Padgett and thus far removed from the motorcade route at the time of the assassination.

How did Oswald ultimately get the job at the Texas School Book Depository—perhaps the only place in Dallas where someone could have looked out of a high window and aimed a rifle at the motorcade with a direct-line shot? On October 14, Ruth Paine was having lunch with some neighbors, one of whom was Linnie Mae Randle, who said that her brother, Buell Frazier, had recently been hired as a schoolbook order filler at the depository. Linnie Mae thought that they might need additional help.

When Paine returned home, she called the depository and spoke to Superintendent Roy Truly. I took Truly's testimony. I asked him, "What did Mrs. Paine say, and what did you say?"

"She said, 'Mr. Truly'—words to this effect, you understand— 'Mr. Truly, you don't know who I am but I have a neighbor whose brother works for you. I don't know what his name is. But he tells his sister that you are very busy. And I am just wondering if you can use another man,' or words to that effect.

"And I told Mrs.—she said, 'I have a fine young man living here with his wife and baby, and his wife is expecting a baby—another baby, in a few days, and he needs work desperately.'

"Now, this is not absolutely—this is as near as I can remember the conversation over the telephone.

"And I told Mrs. Paine that—to send him down, and I would talk to him—that I didn't have anything in mind for him of a permanent nature, but if he was suited, we could possibly use him for a brief time."

BELIN: "Was there anything else from that conversation that you remember at all, or not?"

TRULY: "No. I believe that was the first and the last time I talked to Mrs. Paine."

That afternoon, the "fine young man" came down to Roy Truly's office for an interview. He was hired and went to work the next day, October 16. His pay was $1.25 an hour. This was nearly a month before the determination of the motorcade route in Dallas.

If Marina Oswald's neighbors had not been so friendly and concerned about her welfare, Oswald never would have obtained the job at the depository. If they had waited just one day, Oswald probably never would have taken the job, because the very next day the Texas Employment Commission tried to reach him to tell him of another job that paid $100 more per month. Because Oswald had already been hired at the depository, the Texas Employment Commission referred the job to someone else.

There was another tragic aspect of Superintendent Truly's hiring of Oswald. Originally, it was to be for a "brief time." The Texas School Book Depository Company is a private corporation in the business of selling school books. The books were stocked in the basement and first-floor areas and on the fifth and sixth floors and part of the seventh floor. The books from publishers for whom Oswald filled orders were generally stocked on the first and sixth floors, and depository employees like Oswald would pick up orders on the first floor, put them on a clipboard, and then go to the various storage areas to pick up the books. When schools are opened in the early fall, book orders increase. Then, they rapidly decline. As a matter of fact, one other employee, who was also hired on a temporary basis, was let go on November 15.

But Roy Truly wanted to try to find work to keep the men on the job. So he decided to have some of them lay a new plywood floor. His voice dropped when he testified:

"Actually, the end of our fall rush—if it hadn't existed a week or 2 weeks longer, or if we had not been using some of our regular boys putting down this plywood, we would not have had any need for Lee Oswald at the time, which is a tragic thing for me to think about."

Bonnie Ray Williams testified that as the new floor was laid, he and other employees moved cartons from the west side of the sixth floor to the east side. Oswald was able to readily move a few of these cartons to make a "shield" around the southeast-corner window on the sixth floor so that it could not be seen from other portions of the sixth floor at the time of the assassination. He then took some of the lighter cartons marked "Rolling Readers" and used them as a gun rest right by the window. When we had these examined, we found a palm print and a fingerprint of Oswald's. However, we did not place any great significance on these and other prints of Oswald's on the cartons by the assassination window because it could be argued that he had handled these in the course of his duties as an employee.

There were other tricks of fate. Marina Oswald almost single-handedly might have prevented the assassination. Marina and her husband had a stormy relationship. She was always complaining that he did not make enough money. She ridiculed his political views. The weekend before the assassination, she told him not to come home to see her, ostensibly because Mrs. Paine was planning a birthday party for one of Marina's children.

On Sunday night, November 17, Ruth Paine and Marina Oswald tried to call Oswald at his rooming house in Dallas. They could not reach him because he was registered under the name of "O. H. Lee." When Oswald called his wife and told her why she could not reach him, he used the rationale that he did not want the FBI to know where he lived because they had visited him at his place of employment and he did not like this.* Marina Oswald hung up on her husband. He called back several times the next day, but she refused to talk to him.

Oswald's arrival at the Paine residence on Thursday evening, November 21, marks another crossroads that could have changed the course of history. The events of that evening, according to Marina Oswald's testimony in response to questions by Lee Rankin:

Q. "Did your husband give any reason for coming home on Thursday?"

A. "He said that he was lonely because he hadn't come home the preceding weekend, and he wanted to make his peace with me."

Q. "Did you say anything to him then?"

---

*Oswald had sought to defect to Russia and renounce his American citizenship. When he eventually returned to the United States, the FBI tried to keep track of him.

A. "He tried to talk to me but I would not answer him, and he was very upset."

Q. "Were you upset with him?"

A. "I was angry, of course. He was not angry—he was upset. I was angry. He tried very hard to please me. He spent quite a bit of time putting away diapers and played with the children on the street."

Q. "How did you indicate to him that you were angry with him?"

A. "By not talking to him."

Q. "And how did he show that he was upset?"

A. "He was upset over the fact that I would not answer him. He tried to start a conversation with me several times, but I would not answer. And he said that he didn't want me to be angry at him because this upsets him.

"On that day, he suggested that we rent an apartment in Dallas. He said that he was tired of living alone and perhaps the reason for my being so angry was the fact that we were not living together. That if I want to he would rent an apartment in Dallas tomorrow—that he didn't want me to remain with Ruth any longer, but wanted me to live with him in Dallas.

"He repeated this not once but several times, but I refused. And he said that once again I was preferring my friends to him, and that I didn't need him."

Q. "What did you say to that?"

A. "I said it would be better if I remained with Ruth until the holidays, he would come, and we would all meet together. That this was better because while he was living alone and I stayed with Ruth, we were spending less money. And I told him to buy me a washing machine, because with two children it became too difficult to wash by hand."

Q. "What did he say to that?"

A. "He said he would buy me a washing machine."

Q. "What did you say to that?"

A. "Thank you. That it would be better if he bought something for himself—that I would manage."

The tragedy of all of this is compounded when Marina Oswald later testified that her showing of anger was put on:

Q. "Did the quarrel that you had at that time seem to cause him to be more disturbed than usual?"

A. "No, not particularly. At least he didn't talk about that quarrel when he came. Usually he would remember about what happened. This time he didn't blame me for anything, didn't ask me any questions, just wanted to make up."

Q. "I understood that when you didn't make up he was quite disturbed and you were still angry, is that right?"

A. "I wasn't really very angry. I, of course, wanted to make up with him. But I gave the appearance of being very angry. I was smiling inside, but I had a serious expression on my face."

Q. "And as a result of that, did he seem to be more disturbed than usual?"

A. "As always, as usual. Perhaps a little more. At least when he went to bed he was very upset."

That night Oswald went to bed before his wife. She did not speak to him when she joined him there, although she thought he was awake. The next morning, he left for work before anyone else arose. For the first time, he left his wedding ring in a cup on the dresser in his room. He also left $170 in a wallet in a dresser drawer. This was for him a relatively large sum to leave his wife. He took with him $13.87 and the long brown package that Frazier and Mrs. Randle saw him carry and that he was to take to the depository.

What would have happened had Marina offered to make up with Lee Harvey Oswald? What would have happened if Marina Oswald in reply to the plea of her husband had said, "Yes, let us live together; let us rent an apartment in Dallas tomorrow"?

# 11

# The Obvious Conclusion

One wonderful thing about our jury system is that practicality and common sense generally play such a major role in its operation. Those same ingredients also form a basic part of the instincts of most members of the working press.

Seymour Hersh, who wrote the initial *New York Times* stories in December 1974 alleging unlawful CIA activities in the United States, said one of the most significant factors, from his perspective, disproving the claims of Kennedy assassination sensationalists was that their theories of conspiracy involved so many people that, as a matter of common sense, someone would have let something slip. In turn, this slip would have been discovered, or someone would have confessed to involvement in a conspiracy.

Indeed, the 1986 book *Reasonable Doubt* (Henry Hurt) features the purported assassination confession of Robert Easterling. Who was Easterling? A person who was committed to a mental institution who claims the real assassin departed from the depository by descending from a window by means of a rope ladder (which, of course, must have been invisible) and who claims that the conspirators with whom he was working were planning in early 1963 to shoot the president from that building even though at the time no one knew of any plans of President Kennedy to visit Dallas, much less pass through downtown Dallas in an open limousine as a part of a motorcade.

The back cover of *Reasonable Doubt* contains a quotation from a speech by President Kennedy in February 1962 on the twentieth anniversary of the Voice of America:

> You are obliged to tell our story in a truthful way, to tell it, as Oliver Cromwell said about his portrait, "Paint us with all our blemishes and warts, all those things about us that may not be so immediately attractive."
>
> We compete with . . . those who are our adversaries who tell only the good stories. But the things that go bad in America, you must tell that also. And we hope that the bad and the good is sifted together by people of judgment and discretion and taste and discrimination, that they will realize what we are trying to do here. . . .
>
> We seek a free flow of information. . . . We are not afraid to entrust the American people with unpleasant facts, foreign ideas, alien philosophies, and competitive values. For a nation that is afraid to let its people judge the truth and falsehood in an open market is a nation that is afraid of its people.

It is clear to me that author Henry Hurt in *Reasonable Doubt* does not tell his story "in a truthful way" and instead joins the ranks of the assassination sensationalists and conspiracy buffs who seek to hide the truth. There are dozens of examples. Typically is one that relates to what Hurt calls "most persuasive" evidence of conspiracy. Hurt writes:

> This evidence is highly suggestive of the existence of an ongoing manipulation of Oswald's name and reputation. (It is separate from the evidence showing that Oswald himself was manipulated.) Toward what end remains speculative.
>
> In any accounting of these possibilities, one cannot overlook perhaps the most persuasive of all "other Oswald" sightings. It happened about fifteen minutes after the assassination, well after the official version insists that Lee Harvey Oswald left Dealey Plaza. As discussed earlier,

Roger Craig, a highly respected police officer, saw a man come running toward the street from the direction of the Texas School Book Depository and get into a car driven by a man of Latin appearance. They drove away. This was perfectly corroborated by an independent witness. Later that afternoon, the policeman swore that the man he had seen running from the Book Depository and jumping into the car was now in custody—Lee Harvey Oswald.

Since Hurt asserts that this is the "most persuasive" evidence, it must be examined in light of the record. As a part of that record, the first matter to look at is how reliable a witness is Roger D. Craig. I took Craig's testimony in Dallas. I asked him about his claim that around fifteen minutes after the assassination he had seen a man running toward Elm Street and getting into a light-colored station wagon. The man he saw getting into the car he said was about five feet eight or nine, 140 to 150 pounds. The driver of the car, according to Craig, "struck me as a Negro."

Craig said that later that afternoon he went into the police station to the office of Capt. Will Fritz, the head of the Homicide Division, who was in charge of the investigation. Oswald was in an interrogation room with Captain Fritz and two other people —a representative from the Secret Service and one from the FBI. According to Roger Craig, when he stepped inside the room, Captain Fritz asked Craig whether the suspect (who was Oswald) was the man he had seen. Craig said that Oswald was the same person, and then he said that Oswald interrupted and said, "Everybody will know who I am now."

No one else present remembers Oswald saying to anyone in substance, "Everybody will know who I am now." If he had said this, it would have been akin to an admission of guilt. Since at least three people disagreed with Craig, I was skeptical about whether Craig was accurate in his identification of Oswald as the man running down the hill. Single eyewitness identification at some distance is often inaccurate.

Furthermore:

1. Captain Fritz testified that Craig never even came inside the interrogation room. He said that Craig may have seen Oswald

through the glass, but he did not step inside. Fritz was interrogated by Joseph Ball about whether Oswald said in substance, "Everybody will know who I am now." In response to whether such a thing occurred, Fritz said: "No, sir; it didn't. That man is not telling a true story if that is what he said."

2. Equally relevant is the testimony of Elizabeth Reed, who worked in the second-floor office of the depository and who came back into the building shortly after the assassination—a time that she estimated was about two minutes after the assassination—and saw Oswald walking through her office toward the front stairway to leave the building. When I took her testimony in Dallas, we reconstructed the events, and it did not take much longer than two minutes. Oswald would have been long gone from the scene fourteen or fifteen minutes after the assassination.

3. Further evidence comes from Mary Bledsoe, a former landlady of Oswald's who was riding a bus in the vicinity of the depository a short time after the assassination. The bus was scheduled to leave the corner of St. Paul and Elm Street at 12:30 P.M., heading west on Elm Street toward the depository. It was about seven or eight blocks from the depository when the bus driver, Cecil J. McWatters, testified that Oswald boarded his bus. Mary Bledsoe also testified that Oswald, whom she had known from before, boarded the bus.

4. The most powerful evidence of all was that when Oswald was apprehended, he had a bus transfer in his possession, and the bus transfer was from the bus driven by Cecil McWatters.

Instead of giving his readers relevant information, Hurt fails to disclose relevant facts and makes an outrageous false claim: "A persuasive claim can be made that the conclusions rendered ten months after Kennedy's assassination were largely foregone from the moment of the panel's inception." The very fact that Hurt makes such a suggestion is illustrative of the underlying fallacy in his entire book.

With the knowledge that Oswald had the capacity to kill, and indeed did kill Officer Tippit approximately forty-five minutes after the assassination, and with the additional knowledge that the pistol used in the Tippit murder was purchased by mail order under the same alias and sent to the same post-office box in Dallas as the Kennedy assassination rifle, number C-2766, the evidence in the murder of John F. Kennedy is placed in clear perspective.

The starting point is the testimony of Howard Brennan, who saw the gunman take aim and fire the last shot. Brennan's testimony is reinforced by the newsmen in the motorcade, including Robert Jackson, who saw the rifle being withdrawn. It is also reinforced by Amos Euins, who saw the rifle and the gunman, and by the testimony of the three employees watching the motorcade on the fifth floor, below the assassination window. Harold Norman heard the cartridge cases hit the floor above him and also heard the bolt action of the rifle. His testimony is reinforced by the testimony of Bonnie Ray Williams and James Jarman, Jr.

As Brennan and Euins reported their observations to the police, the depository was searched. In the southeast corner of the sixth floor, immediately above Harold Norman, three cartridge cases were found. In the northwest corner of the sixth floor, near the stairway, a 6.5 mm. Mannlicher-Carcano rifle, serial number C-2766, was found stuffed between boxes. In the presidential limousine, two bullet fragments of sufficient size to be ballistically identifiable were found. In Parkland Memorial Hospital, a nearly whole bullet rolled off a stretcher used to carry Governor Connally.

Scientific ballistic evidence proved that the cartridge cases found at the southeast corner of the sixth floor of the depository, the two ballistically identifiable bullet fragments in the front seat of the presidential limousine, and the bullet found at Parkland Memorial Hospital all came from that rifle, number C-2766, to the exclusion of all other weapons in the world.

Who was the owner of that weapon? Lee Harvey Oswald. Oswald had purchased the rifle through the mail from Klein's Sporting Goods Co. in Chicago. He used the alias of A. J. Hidell, the same alias used to purchase the pistol. This same man, Oswald, closely met the physical description of Howard Brennan as Brennan saw the gunman fire the last shot. Oswald had ready access to the sixth floor of the depository, and he was the only employee who was inside the building at the time of the assassination who had access to the sixth floor and who left the building shortly after the assassination.

There is all of the other evidence: walking seven blocks east to board a bus, then leaving the bus to enter a taxi, taking the taxi to a place several blocks away from his rooming house, the curtain-rod story, the homemade paper bag found by the assassination window that was undoubtedly used to carry the unassembled rifle that contained a fingerprint and palm print of Oswald, the clipboard with his unfilled orders found on the sixth floor by the back stairway, the ballistic testimony, the responses of Oswald during his interrogation in which he denied owning the rifle that he purchased, denied that the picture of him and the rifle was a true picture, denied that he carried a long package into the depository on the morning of November 22, claimed that he was having lunch at the time of the assassination with "Junior" when he was not, denying that he shot Officer Tippit.

Despite Oswald's denials that he shot Officer Tippit and President Kennedy, when you put all of the facts together and couple them with the evidence showing that Oswald murdered J. D. Tippit, there can be no reasonable doubt that Lee Harvey Oswald murdered John F. Kennedy.

# 12

---

# The Paradox of the Birth of the CIA

Today most attacks on the CIA come from the left of the political spectrum. At its birth, however, most of the criticism came from the right.

The origins of the CIA go back to the days before World War II. President Franklin Roosevelt called on William J. Donovan, a New York attorney, to draft a plan for an intelligence service, and that resulted in the creation of the Office of Strategic Services (OSS) during the Second World War. Although the OSS did commendable work, there was lack of overall intelligence coordination. For instance, the FBI had jurisdiction in Latin America as a result of its collection of intelligence dating back to the 1930s, but there was substantial friction between the FBI, the military, and the OSS during the war. This friction was counterproductive to national needs.

In November 1944, General Donovan submitted to President Roosevelt an overall plan for separating the intelligence services from the Joint Chiefs of Staff and creating a centralized intelligence agency under the direct supervision of the president. Donovan's proposal suggested that the new agency would have authority to conduct "subversive operations abroad" but would have "no police or law enforcement functions, either at home or abroad."

Donovan's proposal was opposed by the State Department, the navy, and the FBI. The State Department proposed an interdepartmental committee organization chaired by the secretary of state. The navy wanted its own intelligence service. J. Edgar Hoover wanted the FBI to take charge of all "civilian" intelligence throughout the world and leave "military" intelligence to the armed services. After World War II, the controversy came before Harry Truman, and he made a key decision.

On January 22, 1946, President Truman issued a directive establishing the Central Intelligence Group (CIG), which became the direct ancestor of the CIA. The CIG was a central coordinating agency, but it did not replace the departmental intelligence services already in existence, although the FBI abruptly withdrew its intelligence service from Latin America.

The FBI refused to turn over to the newly established CIG the tremendous sources of information and agent contacts that it had cultivated since the 1930s.

J. Edgar Hoover undermined the national security of this country by refusing to cooperate with the CIG and ultimately the CIA in developing a program for collecting intelligence from Latin America. Hoover never relented, and the CIA had to develop its own sources of intelligence in Latin America without any substantial benefit from what had been cultivated by the FBI for more than a decade.

Legislation was introduced in Congress in 1947 to establish a central intelligence agency. The statute became known as the National Security Act of 1947. In the congressional hearings and debates, most senators and representatives recognized the need for a centralized intelligence agency that would coordinate the collecting of intelligence abroad and would supply the president and his advisers with facts and information necessary for them to make determinations on political, economic, and military conditions abroad. However, there was considerable congressional reservation expressed over abuses that might arise from the creation of this agency. The greatest concerns generally came from conservative Republicans like Rep. Clarence Brown of Ohio. He said in 1947:

> I am very much interested in seeing the United States have as fine a foreign military and naval intelligence as they can possibly have, but I am not interested in setting up here in the United States any particular policy [sic] agency under any President, and I do not care what his name may be, and just allow him to have a gestapo of his own if he wants to have it.
>
> Every now and then you get a man that comes up in power and that has an imperialist idea.

Representative Brown also expressed reservations when he questioned Gen. Hoyt Vandenberg, former air force general who became the director of the CIG. Brown asked Vandenberg whether there should be additional limitations attached to the legislation establishing the new Central Intelligence Agency (CIA) because the CIA "might possibly affect the rights and privileges of the people of the United States. . . ."

General Vandenberg replied:

"No, sir; I do not think there is anything in the bill, since it is all foreign intelligence, that can possibly affect any of the privileges of the people of the United States. . . . I can see no real reason for limiting it at this time."

In the newspapers of this country, the leading skepticism came from the *Chicago Tribune*, which in the late 1940s was the bastion of conservative Republicanism. The *Tribune* referred to the CIA as a possible American "gestapo."

More recently, little criticism has been leveled against the CIA by political leaders who call themselves conservatives despite their traditional concerns about the ever-increasing encroachment of big government, big business, and big labor on the rights of the individual. This is inconsistent with sound conservative philosophy.

There are times when the CIA fails. But there are also instances—the great majority of times—when the CIA does not fail. On the whole, its people are as good as, or perhaps even better than, the people of virtually every other government department or bureau. But because agency activities are inherently secret and because such a wide area of authority rests in the director of central intelligence (DCI), who reports directly to the president, the agency is subject to abuse. The actions of DCI William Casey in the sale of arms to Iran in exchange for hostages and the diversion of profits to the Contras in Nicaragua represent a recent example of how the CIA is subject to abuse by the president or the agency head.

# 13

## The CIA Investigation
## Begins

On December 22, 1974, a front-page story in the *New York Sunday Times* written by investigative reporter Seymour Hersh charged that there had been massive illegal domestic spying by the CIA—something it was forbidden to do. There were other charges also, including claims that the CIA had been illegally opening U.S. mail in direct contravention of federal statutes.

These charges caused immediate national concern—particularly in the aftermath of Watergate. President Ford attempted to meet the problem head-on by appointing, on January 5, 1975, the "Commission on CIA Activities Within the United States," and Vice-President Nelson Rockefeller was named chairman. Other members were Ronald Reagan, former governor of California; John T. Connor, secretary of commerce in the Johnson administration; C. Douglas Dillon, undersecretary of the treasury in the Kennedy administration; Erwin Griswold, former dean of the Harvard Law School and former solicitor general of the United States; Lane Kirkland, secretary-treasurer of the AFL-CIO for many years (who in 1980 was elected president of the labor organization);

General Lyman Lemnitzer, former head of the Joint Chiefs; and Edgar Shannon, former president of the University of Virginia. The presidential order establishing the commission directed that a report be completed in three months.

Within twenty-four hours there were objections to the composition of the eight-man panel. Many people felt that the commission was not independent enough from government to ensure that there would be a full investigation into the charges. Congress started to get into the act to be sure there would be no cover-up.

Sen. William Proxmire charges that the panel was "very one-sided" and asserted that the choice of Vice-President Rockefeller as commission chairman "leaves something to be desired." George Wilson, writing for the *Washington Post*, asserted:

> The public record indicates that some of the members [of the commission] have had dealings with the Agency in the past.
>
> For instance, Vice-President Rockefeller was a member of the President's Foreign Intelligence Advisory Board, which had responsibility for overseeing intelligence activities and making recommendations. C. Douglas Dillon in his work with the Council on Foreign Relations in New York as well as in his capacity as Under Secretary of State had had relationships with the Agency.

Tom Wicker, in the *New York Times* on January 7, wrote: "The 'blue ribbon' commission appointed by President Ford to protect the public against domestic spying by the CIA looks suspiciously like a goat set to guard a cabbage patch. Having the CIA investigated by such a group is like having the Mafia audited by its own accountants."

A *New York Times* editorial on the same day declared, "The commission named by President Ford to investigate charges of domestic spying by the Central Intelligence Agency would inspire greater confidence if so many of its members did not have close ties to the national security establishment."

It was within this framework that President Ford, on January 7, brought forth my name for consideration as executive director of the CIA commission.

I met with Vice-President Nelson Rockefeller in his office in the Old Executive Office Building just west of the White House.

I told him that there would have to be a first-rate legal staff. He concurred. We intensively discussed the nature of the work. I talked about the similarities and dissimilarities between the CIA investigation and our investigation of the Kennedy assassination.

If the commission faced a crisis with the nation's press upon the announcement of its composition, I faced a different kind of crisis of confidence by some members of the commission because of my strong advocacy of individual constitutional rights and my great concern for the right of privacy.

The initial rumblings emanated from a newspaper interview I gave after word of my impending appointment leaked out of Washington. The newspaper story was featured on the front page of the *Des Moines Sunday Register*. The story began:

"David Belin will go to Washington this week with . . . a set of principles about the inviolable rights of individuals in a free society.

" 'I believe that government must be conducted in such a way that regardless of who is president, the rights of individual citizens are not going to be infringed,' says Belin."

By the time I had my first meeting with the commission, my "strict constructionist" comments had been widely publicized. When asked about them, I simply said, "I was accurately quoted, and this is what I believe." If anyone didn't like it, it was too late, for it had already been agreed that my appointment would be formally made as soon as I received the necessary security clearance.

The ramifications of my "strict constructionist" philosophy were magnified by two recommendations that I made to the commission at our first meeting, neither one of which was adopted.

After a few opening remarks to the commission at its January 13, 1975, meeting, I made some initial comments on how I felt the investigation should be conducted. Included was a recommendation that we have as many meetings open to the public as we could, except only for matters involving classified information or agents under cover whose identity should not be disclosed.

I felt the issue of open meetings was important because of the public concern about the CIA and about our investigation and also because of my belief that there is far too much secrecy in government.

The commission did not follow my recommendation.

Another recommendation I made at the first meeting also was overruled. Whenever witnesses testified before the commission, there would obviously be a court reporter present. But I also wanted a court reporter present when witnesses were not there and when the commission members were discussing the course of the investigation with one another. I made a strong argument that everything should be on the record. This is what was done on the Warren Commission. The counterargument was made that this would inhibit full and frank discussion. A vote was taken. Again, my recommendation lost.

There was one initial battle with Rockefeller that I did win. After much argument he finally agreed with my recommendation that we had to have more than ninety days to do a thorough job of our investigation.

# 14

# Eliciting CIA Cooperation

If you had the awesome task of investigating the CIA, what could you do to get the job done with a staff of only ten lawyers?

It quickly became clear that it was essential that we enlist the full cooperation of the CIA. If the CIA wanted to frustrate our investigation, it could make it extremely difficult for us and greatly extend the amount of time the investigation would take.

Therefore, I resolved to use a triple approach to seek the CIA's cooperation. First, I had to convince the agency that it was in its best interest to cooperate with the commission. Second, I had to make sure that it had a respect for the overall abilities of our staff so that the work could ultimately be done even without the agency's full cooperation. Finally, I had to toss in a third factor that would keep them off balance and worry them should there not be full cooperation: the possible use against the CIA of one of the CIA's own tools—the polygraph.

The CIA appointed a special liaison to the commission, E. H. (Hank) Knoche, whose title was "Assistant to the Director." (In 1976, Knoche was appointed deputy director of the CIA.)

CIA Director William E. Colby brought Knoche with him to the first meeting of the commission on January 13 when Colby gave extensive testimony that supposedly disclosed all improper CIA domestic activities.

Two days later, Knoche came to see me at our staff offices at 712 Jackson Place on the west side of Lafayette Square, only a half block from the White House and the Old Executive Office Building where the vice-president's offices were. Precautionary measures had been taken to make sure that our offices could not be "bugged," and the building was under twenty-four-hour guard.

In our first meeting, I told Knoche that I expected the agency to honor the executive order of the president that gave our commission the right to request from every executive department or agency "any information and assistance deemed necessary to carry out its functions under this Order." I also pointed out to Knoche the language of the presidential order that directed that "each department or agency shall furnish such information and assistance to the Commission, to the extent permitted by law."

Then I turned to a matter of great concern to the agency: the question of leaks. I pledged that every member of my staff would be a first-rate attorney outside of government and would be "leak-proof." (Secrecy was indeed maintained throughout the course of our investigation.)

At the end of my conference with Knoche, I decided to lay it on the line. The commission had a problem: We wanted to uncover the truth as quickly as possible. I told Knoche that the CIA had a problem: the preservation of its morale and integrity. After ten or fifteen minutes of discussion back and forth, I got to the heart of the matter:

"You, Mr. Knoche, believe that it is absolutely essential for the United States to have an effective intelligence agency under civilian control. I share that belief. You are concerned that this investigation will not destroy your agency. I share that concern.

"However, if you really care about the CIA, if you really want to do everything possible to see that the CIA is not destroyed by this investigation, then I would urge that you and your colleagues do everything possible to maximize the cooperation that the CIA gives to the commission and that you do everything possible to disclose every improper activity that the CIA may have undertaken which falls within the charter of our commission to investigate improper domestic activities of the CIA.

"I want you to know that if the CIA wants to make it difficult, we will take the time and get it by ourselves. But I want to draw an analogy between this investigation and the investigation of Watergate.

"If everything we now know about Watergate would have been known within the first two or three weeks after the Watergate break-in, it is probable that Richard Nixon would still be president.

"But one of the primary reasons for the downfall of Richard Nixon was that instead of there being immediate and prompt disclosure, there was a cover-up and the facts came out a drop at a time.

"If you want us to extract the facts a tooth at a time, we will be able to do it that way, but most probably we will destroy the agency in the process. On the other hand, if you can do everything possible to open your records to us and make full disclosure of all of the dirty linen, therein lies your best hope to survive this investigation.

"And the worst thing that could happen to the CIA would be for this commission to make its final report and then for the public to find out after the report had been submitted that it was not complete and that there was even more that had not yet come to the surface."

Knoche told me that one problem the CIA faced was that it was compartmentalized in its operations and the director might not know all of the dirty linen.

"Well," I replied, "Mr. Colby better undertake every effort and make sure that his subordinates know the problem so that they undertake every effort to get the information to us as fast as humanly possible."

Knoche called the next day to say he had talked to Colby about the need for full and prompt disclosure. He said Colby understood and wanted to come forward with more information. Supposedly, the reason this information had not been given by Colby at the first meeting of the commission was that his statements in that meeting were in response to the newspaper allegations. Now he wanted to come forward with additional "confessions" of possible improprieties by the CIA.

I immediately contacted the vice-president to let him know that additional information would be forthcoming from Colby—something that the vice-president really did not anticipate, for he had believed Colby's report on January 13 to be a full disclosure.

The only question was whether this would be a complete disclosure or whether it was just another layer or two that Colby felt we would ultimately get, anyway.

I asked for an immediate meeting with Colby during which I made the same presentation. Two more elements were added to complete my case.

The first was a memorandum from me to Colby on January 30. Ron Greene, a brilliant assistant counsel, played a major role in the drafting of this memorandum. I had reviewed an initial report that Colby made to the president on December 24, 1974. I had also reviewed formal statements that Colby had made to the commission at our initial meeting on January 13, 1975, and on January 27. There were other background materials that the CIA provided at the outset of our investigation.

What I did in my memorandum of January 30 to Colby was to take out a dragnet and ask for the CIA to assemble and review all of the documentary evidence that supported this CIA report to the president and to the Rockefeller Commission. I asked that the agency develop

> a summary of each relevant activity or program which will describe the activity or program in question and summarize the nature, extent and location within the agency of the existing documentation concerning it. This summary should include a statement describing the existing documentation concerning both (1) the initiation or approval of the activity or program, and (2) the actual conduct of the activity or program.

I then attached a list of thirty-one areas of inquiry I had gleaned from the reports presented to the president and to the Rockefeller Commission, and I attached to my list CIA code words pertaining to projects and asked for a description of the project or program associated with each code word.

I concluded my January 30 letter to Colby by stating:

> I understand that this request is quite a broad one, and that it will require extensive effort by your staff to give us a rapid response. However, it is essential that the Commission obtain access to this information and documentation if it is to fulfill the mission assigned by the President. Accordingly, I am certain that you will agree that the effort is necessary as part of the Commission's study. I would be happy to meet with your staff to discuss any problems which may arise in compiling this data and to determine an appropriate timetable for a response. We understand that many of the materials are already available, and we would appreciate receiving all of them no later than Friday, February 7, 1975.

That gave Colby and his staff only nine days. But I wanted to let them know that we meant business, and we meant business now.

Not everything was available by February 7. But a large body of material was delivered to us by that date, and additional materials were received shortly thereafter.

There was yet a third tack. I had read that the CIA gave lie-detector tests to a number of its agents to make sure they were not double agents.

Since the CIA itself used this technique, why not suggest that we might be interested in having statements by CIA people tested by a polygraph?

On January 16, 1975, I wrote Knoche:

> As an aid to our investigation, we would appreciate receiving from the Agency a memorandum setting forth a description of the Agency's policies concerning the use of polygraph examinations on CIA employees, contract personnel, or other individuals engaged in activities for or on behalf of the Agency. Copies of any regulations, rules, or

other documents of any type setting forth the Agency's policies should
be included, together with a description of the nature of any changes
in these policies within the past five years. Finally, the memorandum
should include a brief statement concerning the Agency's views relating
to the effectiveness and reliability of polygraph examinations.

We would appreciate receiving a reply by close of business on
Wednesday, January 22, 1975.

On January 22, the information was delivered.

Basically, the CIA, as an aid to investigation, uses a lie detector
to determine the security eligibility of persons for employment by
the agency or of these assigned to the agency. It is also used in
various sensitive agency installations and operations, including on
persons with continued access to very highly classified information.
Every applicant for employment by the CIA is notified at the time
he is given application forms of the agency's intent to use a polygraph examination in the course of his employment processing.
Before he undergoes a polygraph examination, his written consent
is obtained.

In the hands of an expert operator, a polygraph examination
has a very high degree of accuracy, the CIA stated.

After receiving confirmation that the CIA itself uses the polygraph and obtains the consent of all employees to submit to a
polygraph examination and after receiving confirmation that the
CIA believes the polygraph has a high degree of reliability in the
hands of an expert operator, I then told the CIA liaison Henry
Knoche:

"Since the CIA places great reliance and credibility on the polygraph, it may be appropriate for the commission to use the polygraph in the course of its investigation."

I did not say when we might want to use it. I did not say whom
I might want to undertake a polygraph examination. It could have
been Colby. It could have been anyone.

The key was the possibility that I might use it on anyone—and
that possibility, I felt, might have an impact on getting full cooperation from the CIA.

After all, what would happen if a high CIA officer were undergoing a polygraph examination and the operator asked, "Is there anything you know of that has not been disclosed to the Rockefeller Commission that might in any way be deemed an improper activity of the CIA?"

"Under whose orders did you do this?"

"Under whose orders did you not disclose this?"

Ultimately, the CIA realized it was in its best interest to cooperate and to make full disclosure to the commission. I cannot guarantee that we got everything—particularly because of the compartmentalized nature of the agency and the fact that people who might have been involved in improper activities in the past might not be living, might no longer be employed by the agency, or might just have covered up within their own department.

However, I believe we did obtain full disclosure of the various types of improper, unauthorized, and unlawful activities of the CIA within the United States.

As we wrote in our Rockefeller Commission Report:

> The Commission recognizes that no investigation of any governmental intelligence agency can be certain of uncovering every relevant fact. Nevertheless, the Commission believes that its investigation has disclosed the principal categories of CIA activities within the United States which might exceed its statutory authority or might adversely affect the rights of American citizens.

Neither of the two congressional investigations completed subsequent to our work disclosed any unlawful CIA activities within the United States that had not been covered by our investigation. That in itself I felt was independent evidence that we had reached our goal of making a complete report to the president.

Could we have done it without the basic cooperation of the CIA itself? I cannot be sure, except that at the very least it would have taken two or three times as long. And I believe that if there had been matters that we did not discover and that subsequently came to the surface, the ultimate loser would not be the Rockefeller Commission but rather the CIA itself.

I believe my analogy to Watergate was accurate. I also believe it is applicable to other situations, both in the past and those that might arise in the future. There is great virtue in prompt and full disclosure where errors have been made. *The refusal to admit wrong promptly can at times have greater adverse ramifications than the wrong itself.* It applies in relations between people. And it also applies in relations between agencies of our government and the citizens of this nation. In the aftermath of the Iranian arms scandal, President Reagan failed to recognize the importance of this axiom.

It is to the credit of the CIA that the agency people realized it was in their interest to start to cooperate, although at first it was with great hesitancy and suspicion. Nevertheless, they started to reveal everything. And this set the stage for the next confrontation: the question of CIA assassination plans directed against foreign leaders.

How was it that the CIA ever got involved in plots against the lives of foreign leaders? How could a presidential commission appointed to investigate "domestic activities" of the CIA bring within the scope of its authority matters pertaining to CIA operations abroad? What did the Rockefeller Commission investigation disclose? And why weren't the results of that investigation included in the Rockefeller Commission's final report?

# 15

## "The Family Jewels"

**I**t was hard to believe. Page after page of confession. The CIA itself had conducted its own internal investigation in 1973, under the direction of James R. Schlesinger, who was then CIA director. The results of that investigation had been one of the most tightly guarded secrets in Washington.

Here was the perfect example of the disadvantage that is inherent in a cover-up and in lack of prompt disclosure.

What would have happened if the CIA of its own volition in 1973 would have made a public confession of its sins with a pledge not to commit them again? There never would have been a Seymour Hersh exposé capturing the headlines of the *New York Sunday Times*. There never would have been an extensive congressional investigation of the magnitude conducted by the Senate Select Committee. And there probably would not have been an extensive investigation by a presidentially appointed group like the Rockefeller Commission.

In the mid-seventies, the inspector general became a focal point within the CIA for collection of information on questionable activities. In April 1973, James Schlesinger asked the inspector general's office to coordinate the CIA's internal investigation of possible involvement with Watergate matters. He followed this with a May 9, 1973, memorandum to all employees requesting that they report to him any activities that might have been improper.

Out of this internal investigation, the CIA prepared a 693-page document, and it was a summary from this document that was first presented by Hank Knoche. Appropriately, we called it "the family jewels."

As I pored over the first pages of the family jewels, I noticed a section that was blank. I asked Knoche why it was blank. He replied, "Those pages pertain to foreign matters and are not within your jurisdiction, because the commission's jurisdiction only pertains to CIA activities within the United States."

I replied that I was not going to let anyone else determine whether the matter fell within our jurisdiction.

"I don't want the CIA to be the judge of whether an improper activity falls within the jurisdiction of the commission. Let me be the judge—not the CIA."

Knoche was hesitant about what to do. He explained that the matters were extremely sensitive and he did not want me to have any copies of any such documents in my office, particularly when they might involve matters outside our jurisdiction.

I suggested a compromise. Instead of taking anything out of the CIA offices, where it might be subject to possible photocopying, I would go to CIA headquarters in Langley, Virginia, and view the documents to determine whether we had jurisdiction.

What happened next was one of the greatest shocks of my life: learning that my country had participated in assassination plots against foreign leaders in peacetime.

I was outraged. Under ordinary circumstances I would have immediately gone to the commission to advise them of what I had found. But these were not ordinary circumstances.

In the first place, as yet I had not gotten an extension of our original charter, and we faced an April 4 deadline for our report. I knew that getting into this area would prolong the investigation—a circumstance the vice-president strongly opposed. In the second place, there was a serious question in my mind whether we had authority to get into this whole area, since our authority under the presidential order was limited to activities occurring "within the United States." Yet I felt that the nature of what I was seeing was so abhorrent to the principles for which our country stands that there had to be a thorough investigation that would promptly bring the matter before the public. I knew I had access to the file; I did not know whether the congressional committees or anyone else would have access. I resolved to forge ahead without telling any member of the commission.

CIA assassination plans were not covered in any of the areas of investigation I had assigned to the other members of my staff. I decided to assume responsibility for the investigation of assassinations myself.

What I found was a sordid chapter in the history of our country—a chapter in which what we think of as the greatest democracy in the history of mankind adopted the philosophy of communism that the ends justify the means.

The family jewels contained references to CIA consideration of plots to assassinate Cuban premier Fidel Castro, Dominican Republic dictator Rafael Trujillo, and possibly Premier Patrice Lumumba of the Congo. By far the most extensive plans were directed against Premier Castro.

I did not find any evidence of overt activities within the United States involving direct attempts to assassinate any foreign leader. Since the jurisdiction of the Rockefeller Commission was limited to improper *domestic* activities of the CIA, it was necessary to find significant overt activities of conspiracy in this country in order to justify my bringing such evidence before our commission. I did discover the CIA involvement in shipping arms from this country to persons in the Dominican Republic who sought to assassinate Dictator Generalissimo Trujillo (who himself had been involved in an attempt to assassinate the president of Venezuela).

With regard to activities outside the United States, I did not undertake an exhaustive investigation of those areas that had no

domestic aspects and were therefore definitely outside our jurisdiction. However, I did review activities of the CIA directed against
Chile (where General René Schneider, commander-in-chief of the
Chilean army was killed, although not by the CIA); in Indonesia,
where there was some discussion within the CIA about the possibility of an attempt on the life of President Achmed Sukarno,
although I never found that the agency had anything to do with
the death of Sukarno; in the Congo, where it did not appear that
the CIA was responsible for the death of Patrice Lumumba, who
was killed in early 1961; and in Vietnam, where it did not appear
that the CIA participated in the assassination of South Vietnamese
president Ngo Dinh Diem and his brother, Ngo Dinh Nhu, on
November 2, 1963.

The two major areas of domestic involvement involved plans
directed against both Cuban premier Castro and Dominican Republic dictator Generalissimo Trujillo. I assigned my assistant,
Marvin L. Gray, Jr., to concentrate on the Trujillo case, while I
concentrated on Castro.

In the late 1950s, there was increasing internal dissatisfaction
with the government of Cuban leader Juan Batista. As Castro's
influence increased, attempts were made by the Eisenhower administration to persuade Batista to resign and turn over the reins
of government to a group more attuned to the needs and desires
of the Cuban people, particularly in areas of democratic government and social reforms. The former chief of the CIA Western
Hemisphere Division told me that an unofficial ambassador from
this country, with CIA help and encouragement, approached Batista in December 1958, asking that he resign and turn over the
government to new leadership. The request was refused. Had the
United States put more pressure on Batista at that time, the whole
course of American history might have been changed.

Shortly thereafter, Fidel Castro took over the Cuban government. Immediately there was great concern on the part of American
leadership about the presence of a government so closely aligned
with the Soviet Union barely ninety miles from American shores.

In the final months of the Eisenhower administration and continuing into the Kennedy administration, the CIA, with appropriate White House authorization, undertook the development of an operation in support of Cuban exiles seeking to overthrow the Castro government. It culminated in the Bay of Pigs disaster in April 1961.

As plans for the attempted overthrow of the Cuban government were developed, one consideration related to Fidel Castro as the dominant figure. At first, plans were discussed to try to embarrass Castro. They were so amateurish and bizarre that when I first disclosed their substance to the Rockefeller Commission, one of the commissioners commented that the CIA was acting "like a bunch of Keystone Cops." For instance, one plan related to an attempt to spray an LSD drug into a radio studio in which Castro would be delivering a long radio speech. The purpose of the drug was to disorient Castro and make him look foolish to his countrymen. Another plan related to the charismatic character of Castro's beard. The proposal was to make use of a powder that would cause Castro's facial hair to drop out. The powder was to be sprayed in Castro's shoes (I never quite found out how the CIA proposed to have the powder in the shoes in turn get to Castro's person) and as a result cause Castro's hair and beard to fall out.

As evidence of the plots to embarrass Castro unfolded, I remembered my friend Roger Wilkins's admonition to me that people in Washington nibble and nibble at one's integrity and independence and that if you let this happen, before you know it, your integrity and independence will be gone.

There is a corollary: When federal agencies and bureaus go one step too far, they very often try to go even one step beyond that. So it was with the CIA. The plans to embarrass Castro quickly developed into plans to assassinate him.

The plots against Castro basically fell into three chronological categories: 1960–61, which I called the Phase I plans; 1962–63, which I called the Phase II plans; and 1963–65, which I called the Phase III plans. Before I could take oral testimony from the key people involved, I first had to go to the commission. I knew that I would have problems, and I prepared to fight for jurisdiction.

# 16

# The Battle to Investigate Assassination Plots

**T**he presidential order was clear. Section 2 was entitled "Functions of the Commission" and declared that "the Commission shall:

"(a) Ascertain and evaluate any facts relating to activities conducted within the United States by the Central Intelligence Agency which give rise to questions of compliance with the provisions of 50 U.S.C. 403. . . ."

The key words were not "conducted within the United States." Rather, the key words were *"any facts relating to* activities conducted within the United States. . . ."

This was the foundation on which I built my argument. To be sure, the placing of poison pills in Cuba was not an activity within the United States. But there was one activity that did take place in the United States, and that involved the discussions of getting the poison pills to Cuba.

Had those discussions taken place wholly within the confines of CIA headquarters at Langley, Virginia, I would have lost the argument. But the CIA did not limit its plans to CIA employees. Rather, it brought in organized-crime figures.

When a planned murder takes place, there are really two crimes. One of those crimes is the act of murder itself, which takes place in the jurisdiction in which the person is killed. The other criminal act is the planning to commit the crime, which takes place in the jurisdiction in which the plans are made.

My argument was this: The CIA had undertaken plans with non-CIA people within the borders of the United States to commit murder. Even though that act of murder might take place abroad, the planning of that murder was a separate, independent criminal act within the United States that violated the provisions of the CIA's governing charter. The CIA had no authority to plan with others to commit murder. Therefore, it was an unlawful activity within the United States. *Ipso facto*, the Rockefeller Commission had jurisdiction.

Despite the undisputed facts that a group within the CIA had conspired within the United States, I anticipated that a number of the commissioners would hesitate or oppose further investigation of this area. Therefore, while I was searching through the mass of CIA files, I began to meet with individual members of the Rockefeller Commission who I felt would be most open to my arguments. In late February, I spent time with five of the eight commission members to explain what I had found, why I thought it was within the jurisdiction of our commission, and why I felt from a public-policy standpoint it was important that the commission members know about this. I did not ask for permission to continue what I was doing. Rather, I was merely keeping the individual commission members informed.

By the time of our last commission meeting in February, I was far enough along in my investigation and discussions with commission members to bring my findings before the entire commission.

Immediately, there was disagreement, particularly from Nelson Rockefeller, concerning whether I should have even begun my investigation into this area. What disturbed me most was that the discussion only peripherally included the moral reprehensibility of the assassination plots. Rather, the debate centered on whether it was a matter within our jurisdiction.

As the discussion intensified, I felt it would be better to postpone

consideration for at least one week, and I proposed a plan subsequently adopted by the commission. My staff would prepare a
memorandum summarizing the reasons for and against the proposition that we had jurisdiction. At the next week's meeting, I
would bring that memorandum before the commission for their
deliberation, together with my own memorandum.

In the meantime, I was going to continue my own investigation,
and I felt this would give me another week to develop additional
facts.

Before the next commission meeting, I had gained a tremendous
ally—the press. In late 1974, President Ford, in an off-the-record
meeting with some of the top echelon of the *New York Times*,
intimated that the CIA may have been involved in assassination
plots. Off-the-record remarks have a tendency to gradually spread
from one person to another, and eventually Washington news
correspondent Daniel Schorr, who was then working with CBS,
got wind of the story. Schorr, together with Associated Press (AP)
correspondent David Martin, *Washington Post* correspondents
William Greider and George Lardner, Jr., and *New York Times*
correspondents Nicholas Horrock and John Crewdsen, throughout
the first half of 1975 doggedly pursued the investigation of the
CIA by the Rockefeller Commission. On the whole, their reporting
was excellent.

It was Schorr who broke the story about CIA involvement in
assassination plots. On a CBS news telecast on Friday evening,
February 26, Schorr asserted that James Schlesinger, when he served
as DCI, uncovered evidence of agency involvement in the assassination of foreign officials.

Schlesinger did not reply directly. However, an aide who worked
with him during that internal CIA investigation in the post-
Watergate period told the AP, "We never had any indication whatsoever of CIA involvement in assassination."

According to Schorr's news report, at least three assassinations
reportedly took place in the 1960s or late 1950s. Schorr said that
President Ford had told associates that if current investigations of
the CIA "go too far," they could uncover involvement of the

agency in assassinations, which in turn "would embarrass the government and damage relations with at least one foreign country."

The CIA can be very technical in its response. Daniel Schorr's newscast and subsequent newspaper articles gave the CIA an out, for the accusations related to actual "assassinations," which implied success.

In the case of Castro, it was obvious that there had been no successful assassination. In the case of three assassinations that did occur, the CIA could correctly technically claim that it did not assassinate anyone.

Schorr's story opened the floodgates. The *Washington Star* on March 4 carried a report by Jeremiah O'Leary that CIA director William Colby had told President Ford about plans for several assassination attempts against foreigners in which the CIA was involved. Supposedly, this was an "oral addendum" to the fifty-page written report. On March 6, William Greider and George Lardner, of the *Washington Post*, reported the CIA's concern that current investigations "may pursue the alleged involvement of the Agency in three assassination plots aimed at foreign political leaders Fidel Castro in Cuba, Rafael Trujillo in the Dominican Republic, and Patrice Lumumba in the Congo." Nicholas Horrock and John Crewdsen of the *New York Times* developed additional facts. Moreover, by the time of the March 10 Rockefeller Commission meeting, *Time* magazine reported that "sources contend that the CIA enlisted the hired gun help of U.S. Mafia figures in several unsuccessful attempts to kill Cuban Premier Castro both before and shortly after the CIA planned Bay of Pigs invasion of Cuba in 1961."

The momentum was too great to stop. Schorr's story had opened the door. The press had ferreted out additional leads. I was bombarded with press inquiries, but I refused to answer any question. The commission had a position of not divulging anything to the press, and I felt it imperative that I not violate those rules.

Concurrently with the press report, I met individually with commission members and urged that we not ignore the issues. By March 10, the battle was over. A majority of the commissioners voted in support of my recommendation that the Rockefeller Commission had jurisdiction. I was now ready to go ahead with interrogation of persons involved in the events.

My pursuit of the facts in this area was somewhat hampered because Congress did not accede to a request I made to give the Rockefeller Commission the power to subpoena documents and witnesses. I felt it was necessary to have this power should any contingencies arise where we might need it. Indeed, before the investigation was over, I had the need for subpoena power with reference to one witness, Robert Maheu.

A member of the House Judiciary Committee staff advised that at Chairman Peter Rodino's request research had been done. Four reasons were given for denying my request:

1. There is no Congressional representation on the Presidential Panel as there has been in previous Presidential commissions, including the Warren Commission on which President Ford was a member. The Presidential CIA Panel is all from the public sector.

2. The purpose or charge to the Presidential Panel is to look into the possible violation of the CIA charter. This involves an interpretation of Congressional intent and any violation of that intent. This is a question for the Congress to determine and not a public panel.

3. The Warren Commision and others were fact-finding panels and not seeking to determine a violation of a Congressionally-granted charter.

4. The CIA is a creation of the Congress and any investigation of its activities legal or illegal is properly the jurisdiction of the Congress.

The real reason was not any one of the four. Congress itself was undertaking its own investigation of the intelligence agencies, and Congress did not want to help anyone else. Our commission therefore never was granted the power to subpoena.

This same refusal of cooperation by Congress occurred in another area of our investigation where we sought to determine the extent of any CIA involvement in the Watergate affair. Early in our investigation we learned that CIA-related documents were in Watergate files in the possession of the Senate Select Committee. Senator Howard Baker, Jr., supposedly knew where these files were located. Therefore, in early February 1975, I went to call on Baker and took with me a member of my staff, William Schwarzer. We wanted to question Baker generally about any knowledge he might have concerning any CIA involvement in Watergate.

Baker was very cooperative. He concurred in our judgment that we should have access to the files and said they were in the custody of George Murphy of the Joint Committee on Atomic Energy. However, since the files contained classified material, I needed the consent of the CIA.

On February 11, at my request, William Colby wrote Baker, with a copy to George Murphy, stating:

> In connection with requests that I have received from Mr. David W. Belin, Executive Director of the Commission on CIA Activities Within the United States, this is to advise that I have no objection to the release to the Commission of the documentation which was provided to you during the Watergate hearings concerning CIA activities and which is now in the custody of Mr. George Murphy of the staff of the Joint Committee on Atomic Energy.

By the time Murphy was ready to process my letter, the files I wanted had supposedly been turned over to the new Senate Select Committee on Intelligence under the chairmanship of Sen. Frank Church of Idaho. As soon as I found this out, I wrote Church and asked that the documents be made available to a member of my staff.

In the meantime, there appeared to be a jurisdictional dispute in the Senate concerning who would have custody of these documents. Within a few days, I learned that instead of the documents being in the custody of the Senate Select Committee, they had come into the custody of the Senate Rules Committee under the chairmanship of Senator Howard Cannon. William Schwarzer contacted the Senate Rules Committee, explained that for nearly a month we had been trying to get access to these documents, and asked that we be permitted to see them promptly. He followed up this oral request with a letter to Cannon.

Unfortunately, this did not follow Washington protocol. In the first place, Schwarzer was not in a high enough position to write

Cannon. He was a "senior counsel" on the legal staff of the commission. At the very least, the request should have come from me, as executive director.

One member of the Senate Rules Committee staff, John Swearingen, contacted Schwarzer and told him that proper protocol had not been followed. Schwarzer, frustrated by the delay, replied that for several weeks he had been trying to get access to these documents and that the unavailability of the documents was holding up part of our investigation. The response of Swearingen was that access would not be given unless there was a "proper request" made to Cannon.

Furthermore, Swearingen said, the request now would have to be signed by Rockefeller. "Until such request was received, no document would be made available."

The Senate Select Committee had appointed three top people to their staff: William Miller, F. A. O. Schwarz, Jr., and Curt Smothers.

In March they requested that I meet with them to seek my cooperation in turning over materials to the Senate Select Committee as rapidly as possible. I told them that as a citizen I would do everything in my power to be sure that upon the completion of our investigation all the material we had would be turned over to the Senate Select Committee. However, the natural inclinations that I might have as a citizen were susceptible to being changed by the experiences of life in Washington.

I suggested that among the experiences that stood out most in my mind at that time were the frustrations we were having with the Senate Rules Committee and the release of the documents.

Within a few days we were advised that the files we sought would be made available.

Even without the availability of a subpoena, we were able to glean the essential facts of CIA assassination plans. My starting point was with the key CIA people involved, many of whom were no longer with the agency. The first key witness was Sheffield Edwards, who, together with Richard Bissell, had been involved in the earliest development of the plans.

# 17

# CIA Plans to Assassinate Castro – Phase I

**S**heffield Edwards was in his seventies, not very well, and grand-fatherly in appearance, with a warm smile. He was not someone whom you would expect to have been involved in conspiracy to murder.* I began the interview with background questioning after his having agreed (with some reluctance) to allow me to tape-record our conversation.

Edwards was a West Point graduate in the class of 1923. In World War II he served in a command position in the Twelfth Armored Group. After the war, he joined the CIG until it became the CIA in 1947. Originally, he was in charge of the Office of Security and directed a staff of approximately thirty-five people. By the time he retired from the CIA in 1963, his staff had grown to seven hundred.

Edwards said that his first contact concerning a possible plan to try to assassinate Castro "was in the Kennedy administration." (He was wrong; it started in the last few months of the Eisenhower

*Edwards died of natural causes in 1975.

administration, in the fall of 1960.) Richard Bissell, who was then deputy director for plans and was in charge of the whole Bay of Pigs operation, broached the subject.

BELIN: "What did he say to you and what did you say to him?"

EDWARDS: "Yes, I remember that—you had better turn off that thing."

I stopped the tape recorder. Edwards had not understood that I wanted him to relate the substance of his conversation with Bissell.

BELIN: "You wanted me to restate the question. What did he say to you, and what did you say to him?"

EDWARDS: "Bissell asked me if I had any assets that would be available."

BELIN: "Did he say to be available for what?"

EDWARDS: "That would be available into the syndicate."

BELIN: "All right. He asked you and what did you tell him?"

EDWARDS: "I told him I would see."

BELIN: "And subsequently then did you determine an asset that you might have?"

EDWARDS: "Right."

BELIN: "And who was that?"

EDWARDS: "It was Bob Maheu first and then afterwards it was Johnnie Rosselli."

BELIN: "And Johnnie Rosselli was a person that was supposedly involved with the syndicate?"

EDWARDS: "Yes."

BELIN: "Was there anyone other than Rosselli?"

EDWARDS: "Samuel—otherwise Sam Giancana."

BELIN: "And who talked to Rosselli and Giancana? Was it Maheu at first, or you?"

Then Edwards told everything: how organized-crime members had been contacted, how they were going to try to get rid of Castro by placing botulism pills in his food, and how the plan was approved by Allen Dulles, head of the CIA, who later was to become a member of the Warren Commission.

Edwards also testified that he personally briefed Robert Kennedy. With him at the time of that briefing was Larry Houston, general counsel for the CIA.

Edwards said that a memorandum was prepared of the briefing with Attorney General Kennedy.

BELIN: "Was there anything that you knew about this plan to assassinate Castro that you didn't tell Kennedy?"

EDWARDS: "No."

I asked Edwards whether Kennedy told him that he shouldn't do this at all. Again the answer was "No."

BELIN: "Did he in any way say that he disapproved of what had been done in the past?"

EDWARDS: "No."

I asked Edwards if he ever checked whether the botulism pills worked. He said he checked them on some guinea pigs.

BELIN: "And did they work on the guinea pigs?"

EDWARDS: "They sure did."

From other parts of the investigation I determined that in the Phase I plans of the assassination plots there were two passages of pills to Cuba. The first passage was in late February or March 1961, from the syndicate through their courier to a Cuban who worked in the Cuban prime minister's office and had access to Castro. Supposedly the Cuban "asset got scared" and did not try to pass the pill. Pills were subsequently delivered to another "asset" who was in a position to slip the pills to Castro at a restaurant in which the asset worked. This took place in the March–April 1961 period. Castro ceased visiting that restaurant at approximately the same time the pills arrived. After the second attempt failed, the case officer said that the pills were returned to the CIA.

Was it coincidence that Castro stopped going to one of his favorite restaurants? Or is this evidence that as far back as 1961 he knew of these plots?

There is no doubt that Castro knew of the plots and that his knowledge formed the foundation of the warning that he gave in 1963 in September, about ten weeks before the assassination of President Kennedy—a warning that came to the attention of Lee Harvey Oswald. More about that later.

Edwards's testimony about briefing Kennedy was corroborated by the testimony of former CIA general counsel Houston. The memorandum, prepared after Edwards and Houston briefed Robert Kennedy, was dated May 14, 1962. Some background: In the fall of 1960, when plans for assassinating Castro were discussed, crime-syndicate figure Sam Giancana asked the CIA intermediary, Robert Maheu, to arrange for putting a listening device in the room of entertainer Dan Rowan in Las Vegas. Giancana wanted the device because he believed Rowan was having an affair with singer Phyllis McGuire, who was reputed to be Giancana's mistress.

The request by Giancana came when plans were under way for Phase I. Giancana supposedly stated that if he did not get to install the listening device, he would have to go to Las Vegas himself. The case officer said "this would have interrupted the project at a very critical time," and therefore he sought the assistance of Maheu to get a private detective agency to install the listening device.

Maheu passed the request to another private investigator, who contacted Arthur James Balletti. Instead of putting a listening device in the room, Balletti put a wiretap on the telephone. The wiretap was discovered, and Balletti was arrested by a Nevada sheriff. The wiretap was illegal under federal law, and the FBI was brought into the picture. At the time of the incident, the CIA did not know the proposed room-listening device was going to turn into a wiretap.

Edwards had once told Maheu that if Maheu ever got in trouble, he could say to the FBI that he was working on an intelligence operation being handled by the agency. That's what he did, according to an FBI memorandum. Maheu claimed the telephone tap was ordered on behalf of the agency's effort to obtain intelligence through hoodlum elements in Cuba. The FBI then contacted Edwards, who told Sam Papich, the FBI liaison with the agency, that Maheu was involved in a sensitive project and that the CIA would object to prosecution because it would necessitate CIA information and could embarrass the U.S. government. Subsequently, there was a meeting between Edwards and Papich in which

Edwards advised Papich that it would not be in the national interest to prosecute.

To be certain that there would be no prosecution, Edwards and CIA general counsel Houston met on May 7, 1962, with Attorney General Kennedy. Edwards prepared a "Memorandum for the Record" of that meeting. It was dated May 14, 1962 and was entitled "Arthur James Balletti, et al.—Unauthorized Publication or Use of Communications." The opening sentence of the memorandum states: "This memorandum for the record was prepared at the request of the Attorney General of the United States following a complete oral briefing of him relevant to a sensitive CIA operation conducted during the period approximately August 1960 to May 1961."

The memorandum continued:

In August 1960 the undersigned was approached by Mr. Richard Bissell, then Deputy Director for Plans of CIA, to explore the possibility of mounting this sensitive operation against Fidel Castro. It was thought that certain gambling interests, which had formerly been active in Cuba, might be willing and able to assist and further, might have both intelligence assets in Cuba and communication between Miami, Florida and Cuba.

The memorandum then related that an intermediary who was known to the CIA (Robert Maheu) was approached by Colonel Sheffield Edwards "and asked to establish contact with a member or members of the gambling syndicate to explore their capabilities." The approach was to be made "to the syndicate as appearing to represent big business organizations which wished to protect their interests in Cuba." The contact was made with a "syndicate" member who "showed interest in the possibility and indicated he had some contacts in Miami that he might use." The syndicate member, John Rosselli, supposedly told Maheu that the syndicate person "was not interested in any remuneration but would seek to establish capabilities in Cuba to perform the desired project."

The memorandum continued: "Towards the end of September" 1960 contact with another syndicate member from Chicago, Momo

Salvatore (Sam) Giancana, was made, and in turn an arrangement was made through Giancana for the CIA intermediary and his contact

> to meet with a "courier" who was going back and forth to Havana. From information received back by the courier, the proposed operation appeared to be feasible, and it was decided to obtain an official Agency approval in this regard. A figure of one hundred fifty thousand dollars was set by the Agency as a payment to be made on completion of the operation and to be paid only to the principal or principals who would conduct the operation in Cuba.

Maheu reported that Giancana and the other contact

> emphatically stated that they wished no part of any payment. The undersigned [Sheffield Edwards] then briefed the proper senior officers of this Agency of the proposal. Knowledge of this project during its life was kept to a total of six persons and never became a part of the project current at the time for the invasion of Cuba. There were no memoranda on the project nor were there other written documents or agreements. The project was duly orally approved by the said senior officials of the Agency.

The memorandum further read that during the period from September 1960 to 1961 "efforts were continued" by Maheu and the Mafia personnel

> to proceed with the operation. The first principal in Cuba withdrew and another principal was selected as has been briefed to the Attorney General. Ten thousand dollars was passed for expenses to the second principal. He was further furnished with approximately one thousand dollars worth of communications equipment to establish communications between his headquarters in Miami and assets in Cuba. No monies were ever paid [to the syndicate people].

There was expense money paid to Maheu. The memorandum stated that "after the failure of the invasion of Cuba word was sent through" Maheu to the syndicate people "to call off the operation," with the further direction that the syndicate person "was told to tell his principal that the proposal to pay one hundred fifty thousand dollars for completion of the operation had been definitely withdrawn." Only two copies of the memorandum were prepared—one for the attorney general and one to be retained by the CIA.

The deception among the FBI, the CIA, and the Department of Justice is unique. The CIA felt obligated to tell Robert Kennedy in 1962 about the whole story of the Phase I plans. Robert Kennedy was very tight-lipped. He never told his 1962 visitors that he had already known of the operation for approximately one year, for J. Edgar Hoover, on May 22, 1961, had furnished him a memorandum prepared by the FBI from information furnished by Sam Papich. Here is the heart of that 1961 FBI memorandum:

> On May 3, 1961, Colonel Sheffield Edwards, Director of Security, Central Intelligence Agency (CIA), furnished the following information.
>
> Colonel Edwards advised that in connection with CIA's operation against Castro he personally contacted Robert Maheu during the fall of 1960 for the purpose of using Maheu as a "cut-out" in contacts with Sam Giancana, a known hoodlum in the Chicago area. Colonel Edwards said that since the underworld controlled gambling activities in Cuba under the Batista government, it was assumed that this element would still continue to have sources and contacts in Cuba which perhaps could be utilized successfully in connection with CIA's clandestine efforts against the Castro government. As a result, Maheu's services were solicited as a "cut-out" because of his possible entry into underworld circles. Maheu obtained Sam Giancana's assistance in this regard and according to Edwards, Giancana gave every indication of cooperating through Maheu in attempting to accomplish several clandestine efforts in Cuba. Edwards added that none of Giancana's efforts have materialized to date and that several of the plans still are working and may eventually "pay off."

The 1961 FBI memorandum then went into the Balletti situation and reported that Colonel Edwards had no knowledge of the wiretap.

The memorandum concluded with the following paragraph:

> Colonel Edwards advised that only Mr. Bissell (Deputy Director of Plans, CIA) and two others in CIA were aware of the Giancana-Maheu

activity in behalf of CIA's program and that Allen Dulles was completely unaware of Edwards' contact with Maheu in this connection. He added that Mr. Bissell, during his recent briefings of General Taylor and the Attorney General in connection with their inquiries into CIA relating to the Cuban situation told the Attorney General that some of the CIA's associated planning included the use of Giancana and the underworld against Castro.

Subsequently, on March 6, 1967, J. Edgar Hoover sent to the attorney general a letter with an accompanying March 6, 1967, FBI memorandum entitled "Central Intelligence Agency's Intentions to Send Hoodlums to Cuba to Assassinate Castro." The memorandum referred to the Balletti wiretap matter and stated that the FBI

> checked matter with CIA on 5/3/61 and learned CIA was using Robert Maheu as intermediary with Sam Giancana relative to CIA's "dirty business" anti-Castro activities.
> By letter 5/22/61 we furnished former Attorney General Kennedy a memorandum containing a rundown on CIA's involvement in this. The originals of the letter and memorandum were returned to us for filing purposes. A copy of that memorandum is being attached to instant letter being sent to Attorney General.
> On 5/9/62 Kennedy discussed with the Director a number of matters, including admission by CIA that Robert Maheu had been hired by that Agency to approach Sam Giancana to have Castro assassinated at a cost of $150,000. Kennedy stated he had issued orders that CIA should never undertake such steps again without first checking with the Department of Justice and stated because of this matter it would be difficult to prosecute Giancana or Robert Maheu then or in the future.

The 1967 Hoover memorandum stated that the FBI had learned on June 20, 1963, that the CIA contacts with the Mafia had "continued up until that time when they were reportedly cut off." The FBI memorandum also stated that it appeared that one Mafia member involved in the plans "is using his prior connections with the CIA to his best advantage."

A contemporaneous FBI memorandum dated March 6, 1967,

stated that Robert Kennedy, following his briefing in May 1962, informed the FBI on May 9, 1962, about the briefing. "He [Robert Kennedy] indicated that a few days prior thereto he had been advised by CIA" that an intermediary had been hired by the CIA to approach Sam Giancana with a proposition of paying $150,000 to hire some gunman to go into Cuba and kill Castro. The memorandum further continued:

> Mr. Kennedy stated that upon learning CIA had not cleared its action in hiring [the intermediary] and Giancana with the Department of Justice he issued orders that CIA should never again take such steps without checking with the Department of Justice.
>
> Mr. Kennedy further advised that because of this matter it would be very difficult to initiate any prosecution against Giancana, as Giancana could immediately bring out the fact that the United States Government had approached him to arrange for the assassination of Castro.

Kennedy was absolutely right. But why didn't he tell this directly to the CIA in May 1961, when the FBI first told him about the CIA collaboration with the Mafia in assassination plots directed against Castro?

One further question: Did Robert Kennedy tell his brother John about these plots and the involvement of the CIA?

# 18

## Executive Action Capabilities and the Phase II Plans

One particularly difficult assignment with the Rockefeller Commission involved the interrogation of William K. Harvey, the key CIA case officer in the Phase II plans.*

After Harvey retired from the CIA, he moved to Indianapolis and resumed his law practice. He was a very tough witness and initially very reluctant to testify.

After more than an hour of background discussion, he started to open up. After another hour of discussion, I asked if I could put on tape a question-and-answer summary of our conversation so that I would have an accurate record.

Harvey agreed. The recorded interview began. He was born in 1915 in Danville, Indiana. Harvey was smart. He was associate editor of the *Indiana Law Review* and was a member of the Order of the Coif, which meant that he graduated in the upper 10 percent of his law-school class. After briefly practicing law in Kentucky, he joined the FBI in the fall of 1940 and remained with them until

*William Harvey died of a heart attack in 1976.

he joined the CIA in 1947. Much of his time he spent overseas, and he had a reputation as a hard-nosed CIA operative. There were stories inside the CIA that Harvey had been involved in seeking to dig a tunnel under the Berlin Wall while he was stationed in Germany.

Harvey came back to the United States from Germany in 1959 and spent most of the next four years in Washington before going abroad again. In 1967 he retired and moved back to Indiana.

Before the taped session, Harvey said that either in late 1961 or early 1962 he talked with someone in the CIA concerning what that person called a request from the White House for the agency to develop what was called an "executive action capability"— assassination or liquidation of leaders in foreign countries. According to Harvey it was Richard Bissell with whom he had this conversation.

He also said that he first learned about the Castro operations from Bissell, who asked him (Harvey) "to discuss it with [Sheffield] Edwards and take it over." Harvey stated that Edwards briefed him and told him to get in touch with the Phase I case officer.

The Phase I case officer mentioned to Harvey the contact with Robert Maheu, whom Harvey knew. They had been in the same FBI training class. However, Harvey said he had not very much contact with Maheu after he (Harvey) left the FBI in 1947.

Harvey said that as he went through the analysis of the Phase I plan, he decided the plan was "a damned fool idea to start with" and had been handled in an "incredibly amateurish" fashion.

BELIN: "You also stated to me today that you thought we were dealing with what you referred to as a huge hand grenade, that you could not afford to have go off, so far as outside knowledge of it is concerned."

HARVEY: "That is correct. It was not just a question of my not being able to afford that it go off, but in the aftermath of the Bay of Pigs failure, that was not the kind of an explosion that the government, the Agency, or anyone else could well afford."

BELIN: "And one of the concerns you had, I believe, was that so many people seemed to know about the plan. Is that correct?"

HARVEY: "That is correct."

BELIN: "Do you have any opinion as to whether or not Castro might or might not have known about it?"

HARVEY: "Given the capabilities of Castro's security apparata and the general sieve-like character of the Cuban community in exile and the number of people who knew at least something about this particular incident or operation, before I had any connection with it, or later as a result of things that occurred before I had any connection with it, I think and thought at the time that it was quite conceivable that it had been penetrated. I cannot honestly state that I had at that time any firm reason to believe that Castro was aware of this operation."

Harvey was a man who worked alone. One of his first requirements was to have everyone else "stay completely out of the operation." So Harvey instructed Edwards to tell the Phase I case officer to stay out.

Harvey also said he was concerned about possible action by the Cuban exile community to blackmail the U.S. government or any individuals involved in the operation.

The Phase II plans involved two possibilities: "rifle fire and the use of poison." Harvey was working with organized-crime figure John Rosselli. Arms were sent into Cuba. The assassination plot never succeeded.

Although the Phase II plans did not succeed, I was concerned about who authorized these attempts to kill Castro. I uncovered incriminating documents. One was a copy of minutes of an August 10, 1962, meeting of what was known as the "Special Group (Augmented)." This was a group of senior people in the Kennedy administration who were involved in overall planning of operations directed against Cuba. The word "augmented" was used to indicate the addition of Robert Kennedy as a member of the group. Along with Kennedy were the secretary of state, Dean Rusk, the secretary of defense, Robert McNamara, the assistant to the president for national security, McGeorge Bundy, Gen. Maxwell Taylor, and several other people—one of whom turned out to be a member of the Rockefeller Commission, Gen. Lyman Lemnitzer.

In 1962, Lemnitzer was chairman of the Joint Chiefs of Staff. The coordinating officer of the Special Group (Augmented) was Brig. Gen. Edward Lansdale.

John McCone was appointed by President Kennedy as DCI after the Bay of Pigs fiasco. I asked Harvey about the participation of McCone in these assassination plans:

BELIN: "Mr. Harvey, did John McCone know at this time what was going on?"

HARVEY: "To my knowledge, he did not."

BELIN: "You were at a meeting of the Special Group (Augmented) in the Department of State in August of 1962 when someone brought up the possibility of liquidation of Castro, is that correct?"

HARVEY: "That is correct."

BELIN: "Do you remember what Mr. McCone did at that time?"

HARVEY: "Yes. He got rather red in the face and made a comment, 'Well, that's not something that should be discussed.' Now, please don't hold me to these words."

BELIN: "That's to the best of your recollection?"

HARVEY: "The best of my recollection is I was at that meeting with John McCone. To the best of my recollection the remark that he made was a clear effort to stop any such proposals, suggestion or any discussion thereof at that meeting within that forum immediately."

BELIN: "Earlier, before that meeting, had you had any discussions with Richard Helms about whether or not McCone should be advised of what was going on after McCone became DCI?"

HARVEY: "Yes, I had."

According to Harvey, they thought it best not to tell McCone.

Colonel Edwards told me that he did not know at the time of the May 7, 1962, briefing of Attorney General Kennedy that the Phase II case officer, William Harvey, was undertaking another plan along the lines of Phase I. Therefore, Edwards said he did not tell Robert Kennedy at the time of the briefing that there was a Phase II plan under way.

Richard Helms knew about Phase II, but he was most reluctant as a witness to talk about it.

When I asked Helms whether he remembered any discussions with Harvey concerning the furnishing of either arms or poison pills to Cuban exiles to further assassination plans, Helms replied: "I don't have any question that we tried to line them [up] in Cuba, to bring down this government or to kill anybody they could lay their hands on." But he did not recall that "a specific project was approved which was designed for a man to go to point B and actually shoot or poison or do something to Castro."

Helms testified before the commission that he "was not aware of the CIA ever having assassinated any foreign leader. I certainly never authorized the execution of any such operation while I was Director or Deputy Director and when I was Deputy Director for Plans I don't remember it coming forward. I certainly never recommended such an action to the then Director."

Helms said that although he had no recollection of any discussion with Harvey not to tell the DCI, McCone, in 1962 about the existence of plans, "I have no reason to cavil" that this was the fact.

When I first interrogated John McCone about assassination plans directed against foreign leaders, he said that he never knew about the Phase II plans until meeting with me in April 1975. Furthermore, McCone stated that the only knowledge he ever had of the Phase I plan was knowledge he received on August 16, 1963, from Richard Helms when he was given a copy of the May 14, 1962, "Memorandum for the Record" delivered to Attorney General Kennedy.

McCone was the DCI. He was the top officer in the agency and reported directly to the president. Yet, inside the agency, officers were hiding from McCone the Phase II plans that were under way at that very time—something that Harvey himself referred to as a potential "explosion" that neither "the government, the Agency, or anybody else could well afford."

Hiding these facts from McCone, the DCI, was one of the most damning facts I discovered in my investigation. The ramifications of an agency out of control were very grave.

# 19

# The Amnesia Syndrome – McNamara, Bundy, and Taylor

There was little doubt in my mind that Robert McNamara was not telling me the truth. He was nervous and ill at ease—hardly what you would expect from a person who had been the chief executive officer of Ford Motor Company, secretary of defense in the Kennedy and Johnson administrations, and chairman of the World Bank.

Within a few minutes, he started to apologize for his lack of memory. Then he claimed that he had worked so hard during the Vietnam War period when he was secretary of defense that he had lost virtually all memory of what took place in the Kennedy administration.

The words just did not ring true.

It was not until October 1987 that the nation had proof that McNamara had not lost his memory about what took place in the Kennedy administration, which in turn makes me suspicious that he was covering up crucial information about the assassination plots during my interrogation. The evidence came out because of the twenty-fifth anniversary of the Cuban missile

117

crisis—an event that took place in October 1962, when, for a few days, we seemed on the brink of nuclear war. The participants got together for a twenty-fifth anniversary celebration, amid much fanfare from the press. McNamara came forward with pinpoint memory of what took place during those critical days. This was a far cry from the amnesia that he claimed he had suffered from in 1975.

Why did Robert McNamara try to cover up what actually took place? The answer was clear: Top officials inside the Kennedy administration were directly aware of the assassination plots against Fidel Castro; moreover, some of those officials were actively encouraging his liquidation. I believe that Robert McNamara was one of those parties. I also believe Robert Kennedy was another. And, if Robert Kennedy knew, I believe it is reasonable to assume that his brother, President John F. Kennedy, also knew and approved of the plans.

The critical document implicating Robert McNamara was an August 14, 1962, memorandum prepared by William K. Harvey for Richard Helms, who was then deputy director of plans for the CIA. Attached to Harvey's memorandum was a copy of an August 13, 1962, memorandum prepared by General Lansdale, who was the coordinating officer of the Special Group (Augmented).

In contrast to the amnesia claims of McNamara, Harvey's memorandum spoke loud and clear. Here is what Harvey wrote:

1. Action. None. This memorandum is for your information.

2. Reference is made to our conversation on 13 August 1962, concerning the memorandum of that date from General Lansdale. Attached is a copy of this memorandum, excised from which are four words in the second line of the penultimate paragraph on page 1. These four words were "including liquidation of leaders."

3. The question of assassination, particularly of Fidel Castro, was brought up by Secretary McNamara at the meeting of the Special Group (Augmented) in Secretary Rusk's office on 10 August. It was the obvious consensus at that meeting, in answer to a comment by Mr. Ed Murrow, that this is not a subject which has been made a matter of official record. I took careful notes on the comments at this

meeting on this point, and the Special Group (Augmented) is not expecting any written comments or study on this point.

4. Upon receipt of the attached memorandum, I called Lansdale's office and, in his absence, pointed out to Frank Hand the inadvisability and stupidity of putting this type of comment in writing in such a document. I advised Frank Hand that, as far as CIA was concerned, we would write no document pertaining to this and would participate in no open meeting discussing it. I strongly urged Hand to recommend to Lansdale that he excise the phrase in question from all copies of this memorandum, including those disseminated to State, Defense, and USIA. Shortly thereafter, Lansdale called back and left the message that he agreed and that he had done so.

The attached Lansdale memorandum, dated August 13, 1962, had excised from it a phrase. The blank space was the approximate size of the phrase "including liquidation of leaders."

Sometime after his 1961 appointment to serve with Secretary McNamara, Lansdale had a discussion with President Kennedy.

LANSDALE: "I do not recall exactly on what. He asked me if I would think about the situation in Cuba and if I could come up with any suggestions or recommendations from such a study. It was a rather vague assignment by him, but it was to be done for him personally."

Lansdale "suggested an intermediary" to whom he would report, and Lansdale said that the president "appointed his brother, who was the Attorney General."

According to Lansdale, he made written recommendations in late 1961 or early 1962 to the president, "to see if there was a possibility of using Cuban refugees to help them get their political thinking together to see if there would be any feasibility of a revolution in Cuba." He said that he thinks he gave the written report to the attorney general for delivery to the president and that he later saw the paper "in the files of the president . . . he received it and he had possession of it."

In early 1962 there were discussions about Cuban exiles possibly going back inside Cuba to harass the regime. Lansdale testified that the possibility of these exile groups trying to assassinate Castro "might well have been mentioned." However, he said, "I don't recall a single instance of any serious action being undertaken" on any plan for assassination. He went on to say that whatever discussions took place concerning assassination related to possibilities rather than actualities.

I asked about the development of an "executive action capability."

Lansdale said that if there was a direction to submit papers, it was an authorization to submit papers and not necessarily an authorization to carry out the action. Lansdale admitted that "there might well have been" a request that the CIA come up with, as a possibility, a plan for liquidation of leadership.

If that request was made, he said that it could have been one of his requests and that he "quite probably would have discussed it with the secretary of defense" and "possibly the attorney general, with whom I was in contact."

Lansdale said that at no time during 1960, 1961, 1962, or 1963 did he know of the existence of any plans for the assassination of any Cuban leader or any other leader.

Despite the existence of the Harvey memorandum of August 14, 1962, and Lansdale's own memorandum of August 13, 1962, with the blank space, Lansdale testified that he never heard any discussion of "executive action capability" to liquidate any foreign leaders.

The documents indicated Lansdale was not telling the truth.

From Lansdale, I went back to Robert McNamara. Before we went on the record, he repeated his statement that he had lost virtually all memory of what took place in the Kennedy administration. He said he had no recollection of even being present at the August 10, 1962, meeting.

"I'm not suggesting I wasn't but I have no recollection of it. I do seem to recall that there was such a group; I doubt very much if I was a member of it." He said he "might have been a participant" at one or more meetings. In fact, the minutes record his being there. When asked whether he heard anyone discuss the possibility of assassinating Castro or any other foreign leader,

McNamara replied: "No. I should interject here another point I made earlier, as I have no notes—I did not take notes of any meetings I attended with rare exceptions, and I have no other basis for refreshing my memory, and my memory of those years is very bad. I'm not saying this to in any way qualify what I'm saying except that it is a fact that my memory is poor in relation to the period."

McNamara: "I am almost certain that were an assassination contemplated, which seems to me . . . extremely unlikely, if it were contemplated or any action been taken to move in that direction, it would have had to receive the approval of not just Mr. Bundy but other officials at that same level, including my deputy, I think, and my deputy never would have approved anything like that without discussing it with me."

McNamara said he "couldn't imagine anything relating to a CIA operation that was known to the President and was not known to Mr. Bundy. I can imagine something with respect to CIA known to Mr. Bundy, not known to the President either because they were not that important or conceivably because it was thought desirable to protect the President from certain knowledge . . . I can't imagine Mr. Bundy himself supporting assassination. I can't imagine him supporting assassination of a foreign leader, without mentioning it to the President, even though to do so would by that action involve the President. I say I can't imagine him supporting assassination of a foreign leader without the President's knowledge because it is the President who would pay if that action were undertaken and it ever became known. Mr. Bundy recognized, more than the rest of us, the importance of protecting the presidency as well as the particular president, and particularly protecting his ability to govern."

What about McGeorge Bundy? Head of the Ford Foundation, former dean at Harvard, a member of the eastern establishment power structure, and close adviser to President Kennedy. He was assistant to the president for national security affairs, the position Henry Kissinger first held in the Nixon administration.

Called before the Rockefeller Commission, Bundy said that he was never aware of any "actual decision" to assassinate any foreign leader. However, he said that he did "have a vague recollection of the existence or the possible existence of contingency planning in this area. I am sorry to say I cannot help you much with details about it because I can't fish them out of my memory, but I could not exclude that there were contingency plans, and a contingency capability of some sort, or plans for such a capability at some time." He said he did not know of any case in which plans went beyond the contingency stage, "and I know of no such authorization or any involvement by anybody in the White House staff or anybody else, for that matter."

When asked whether he ever heard any discussion concerning a plan to assassinate Cuban leaders, Bundy replied, "Not that I can remember. . . . I certainly cannot exclude the possibility that you could have had the kind of discussion in which one or another individual would have said it would be, that there is a possibility that thus and such a Cuban group, if landed and infiltrated, might have as one of its missions the following, which might have included an attack on one or another Cuban leader. I do not have any direct recollection that this did happen, but I cannot exclude that it did happen."

Bundy testified that he did not know of any decision to undertake a plan of assassination. "That contingent capability may have been authorized in this field I cannot exclude, although I have no direct recollection of it. It is the decision to go ahead that I am sure I do not remember."

Bundy said that he would have been "surprised" if any effort to assassinate a foreign leader had been undertaken without his approval as the president's assistant for national security affairs, and he said that he himself would "not have authorized anything of that kind without much higher authority than my own. I could not exclude that there would be communication with the president by other channels. Neither President Kennedy nor President Johnson always used any one channel."

The director of central intelligence had direct access to the president, according to Bundy. He said that based on his experience,

"I would not have expected . . . the Agency would have undertaken anything like an attack on the life of a foreign leader without direct order from higher authority. . . . It did not happen in the time I was there . . . but I can conceive of the President saying to somebody, 'I do not want to make this decision' but giving some indication of the kind of decision he wanted made."

Bundy's testimony did not ring true in light of other evidence. A 1967 CIA inspector general's report quoted Richard Bissell telling William Harvey early in the Kennedy administration that "the White House has twice urged me to create" an executive action capability. Moreover, Bundy, like McNamara, seemed ill at ease during portions of his testimony. He seemed worried as he left the commission hearing room.

Early the next morning I received a telephone call from him. He said he had been thinking about the matter overnight and wanted to come in and make some additions and modifications to his testimony.

Bundy said that in thinking about the matter overnight, "I have had a vague recollection, which I cannot pinpoint in time, that there was discussion that I knew about at some time of a proposal or scheme or project" in relation to the Castro regime "that did involve poison, and the characteristic that sticks in my memory is that it would have involved a rather large scale use of poison and, as I recollect it, it never came anywhere near approval." Proposals under the overall plan with regard to Cuba "which did come from time to time (mostly not with respect to assassination) were reviewed in the first instance for practicability and only after that for wisdom or political rightness, and I recall no proposal for liquidation that ever got past the first stage to the second."

Bundy said, "I simply have no recollection of plans" that "existed in January or February 1961" that involved the attempted poisoning of any Cuban leader. "I believe my memory tells me in a more general way that my knowledge of a scheme or idea of using poison probably relates to the year 1962."

BUNDY: "I am absolutely certain that I never knew of or believed that there was any authorization to go ahead with an effort to liquidate Castro, or any other Cuban leader."

With reference to his testimony concerning an "executive action capability," Bundy said, "I recall the words 'executive action capability' more clearly today than I did yesterday . . . but I do not have any recollection as to what I knew about that or who requested it or how much was done under it. I don't recall having any particular continuing interest in or information about that particular activity," which was "something like" a "plan to have some kind of stand-by capability for action against individuals."

Another important member of the Special Group (Augmented) was Gen. Maxwell Taylor. President Kennedy asked Taylor on April 22, 1961, to work with Robert Kennedy and conduct a reevaluation of military, paramilitary, guerrilla, and antiguerrilla activities that fall short of outright war, with particular attention to Cuba. Within months, Operation "Mongoose" was hatched. The goal, in the words of a November 30, 1961, memorandum from President Kennedy to Secretary of State Rusk, was to "use our available assets . . . to help Cuba overthrow the Communist regime."

According to written memoranda, Taylor was at the August 10, 1962, meeting of the Special Group (Augmented). In testimony, though, Taylor said that he had no recollection of any assassination plan being discussed, although he said that it might have been.

Taylor also stated that he was not aware of the existence of any plans to assassinate Castro. He said that he did not have any discussions with the president concerning the possibility or the existence of any such plans. However, "in the case of Bob Kennedy and Allen Dulles, we talked about so many things at the time of the Bay of Pigs as we sat around the table I couldn't say—that the desirability of the disappearance of Castro or what would happen if he were assassinated in Cuba—that was not raised, I don't recall." He said he didn't recall any conversations about assassination with Bundy or Walt W. Rostow, Bundy's assistant who succeeded Bundy in the Johnson administration, "I couldn't say that discussion in the abstract—'wouldn't it be a nice thing if someone bumped Castro off'—that could well have been said, but I just don't recall it."

Taylor said that he never knew of any authorization for the CIA to undertake any assassination. He also said he had no knowledge of the phrase "executive action capability" or any proposal for the CIA to develop a general standby capability to assassinate foreign leaders.

I then went to Gen. Lyman Lemnitzer, a member of the Rockefeller Commission who was present at the August 10, 1962, meeting. In an affidavit, he declared he had no recollection of the question of the liquidation of Castro or other Cuban leaders being discussed.

The picture was clear. President Kennedy directly asked General Lansdale to come up with "suggestions or recommendations" about "the situation in Cuba" and to do this for him "personally." Lansdale suggests "an intermediary," and President Kennedy appoints his brother, the attorney general. With the addition of Robert Kennedy, General Lansdale's group becomes known as the "Special Group (Augmented)," with the "Augmented" person being Robert Kennedy.

Lansdale works under Robert McNamara. There is a meeting of the Special Group (Augmented) on August 10, 1962. A written memorandum of that meeting is prepared summarizing the discussions, and in it Lansdale puts as part of the alternatives discussed the phrase "including liquidation of leaders."

That this was discussed is documented by the William Harvey memorandum of August 14, 1962. Despite the memorandum, Lansdale claims he never heard of any discussions to liquidate foreign leaders. McNamara said he had no recollection of anything and did not even remember being present at the August 10 meeting, although the minutes record his being there.

Bundy walked a tightrope and said he was never aware of any "actual decision" to assassinate any foreign leader. "I never knew of or believed there was any authorization to go ahead with an effort to liquidate Castro, or any other Cuban leader." Maxwell

Taylor said he had no recollection of any assassination plan being discussed, but he admitted that it might have been discussed with the president. He also admitted that the possibility or desirability of the assassination of Castro may have been discussed with Robert Kennedy.

Based on the documentary evidence, the testimony of Harvey and his memoranda, and the admissions of Lansdale, McNamara, Bundy, and Taylor, it was clear that if this information were all put before a jury, there would be little doubt what they would conclude. The highest officials of the Kennedy administration were intimately involved in the discussions of CIA plans to assassinate Fidel Castro. Robert Kennedy was also intimately involved with those plans, and I believe his brother also knew.

At the Rockefeller Commission, there were knowing looks from several members, who referred to the "amnesia syndrome" of much of the leadership of government during the Kennedy and Johnson years, particularly with reference to Cuba and Vietnam. Ironically, one member of the commission, Ronald Reagan, would within a few years become president and witness the same syndrome in his administration.

There is one interesting sidelight that took place during the interrogation of John McCone about the August 10, 1962, meeting. McCone said he vividly remembered the meeting because he was about to leave for a trip to Europe—I believe he said it was on a delayed honeymoon with his wife.

Shortly before he was to leave, he heard that missiles were being installed in Cuba. When he discussed this with McNamara, Rusk, and others, he was assured that they were defensive missiles.

McCone said he was sure they were not just defensive missiles. Information from the CIA, including photos interpreted by CIA experts, led McCone to conclude that McNamara, Rusk, and the rest were wrong.

McCone contacted someone in whom he had great confidence to ask how to best present his case to the president. He was told that his best course of action would be through the Congressional Armed Forces Committee and that the best person to contact on that committee was a congressman from Michigan—Gerald

Ford—who also was very concerned about the "nature" of the Russian missiles.

McCone said he reached Ford and that Ford helped pave the way toward convincing Kennedy that the missiles were offensive in character. By September, the suspicions of McCone were confirmed, and the president acted decisively in the Cuban missile crisis to force the dismantling of the Russian missiles. What would have happened if there had not been a CIA, independent of the State and Defense departments, to bring such matters to the attention of the president?

After President Ford studied the Rockefeller Commission Report, he directed his staff to prepare a comprehensive executive order governing U.S. foreign-intelligence activities. The final executive order (No. 11905) was published on February 19, 1976. Here are the salient sections pertaining to CIA involvement in assassination plots:

Section 1. *Purpose.*   The purpose of this Order is to establish policies to improve the quality of intelligence needed for national security, to clarify the authority and responsibilities of the intelligence departments and agencies, and to establish effective oversight to assure compliance with law in the management and direction of intelligence agencies and departments of the national government. . . .

Sec. 5. *Restrictions on Intelligence Activities.*   Information about the capabilities, intentions and activities of other governments is essential to informed decision-making in the field of national defense and foreign relations. The measures employed to acquire such information should be responsive to the legitimate needs of our Government and must be conducted in a manner which preserves and respects our established concepts of privacy and our civil liberties.

Recent events have clearly indicated the desirability of government-wide direction which will ensure a proper balancing of these interests. This section of this Order does not authorize any activity not previously authorized and does not provide exemption from any restrictions otherwise applicable. Unless otherwise specified, the provisions of this section apply to activities both inside and outside the United States. References to law are to applicable laws of the United States.

(a) *Definitions.*   As used in this section of this Order, the following terms shall have the meanings ascribed to them below: . . .

(4) "Employee" means a person employed by, assigned or detailed to, or acting for a United States foreign intelligence agency. . . .

(g) *Prohibition of Assassination.*   No employee of the United States Government shall engage in, or conspire to engage in, political assassination.

(h) *Implementation.*

(1) This section of this Order shall be effective on March 1, 1976. Each department and agency affected by this section of this Order shall promptly issue internal directives to implement this section with respect to its foreign intelligence and counter-intelligence operations.

(2) The Attorney General shall, within ninety days of the effective date of this section of this Order, issue guidelines relating to activities of the Federal Bureau of Investigation in the areas of foreign intelligence and counterintelligence.

Of course, there are two major problems with this presidential order. The first is how one can make certain that the presidential order is followed. CIA director William Casey and Lt. Col. Oliver North were not following federal statutes when they were involved in the Irangate scandal and the improper diversion of funds to the Nicaraguan Contras.

Moreover, inside the CIA people were developing scenarios to show why the presidential order was not necessarily appropriate for all occasions. The example most often cited was Adolf Hitler. "Would not the world have been better off if we had had a CIA in 1938 and someone had gone over to assassinate Adolf Hitler?"

Another problem, of course, is in the definition of what is prohibited: "*Political*" assassination.

The order did not issue an absolute prohibition against any conspiracy or plot to murder, nor was there any prohibition of "military" assassination.

The "opposition," to use a favorite CIA word, has no such limitations on the activities of their secret intelligence agencies. Why should we? Is it not necessary to "fight fire with fire"?

The answer, of course, is that we cannot let the ends justify the means and adopt the same standards followed by the "opposition." If we let ourselves fall into such a trap, we will be undercutting the very foundations of our democratic society that we so dearly prize.

Yet there is still that question to be answered: What would we do if there were another Adolf Hitler who came into power and threatened world domination?

# 20

# The Phase III Plans

The Bay of Pigs fiasco was over, and Castro was still in power. The Cuban missile crisis was over, and Castro was still in power.

Inside the CIA there was frustration. In the White House there was frustration. Richard Helms asserted that Castro was becoming almost an "obsession" with the Kennedy administration in general and Robert Kennedy in particular.

Whether this White House pressure had anything to do with the continuing plans inside the CIA is a matter of speculation. However, there is no doubt that inside the agency Fidel Castro was not a forgotten man.

During 1963 several schemes were developed inside the agency for possible use against Castro. Helms testified he was vaguely aware of some of these, which he called "harebrained." There was no indication that any extended beyond the discussion stage. One involved discussions inside the CIA of having General Donovan, who was negotiating with Castro for the release of the Bay of Pigs prisoners, give Castro a contaminated skin-diving suit. The CIA plan was to dust the inside of the suit with a fungus producing madera foot, a disabling and chronic skin disease, and also to contaminate the suit with tuberculosis bacilli in the breathing apparatus. There is no evidence that Donovan knew of any such schemes, and that idea itself was dropped because Donovan of his own volition gave Castro an uncontaminated skin-diving suit as a gesture of friendship.

There were also discussions about preparing a booby-trapped seashell to be submerged where Castro skin-dived. The seashell would be loaded with explosives to blow when it was lifted. After investigation, it was determined that there was no shell in the Caribbean large enough to hold a sufficient amount of explosive and spectacular enough to attract the attention of Castro. Also, a midget submarine that was to be used to place the shell did not have a long enough operating range.

Meanwhile, a more promising situation arose. It involved a high-ranking Cuban official who had been an early Castro supporter and a member of a group that helped overthrow Cuban dictator Juan Batista. Shortly after Castro took over the government, this Cuban became disenchanted because of "the harsh police state policies that were being carried out."

At first, the Cuban wanted to defect, and the CIA made contact with him. From the standpoint of the CIA, the man was far more valuable inside Cuba. The CIA sought to persuade him to stay, saying he would be able to do something significant. Inside the CIA, he became known as AM/LASH. Knowledge of his activities was confined to a select few.

In 1963 a CIA employee fluent in Spanish was assigned to the Special Operations Group on Cuba. This employee, the Phase III case officer, was assigned "to collect intelligence and to try to organize a group of military officers inside Cuba who were opposed to the Cuban regime—the Castro regime."

In late 1963, the Phase III case officer met with AM/LASH outside of Cuba. At this first 1963 meeting, the case officer testified, there was no discussion about assassination of any Cuban leader.

At a subsequent 1963 meeting, in Europe, the case officer said, discussions concerned "getting into more detail on the organization of a group inside Cuba which could be used in an internal coup against the Castro government."

THE CASE OFFICER: "The subject of assassination was never raised by me. It was never discussed in that context. In discussing the coup and how a coup would be carried out, this particular contact did raise the possibility and in his mind the very real possibility that there would be bloodshed, and that somebody would be killed. Their, or his, opinion was that to even get the internal revolt, a coup, under way that the leadership—the top leadership—would have to be neutralized. Specific assassination of any of the people, it was not discussed in those particular terms."

According to the case officer, AM/LASH held a relatively high position in the Cuban government. The Cuban "requested a meeting [with] a high level policymaker in Washington, specifically mentioning Robert Kennedy as one of the people with whom he would like to talk, to get some assurance that Washington was serious about proceeding with this type of an operation."

The Cuban also said "that they would need some help in arms probably in getting started, in kicking off the coup." The Cuban mentioned high-powered rifles and scopes and said "they felt that they could capture sufficient arms to carry on once they started."

Inside the agency it was agreed that Desmond Fitzgerald, chief of the special affairs staff, would meet with AM/LASH. Fitzgerald had replaced William Harvey as head of the covert Cuban operations. The CIA developed a plan whereby Fitzgerald would represent himself as the personal representative of Robert Kennedy. There was disagreement in testimony about whether Robert Kennedy knew about this meeting.

Fitzgerald met AM/LASH in Europe and "assured him . . . that the U.S. Government was serious about this operation . . ." and "that the U.S. Government was prepared to support the coup and that when they launched the coup as soon as they established themselves in any reasonable manner inside Cuba that the U.S. Government would support them."

There was another meeting that was planned for Europe. The day was prophetic: November 22, 1963: AM/LASH wanted the

CIA to develop a special device. There was disagreement within the agency whether this device was to be used to assassinate Castro, using a deadly poison, or whether it was to be used for self-defense. Although the CIA did not develop the precise device requested by AM/LASH, it did develop a ballpoint pen that had a hypodermic needle inside. When you pushed the lever, the needle came out and poison could be injected into someone. The Phase III case officer showed the pen to the Cuban contact on November 22, 1963. The Cuban contact declined the gadget "because of the close proximity with which he would have to get to a person if anything developed in the form of a confrontation with him." Instead, the Cuban asked for weapons, and the case officer told the Cuban "that a cache of weapons would be put down for him in Cuba."

One or two caches of weapons, including high-powered rifles with scopes, were subsequently placed down in Cuba. In addition, the Phase III case officer said he delivered money to help the Cuban contact with his living expenses while in Europe. "It was around $1,000 at one time, no more than that."

The case officer broke off contact with the Cuban in late 1964 and was reassigned. The Cuban contact then was turned over to a Cuban exile group whose goal was to assassinate Castro. The CIA tried to arrange the meeting between the Cuban exile group and AM/LASH in a way that would leave the CIA out of the picture. However, there was a major problem: Too many people were starting to know about AM/LASH and his plan. Furthermore, there was little doubt by knowledgeable people inside the CIA that Castro penetrated many activities of the Cuban exile community.

After CIA support was withdrawn, a Cuban leader was arrested in March 1966. According to a *Prensa Latina* news release, the man confessed to receiving rifles with telescopic sights from the CIA to be used for the assassination of Castro. The man also claimed he received $100,000 for this plan.

Naturally, Secretary of State Rusk was concerned about this news story. So the CIA sent a memorandum to Rusk shortly after the story appeared. In this memorandum the CIA said that the contact it had made with the high government official in Cuba was in order to collect intelligence of military activities and objectives in Cuba. The agency said: "There is no truth to the allegations that the CIA paid $100,000 or any other sizable sum of money" as claimed in the Cuban newspapers following the confession. The CIA also said "the Agency was not involved" with either of two men arrested by Cuba "in a plot to assassinate Fidel Castro as claimed in the *Prensa Latina* news release, nor did it ever encourage either of these two persons to attempt such an act. . . ." The memorandum to Rusk was signed by Richard Helms and was dated March 6, 1966.

Helms may have been right when he said the CIA never paid $100,000. He might also have been technically correct in saying that "the Agency was not involved" in any plot to assassinate Castro, with Helms assuming this meant in 1966, or even in 1965, when the involvement was with Cuban exile groups. But what Helms did not tell Rusk—a member of the NSC, which has authority over the CIA—was the whole truth behind AM/LASH, nor did Helms tell Rusk about the Phase I or Phase II plans.

There is one final footnote—a footnote that appears in no CIA documents but which was told to me by a CIA officer. AM/LASH may have been a double agent. His arrest did not take place until months after his direct association with the CIA had been terminated. Though he was arrested for plotting the death of Castro, he was not executed. AM/LASH was merely imprisoned—in stark contrast to what ordinarily happens in totalitarian regimes when a key person is arrested in an unsuccessful plot to assassinate a dictator.

# 21

## The CIA's Spying on American Citizens

### Intercepting U.S. Mail

U.S. statutes forbid opening U.S. mail, as any nation must that operates under the rule of law. Yet our investigation disclosed that over a period of twenty years the CIA engaged in a program that led to the illegal interception of mail.

The CIA mail-intercept program is probably the best illustration of the importance of having adequate supervision and control over a secret intelligence agency. The reason is threefold:

1. The mail-intercept program transcended both Democratic and Republican administrations.

2. The CIA program was a typical example of one potential illegality leading to another.

3. The CIA program was directly in violation of federal statutes.

The idea for the program occurred barely five years after the CIA was formed, in the last year of the Truman administration. The CIA recognized that mail was a potential source of intelligence. It also recognized that there were federal statutes involved.

What did the CIA do? In a planning memorandum dated July 1, 1952, the chief of the Special Security Division wrote:

> I believe we should make contact in the Post Office Department at a very high level, pleading relative ignorance of the situation and asking that we, with their cooperation, make a thorough study of the volume of such mail, the channels through which it passes and particularly the bottlenecks within the United States in which we might place our survey team.

The plan was really to deceive the Post Office Department into thinking the CIA was only going to try to examine the outside of the mail. From the very beginning, the intent was to go much further. The last paragraph of the July 1 memorandum stated:

> Once our unit was in position, its activities and influence could be extended gradually, so as to secure from this source every drop of potential information available. At the outset, however, as far as the Post Office is concerned, our mail target could be the securing of names and addresses for investigation and possible further contact.

Inside the CIA, the wheels started to turn. One thing the CIA determined was that the FBI maintained no records of correspondence between U.S. and Soviet citizens. Therefore, CIA officials discussed advising the FBI of what they planned to do, noting that any mail operation would require the cooperation of both the Post Office Department and the FBI. Inside the CIA, a memorandum referred to the sensitivity of the operation as "patently obvious."

On November 6, 1952, the CIA contacted the chief postal inspector and asked him to work with one or two CIA employees. The CIA told the post office that its intention was to examine the outside of envelopes.

By December 1952 the CIA was surveying how all mail passing to and from the Soviet Union was handled through New York. By February 1953, unbeknownst to the Eisenhower administration or the Post Office Department, CIA employees were unlawfully opening mail. However, gleaning information this way was not enough. CIA officials decided to photograph both sides of all first-class mail to and from the Soviet Union.

The agency, however, ran into problems with postal inspectors. They were unwilling to go forward without authorization from higher officials in the Post Office Department. The CIA didn't want to be thwarted. Allen Dulles, the CIA director, and Richard Helms, chief of operations in the plans directorate, in May 1954 met with Postmaster General Arthur Summerfield and three of Summerfield's assistants.

Dulles told Summerfield how important the mail program was and asked that it be allowed to continue. At this meeting, Dulles never leveled with Summerfield that the CIA planned to open mail, not just examine the covers. Summerfield, on the basis of the information given, gave the go-ahead.

The next step was to find out how to circumvent the statute that says no one can open the U.S. mail. The CIA came up with a unique answer, combining bribery with patriotism: Find a postal employee who will turn his back on what you do, tell him it is for the good of the country, and pay him off. The plan worked. The CIA found a cooperative employee in a low-echelon position in New York, through which all mail to and from Iron Curtain countries passed.

By late 1955, the CIA had eight full-time employees and several part-time employees engaged in opening mail.

Everything was going smoothly—except for one problem: Not enough mail was being opened. This led to the next step: approval within the CIA of a new counterintelligence program to work in conjunction with the mail project.

Despite recognition of the legal problems, the expansion proposed by the CIA counterintelligence staff was adopted and was ready to go in late 1956.

Although at one time the CIA had talked about telling the FBI what it was doing and although the FBI had responsibility for counterintelligence inside the United States, the CIA did not trust the FBI. Therefore, the CIA kept the FBI in the dark about the mail-opening project. The FBI found out by happenstance. In January 1955 the FBI, on its own, approached the Post Office Department about monitoring mail to and from the Soviet Union.

The Post Office Department was aware of what they thought was a CIA program to photograph the covers of envelopes going to and from the Soviet Union, so they brought the FBI to the CIA.

Within weeks, a cooperative plan was worked out. The CIA agreed that it would send to the FBI purloined items of internal-security interest. In turn, the FBI would provide the CIA with lists of persons or matters in which the FBI was interested. FBI and CIA personnel agreed the mail project should be continued by the CIA alone so far as the actual opening of mail and photographing of covers were concerned. However, gradually the primary beneficiary of the project became the FBI.

By 1959 the CIA was examining the covers of millions of items of mail each year. In 1959 alone it opened over thirteen thousand letters—thirteen thousand violations of the law.

By the end of 1960 the CIA installed a small laboratory for technical examination of letters in an effort to uncover foreign-espionage techniques of communication. Everything was done right on location in New York City. Envelopes of letters selected during the initial scanning process were photographed. Then the most important letters were opened, their contents photographed, and the letters resealed. The watch lists were primarily provided by the FBI and also by the counterintelligence staff or other components of the CIA. There were several hundred names on the watch lists, including both foreigners and U.S. citizens.

With the inauguration of John Kennedy in January 1961, there was a new postmaster general. His name was J. Edward Day. A meeting was set up on February 15, 1961, among Day, Allen Dulles, and Helms.

What happened at that meeting is not entirely clear. Dulles is dead. Helms's memory is not precise. However, a memorandum by Helms on February 16, 1961, stated that Day was advised of the "background, development and current status" of the mail project, "withholding no relevant details." On the other hand, Day said that when Dulles came to visit him, Dulles said he had something "very secret" to talk about. Day said he told Dulles he would rather "not know about the secret," and according to Day, Dulles did not tell him anything about it.

Inside the CIA, the inspector general's office forms a vital part of the internal auditing and controls. The inspector general is appointed by the agency director and is charged with reviewing employee grievances, supervising equal-employment practices, investigating reports of wrongdoing, and performing special management reviews of CIA activities. When the inspector general found out about the mail-opening program in 1960, he had two choices: He could close the operation. Or he could look for the best way to retreat if knowledge of the plan outside the agency created a "flap." He chose the latter. The inspector general's office recommended the preparation of an "emergency plan" and "cover story" in case knowledge of the plan leaked.

On February 1, 1962, the deputy chief of counterintelligence wrote the director of security asserting that "the effort was worth the risk," although acknowledging that "a flap would put us [the project] out of business immediately and give rise to grave charges of criminal misuse of the mails by government agencies." The memorandum acknowledged that if there was a major leak, there would be a formal "charge of violation of the mails."

> Since no good purpose can be served by an official admission of the violation, and existing Federal Statutes preclude the concoction of any legal excuse for the violation, it must be recognized that no cover story is available to any government agency.
>
> Unless the charge is supported by the presentation of interior items from the project, it should be relatively easy to "hush-up" the entire affair, or to explain that it consists of legal mail cover activities conducted by the Post Office at the request of authorized Federal Agencies. Under the most unfavorable circumstances, including the support of charges with interior items from the project it might become necessary, after the matter has cooled off during an extended period of investigation, to find a scapegoat to blame for unauthorized tampering with the mails.

On September 26, 1963, the CIA officer in charge of the mail project wrote a memorandum to another officer in the Operations Division. "There is no legal basis for monitoring postal communications in the United States except during time of war or national emergency," he wrote.

Inside the CIA, the general counsel has jurisdiction in matters involving the law. However, the Rockefeller Commission found nothing in all of the records of the CIA to indicate that the agency's legal counsel was ever asked to give an opinion on the mail-intercept program. The reason is obvious: The opinion would have said that the project was unlawful.

In November 1964, Lyndon Johnson was elected, and a new postmaster general was appointed. The intercept program continued. The CIA talked about perhaps advising Johnson of the program, but this was rejected; instead, internal instructions were given "to arrange to pass this information through McGeorge Bundy to the president" after a then current investigation by a Senate subcommittee concerning governmental agencies engaged in "snooping into the mail" was completed.

Richard Nixon was elected in November 1968. A new postmaster general was appointed. The program continued. The new postmaster general, Winton Blount, refused to testify before the Rockfeller Commission on this matter. However, the record shows that he was looking for a new chief postal inspector and that he went to none other than Richard Helms for a recommendation. By now, Helms was the DCI. He suggested the names of three or four persons, one of whom was William J. Cotter, who had been with the CIA since 1951.

Cotter left the CIA on April 8, 1969, to be sworn in as chief postal inspector. He was worried. As he was leaving the CIA, he expressed concern that his new position might force him to disclose the existence of the mail project. What could be done? Cotter indicated he did not plan to make any inquiries about the project and planned to do nothing about it unless someone mentioned it to him. He thought he might ultimately have to disclose it to the postmaster general.

In a July 1969 review of the counterintelligence staff by the CIA inspector general, for the first time there was an express recommendation that the CIA get out of the mail-interception program either by canceling the project or by transferring it to the FBI. The inspector general's recommendation was not followed.

Things went smoothly until January 1971, when Cotter received a letter from an association of American scientists inquiring whether first-class mail was being opened with acquiescence by the Post Office Department. Cotter advised the CIA of his concern. He was loyal to the CIA, but he could not deny knowledge of the project under oath. Furthermore, Cotter felt his highest loyalty belonged to the postmaster general. Helms talked with Cotter, and it was agreed Helms would go to Postmaster General Blount—but first Helms wanted to talk with the attorney general of the United States, John Mitchell.

On June 1, 1971, Helms met with Mitchell. According to Helms, Mitchell concurred in the value of the operation and expressed no objections to its continuation.

Mitchell also encouraged Helms to brief Blount, and on June 2, Helms met with Blount. No major objection was raised, according to all CIA records, and the project continued. But Cotter grew increasingly uneasy. Finally, in early 1973, he demanded that unless the CIA obtained higher-level approval for the project by February 15, 1973, it would have to be terminated.

By then, James Schlesinger was the DCI, and Cotter's ultimatum was directed to his attention. The counterintelligence staff under James Angleton argued that the project should be continued because of its importance to the FBI and the CIA. Schlesinger determined that the project should be turned over to the FBI and should not be handled by the CIA because "the product to the CIA" from the mail project was not "worth the risk of CIA involvement" and the flap that would result if it were discovered.

The great majority of high CIA officials I interviewed shared the view of James Schlesinger that the net intelligence gain derived from the mail-interception program was not worth the risk of CIA involvement in a project that was specifically forbidden by federal statute.

Schlesinger did agree to ask Cotter to deter termination while the CIA took it to a "very high level," but Cotter refused, and the project was closed on February 15, 1973.

By then the interception had become massive. For instance, in

1972 the New York mail intercept examined the outside of over 2,300,000 items, and photographs were taken of 33,000 items. Of these, 8,700 were opened and their contents analyzed—the majority made on the basis of the watch lists. By the end of 1972, the active watch-list names totaled 600. Initially, only mail coming into the United States had been intercepted, but during the latter years, both incoming and outgoing mail was opened. But file data were provided going back to 1955 in a compartmentalized, computerized record system containing almost 2 million entries.

The main program was developed in the New York City operation. However, there were three minor programs outside New York: a 1954–55 project in Hawaii, a three-week program in New Orleans in 1957, and a 1970–71 program in San Francisco.

For the FBI, the primary value of the project was in internal-security matters. For instance, a U.S. citizen on the FBI watch list was suspected of having contacts with KGB intelligence. This could possibly be verified by opening the suspect's mail directed to the Soviet Union. From the standpoint of the CIA, the mail-opening project provided a useful source of technical communications intelligence on such matters as secret writing, censorship techniques, and confirmation of otherwise questionable information. The counterintelligence staff felt that they gained strategically important counterintelligence leads.

To be sure, there was some intelligence benefit from the mail openings, but the benefit was not nearly so great as the CIA or FBI would have one believe. And the benefit occurred at a high price: violation of a federal statute. This is wholly apart from constitutional questions under the Fourth Amendment, which guarantees citizens freedom from unreasonable search and seizure, and under the First Amendment, which guarantees rights of free speech.

Who was to blame? Lots of people. The top officers of the CIA knew the federal law and yet initiated and continued the project. The top officers of the Post Office Department—some knowingly and others unwittingly—acquiesced. So did at least one attorney general, and perhaps others. The oversight arms inside the CIA, which did not close down the project even though they knew it was unlawful, bear a share of the blame. Congress, for failing to exercise proper oversight, can be faulted, as well.

Ironically, the CIA, in its unlawful mail-interception project, had adopted the tactics of the "opposition" that the end justified the means, however illegal.

## Operation "CHAOS"

The name of the CIA operation was "CHAOS." Like the unlawful opening of U.S. mail, Operation CHAOS was a creature nurtured and developed in both Democratic and Republican administrations. However, there was a major difference between CHAOS and the mail program. The impetus and pressure to expand the mail program came from within the CIA. The pressure for CHAOS emanated from the White House.

· When President Eisenhower left office in January 1961, there were fewer than nine hundred American troops in Vietnam. President Kennedy increased our presence to nearly twenty thousand troops. Lyndon Johnson called for more escalation, until there were more than five hundred thousand American troops in Vietnam. But despite the fact that the Johnson administration (through deceptive claims) had gotten overwhelming support from Congress in rushing through the Gulf of Tonkin resolution, on college campuses and elsewhere there was more and more unrest about the war. A new phrase came into being: "American dissidents."

Demonstrations increased in 1967. On January 21, nearly two thousand people marched in front of the White House, demanding a halt to the bombing of North Vietnam and calling for a deescalation of the ground war in South Vietnam. On April 15, massive demonstrations and parades were held in New York and San Francisco to protest U.S. policy in Vietnam. The summer of 1967 was marked by some of the worst protest disturbances in our recent history; thousands were arrested, and 83 people were killed, 1,897 people injured, and hundreds of millions of dollars of property destroyed.

It was in this context that President Johnson, on July 2, 1967, formed the Kerner Commission—the National Commission on Civil Disorders—and directed it to investigate and make recommendations concerning the origins of the civil disorders. The president instructed all departments and agencies to assist the Kerner Commission by supplying information to it.

Inside the White House, there was dissatisfaction with whether the FBI could handle this alone. So the president went to Richard Helms, the DCI, to pressure the CIA to determine whether there were any substantial foreign connections with the racial violence and civil disturbances.

An FBI memorandum stated:

> The White House recently informed Richard Helms, Director, CIA, that the Agency should exert every possible effort to collect information concerning U.S. racial agitators who might travel abroad . . . because of the pressure placed upon Helms, a new desk has been created at the Agency for the explicit purpose of collecting information coming into the Agency and having any significant bearing on possible racial disturbances in the U.S.

On August 15, 1967, an internal directive in the CIA established an operation for overseas coverage of subversive student activities and related matters. On August 29 the Kerner Commission requested CIA information on civil disorders. At first, the CIA offered to supply only information on foreign connections with domestic disorders. That was lawful. However, once again, the CIA moved from legal to illegal investigative procedures and then from one illegality to the next.

Inside the CIA, an officer already was developing a computer system to categorize, store, and retrieve information on Americans abroad who were part of the "New Left."

A crash program was undertaken to study the "international connections of the United States peace movement." The CIA collected all available government information on dissident groups. All field stations of the CIA's clandestine service were asked to provide any information they had. This was of little consequence. Most information came from the FBI.

**DEALEY PLAZA -- DALLAS, TEXAS**

1. TEXAS SCHOOL BOOK DEPOSITORY
2. DAL-TEX BUILDING
3. DALLAS COUNTY RECORDS BUILDING
4. DALLAS COUNTY CRIMINAL COURTS BUILDING
5. OLD COURT HOUSE
6. NEELEY BRYAN HOUSE
7. DALLAS COUNTY GOVERNMENT CENTER (UNDER CONSTRUCTION)
8. UNITED STATES POST OFFICE BUILDING
9. PERGOLAS
10. PERISTYLES AND REFLECTING POOLS
11. RAILROAD OVERPASS (TRIPLE UNDERPASS)

The Dealey Plaza area, Dallas, Texas. The motorcade turned right from Main Street onto Houston Street and then made a reflex-angle turn left from Houston onto Elm Street. *Warren Commission Exhibit No. 876, courtesy of The National Archives.*

President John F. Kennedy, Jacqueline Kennedy, Governor John Connally, and Nellie Connally in the presidential limousine in the Dallas motorcade minutes before the assassination. There were two Secret Service agents in the front seat: William Greer, the driver, and Roy Kellerman. *Warren Commission Exhibit No. 697, courtesy of The National Archives.*

The presidential limousine shortly after the first shot struck President Kennedy. Secret Service agents in the follow-up car are standing on the running board and looking toward the rear, from where they thought they heard the shots coming. The building in the background is the front of the Texas School Book Depository. *Warren Commission Exhibit No. 203, courtesy of Wide World Photos.*

Simulated view from the point of J. D. Tippit's squad car to William W. Scoggins's cab. The house on the left with the porch is where Barbara and Virginia Davis saw Oswald cutting across their lawn running toward the cab as he tossed cartridge cases into the bushes. *Warren Commission Exhibit No. 534, courtesy of The National Archives.*

**PHOTOGRAPH FROM ZAPRUDER FILM**

**PHOTOGRAPH FROM RE-ENACTMENT**

**PHOTOGRAPH THROUGH RIFLE SCOPE**

| | |
|---|---|
| DISTANCE TO STATION C | 151.4 FT. |
| DISTANCE TO RIFLE IN WINDOW | 188.6 FT. |
| ANGLE TO RIFLE IN WINDOW | 20°23' |
| DISTANCE TO OVERPASS | 336.4 FT. |
| ANGLE TO OVERPASS | +0°24' |

## FRAME 222

Reconstruction of the location of the motorcade at the approximate moment when the first shot struck President Kennedy in the neck and exited at a speed of about 1,775 feet per second, striking Governor Connally, who was directly in line with President Kennedy and with the rifle in the southeast corner window of the sixth floor of the depository building. *Warren Commission Exhibit No. 894, courtesy of Henry Zapruder.*

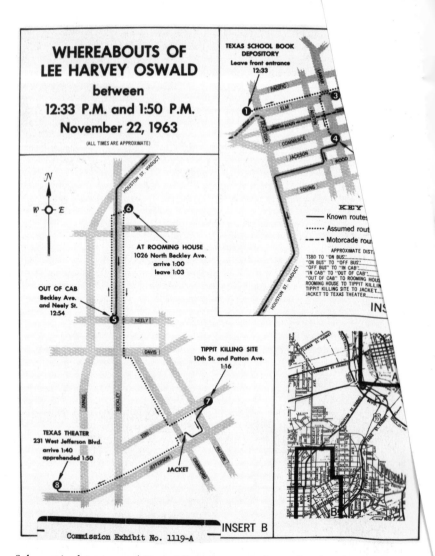

**WHEREABOUTS OF LEE HARVEY OSWALD between 12:33 P.M. and 1:50 P.M. November 22, 1963**

(ALL TIMES ARE APPROXIMATE)

**TEXAS SCHOOL BOOK DEPOSITORY**
Leave front entrance
12:33

AT ROOMING HOUSE
1026 North Beckley Ave.
arrive 1:00
leave 1:03

OUT OF CAB
Beckley Ave.
and Neely St.
12:54

TIPPIT KILLING SITE
10th St. and Patton Ave.
1:16

TEXAS THEATER
231 West Jefferson Blvd.
arrive 1:40
apprehended 1:50

JACKET

**KEY**
—— Known routes
········ Assumed rout
– – – Motorcade rou

APPROXIMATE DIST
TSBO TO "ON BUS"
"ON BUS" TO "OFF BUS"
"OFF BUS" TO "IN CAB"
"IN CAB" TO "OUT OF CAB"
"OUT OF CAB" TO ROOMING HOUS
ROOMING HOUSE TO TIPPIT KILLIN
TIPPIT KILLING SITE TO JACKET
JACKET TO TEXAS THEATER

INSERT B

Commission Exhibit No. 1119-A

Schematic drawings of Oswald's movements from the time he left the depository building shortly after the assassination to the time of his apprehension at the Texas Theatre. *Warren Commission Exhibit No. 1119-A, courtesy of The National Archives.*

Simulation of Howard Brennan as he sat on the retaining wall facing the depository building, where he saw a gunman in the southeast corner sixth-floor window take aim and fire the last shot. In the southeast corner fifth-floor windows were other Texas School Book Depository employees watching the motorcade, including Junior Jarman, with whom Oswald claimed he was having lunch at the time of the assassination. *Warren Commission Exhibit No. 477, courtesy of The National Archives.*

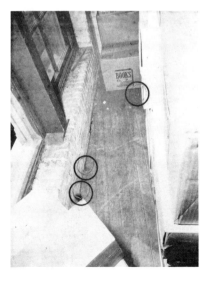

The southeast corner sixth-floor window of the depository building shortly after the assassination. The open window is where Brennan saw the rifleman. The boxes by the window were used as a gun rest by Oswald; the cartridge cases from his rifle are circled. *Warren Commission Exhibit No. 512, courtesy of The National Archives.*

Lee Harvey Oswald, with his pistol in its holster, holding his rifle and a copy of the *Militant* newspaper. This picture was taken in the backyard with Oswald's own camera. *Warren Commission Exhibit No. 133-A, courtesy of Tony Spina and the* Detroit Free Press.

The Mannlicher-Carcano rifle No. C-2766, purchased through the mail by Oswald under the alias A. J. Hidell. *Warren Commission Exhibit No. 139, courtesy of The National Archives.*

Oswald's revolver, which he had ordered through the mail under the alias A. J. Hidell. *Warren Commission Exhibit No. 134, courtesy of The National Archives.*

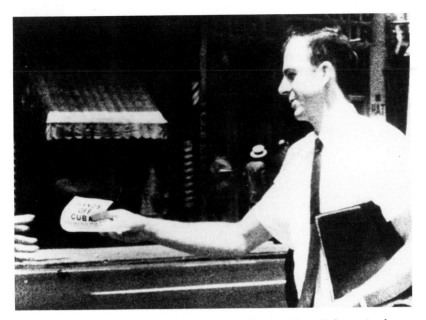

Oswald passing out a "Hands Off Cuba" flier in New Orleans in the summer of 1963. *Garner Exhibit 1, courtesy of The National Archives.*

A copy of a "Hands Off Cuba" sheet shows Oswald's name clearly stamped on the bottom. *Warren Commission Exhibit No. 2966-A, courtesy of The National Archives.*

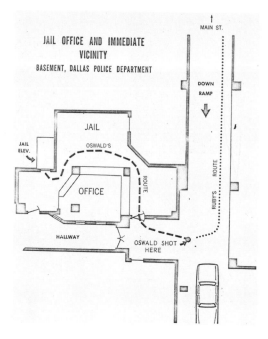

Diagram of the jail, office, and immediate vicinity in the basement of the Dallas Police Department, where Jack Ruby shot Oswald. *Warren Commission Exhibit No. 2177, courtesy of The National Archives.*

The instant Jack Ruby darted forward to shoot Oswald. Ruby (right foreground) is in the dark suit and light hat with a dark band. *Pappas Exhibit No. 1, courtesy of Bob Jackson and the* Dallas Morning News.

By November 15, 1967, the CIA had completed its study. Helms delivered it to Johnson.

The study showed exactly what the White House did not want to believe: that there was little evidence of foreign involvement or foreign financial support of the peace activities in the United States.

The president was not satisfied. So within five days a new CIA study was launched. This was called "Demonstration Techniques," and it concentrated on antiwar demonstrations in the United States and abroad. The use of the CIA's computer resources was broadened.

Updated versions of the peace-movement study were sent to the president on December 22, 1967, and January 5, 1968. The results were the same: no substantial foreign connections or financial support.

The information gathered from these studies and the computer bank became the foundation for what developed in 1968 into Operation CHAOS: the collection of information and files on activities of American citizens. The CIA worked hand in hand with the FBI.

Inside the CIA, there was knowledge that the agency was dangerously close to violating its charter. Therefore, CIA officials took extreme precautions within the agency to limit who had access to these information banks on activities of American citizens. In July 1968 cables were sent to all CIA field stations directing that information on dissident groups abroad be sent through a single restricted channel on what was called an "eyes only" basis to the chief of Operation CHAOS. "Eyes only" meant that no copies were to be made.

The antiwar demonstrations continued in 1968. There were growing White House demands for greater coverage of the activities of dissident groups and student unrest. CIA top officers commissioned the preparation of a new analytic paper for the president. This was entitled "Restless Youth." The paper was produced in two versions—the first for the Johnson administration and the second for the Nixon administration.

The Johnson-administration version was delivered to two people: Johnson and his special assistant for National Security Affairs, Walt W. Rostow. Helms was aware that the CIA was exceeding its jurisdiction, so he wrote a covering memorandum when he delivered the paper to Johnson on September 4, 1968: "You will, of course, be aware of the peculiar sensitivity which attaches to the fact that the CIA has prepared a report on student activity *both here* and abroad." [italics mine] This was the key to the illegal activity—that it pertained to a report on student activities in the United States as well as abroad.

What was the conclusion of "Restless Youth"? Again, the CIA found that there was no substantial foreign direction or foreign financial support of peace activities within the United States. Rather, the primary causes of student unrest were social and political alienation at home.

In January, Richard Nixon was inaugurated. Henry Kissinger became his assistant for national security affairs. Four weeks later, Helms gave Kissinger a copy of the first version of "Restless Youth." In a covering memorandum, Helms pointed out to Kissinger the impropriety of the CIA's involvement in the study:

> In an effort to round-out our discussion of this subject, we have included a section on American students. This is an area not within the charter of this Agency, so I need not emphasize how extremely sensitive this makes the paper. Should anyone learn of its existence it would prove most embarrassing for all concerned.

What did the Nixon administration do in the face of specific knowledge that the CIA was exceeding its charter? It picked up where the Johnson administration left off. Instead of curtailing the CIA's improper activities, it directed that they be increased—and with the same rationale. Just as Lyndon Johnson felt that the conclusions of the CIA were based on inadequate intelligence capabilities within the dissident movement, the Nixon administration took up the same battle cry.

According to Helms, Nixon felt that the previous reports showed only one thing: inadequacy of intelligence-collection capabilities within the protest movement. Therefore, Nixon directed that one of his staff assistants, Tom Charles Huston, write to the CIA. And so Huston did—on June 20, 1969, asking for the preparation of a report to the president on foreign Communist support of revolutionary protest movements in the United States. Huston demanded a reply within ten days, and on June 30, 1969, the CIA responded with a report entitled "Foreign Communist Support to Revolutionary Protest Movements in the United States." What did the report conclude? The same thing as previous reports. While the Communists encouraged the peace movement with propaganda and exploitation of international conferences, there was meager evidence showing Communist funding of such movements and no evidence of Communist direction and control.

White House pressure intensified, and there was a gradual increase in the staff of Operation CHAOS, so that by late 1969, the Operation CHAOS staff totaled thirty-six people. Eventually, it totaled fifty-two. There was further isolation within the CIA. The location of Operation CHAOS workers was a vaulted basement area. Because the CIA knew it was engaged in activities beyond its charter, extreme security measures were undertaken to make sure that word did not leak. However, some within the CIA did question whether the operation was proper. Their voices were not raised very loudly, and they were effectively silenced. On September 6, 1969, Helms sent a memorandum to all deputy directors in the CIA assuring them that the CHAOS operation was within the statutory authority of the CIA and directing them to support it.

In response to White House pressure, there was a major change in CHAOS. Until late 1969 most information being compiled and fed into the computer was received from CIA field stations abroad or from reports issued by other government agencies, principally the FBI. In October 1969 the CIA started to recruit its own agents to work directly for the operation. Eventually, more than twenty agents became part of the operation. Although most of them were used abroad, three agents were used in the United States.

Operation CHAOS also was furnished the information gained from the unlawful mail-opening program. In return, Operation CHAOS provided watch lists for U.S. citizens' mail to be monitored and intercepted by the mail-opening operation.

Ultimately, names of 300,000 American citizens and organizations were stored in the CHAOS computer.

From these names, there were 7,200 separate personality files developed on citizens of the United States. Most of these files consisted of FBI reports or materials such as news clippings. There were also nearly a thousand "subject" files on numerous organizations, such as Students for a Democratic Society, Women's Strike for Peace, American Indian Movement, the Black Panther Party, Clergy and Laymen Concerned About Vietnam, and Grove Press, Inc.

The Grove Press file indicated how far the CIA went to respond to presidential pressures that there must be foreign conspiratorial direction for the peace movement. Grove Press published a book by Kim Philby, a British intelligence officer who turned out to be a Soviet agent. Therefore, Grove Press became a part of the Operation CHAOS computer-system bank. The Operation CHAOS analysts (who eventually totaled more than fifty) collected all available information on Grove Press. Among the other business endeavors of Grove Press was an X-rated motion picture with heavy sex orientation—*I Am Curious Yellow*. When the Rockefeller Commission went into the CHAOS files and looked at Grove Press, it found that the analysts had dutifully clipped and photographed several film critics' reports on the film.

Month after month, Operation CHAOS plodded along, cramming more and more information into the data banks. Inside the agency, steps were taken to assure that people did not question the propriety of the operation.

Helms even instructed the head of Operation CHAOS to avoid disclosing part of his activities to his administrative superior, James Angleton, the counterintelligence chief of the CIA. Instead, the DCI took direct supervisory responsibility for the overall operation.

The inspector general staff in one field survey in November 1972 was prevented from reviewing Operation CHAOS files or even discussing any operations about Operation CHAOS.

The CIA's general counsel was never consulted about the propriety of Operation CHAOS. Finally, unlike almost every other program within the CIA clandestine service, Operation CHAOS was never subjected to an annual review and approval procedure, nor was there any formal review of the operation's budget.

However, there was a middle-management group within the agency that had been organized to discuss and develop possible solutions to various CIA problems. In 1971 it questioned the propriety of Operation CHAOS.

The questions were squelched by Helms. In a memorandum for the record on December 5, 1972, Helms stated:

"CHAOS is a legitimate counterintelligence function of the Agency and cannot be stopped simply because some members of the organization do not like this activity."

What happened to Operation CHAOS? Its activities receded as the war wound down. Then, when James Schlesinger became DCI, he undertook an exhaustive study to determine areas of "questionable" activities by the agency. The report was turned over to William E. Colby when he became DCI. In turn, Colby directed that Operation CHAOS be "restricted to the collection abroad of information on foreign activities relating to domestic matters. Further, the CIA will focus clearly on the foreign organizations and individuals involved and only incidentally on their American contacts."

In March 1974, Operation CHAOS was terminated. Millions of dollars had been spent. There were no adequate internal controls. Most of the files had little if any value to ongoing intelligence activities. CHAOS had been an unproductive, expensive, unlawful enterprise that involved the CIA in collecting information on domestic activities of American citizens.

No disclosure ever was made to the American public by the CIA that it had done anything wrong. Rather, employees who had been ignored once too often went to Seymour Hersh of the *New York Times*, who then ferreted out the facts. Hersh wrote about Operation CHAOS and other unlawful CIA activities. The story was published December 22, 1974, and out of it came the presidential appointment of the Rockefeller Commission to investigate possible unlawful activities of the CIA.

If the CIA had leveled with the congressional oversight committees as well as with the American public in the spring of 1974 when Operation CHAOS was terminated, the existence of the program would have attracted far fewer headlines. But the CIA chose to keep the existence of Operation CHAOS a secret, and word eventually leaked to the press.

Operation CHAOS originated due to pressure from the White House. The isolation of Operation CHAOS within the CIA and its insulation from supervision by the regular chain of command as well as its insulation from investigation by the Office of General Counsel and the inspector general's office all contributed toward the excesses of this CIA program.

Regardless of why the minutes were being withheld, the real question was what to do. One choice was public confrontation. But that could have diverted the attention from the entire Rockefeller Commission Report, which would not have been fair to the commissioners or the public.

I had already come across evidence implying that the president (in this case, President Kennedy) knew about the assassination plans in general; I had also come across evidence indicating he did not know of the details—just as was the case with President Reagan's knowledge or lack of knowledge about the sale of arms to Iran and the illegal diversion of funds to the Nicaraguan Contras. Either case was bad: On the one hand, the president directing assassination plans in peacetime; on the other hand, an agency out of control.

Furthermore, I thought that perhaps the most important finding had been that Kissinger had again failed to understand the democratic process. Despite a presidential order directing full cooperation with the Rockefeller Commission, the NSC had in effect tried to stonewall by failing to respond, failing to respond, failing to respond—and finally, when they did respond, failing to deliver everything in their possession.

Kissinger knew—and the NSC knew—that the Rockefeller Commission was under a time restriction. Our original deadline of April 6 had been extended to June 6. The initial response from the NSC did not come until May 9. The advice that we would not be given direct access to the documents did not come until May 9.

I made additional oral requests after May 9, saying that I knew that we had not received everything. Weeks before, we had seen CIA files that referred to other meetings involving Bundy, Vance, Robert Kennedy, and others during which there were discussions about assassination plots by the Cuban exile community and also possibly the Mafia.

There is one final aspect of the confrontation that is the most damning of all. In June 1975 someone gave me a copy of a memorandum inside the files of the NSC. It was dated April 1975. The memorandum referred to my request for access to the files of the

NSC. It stated that Kissinger's office had already determined it would not comply with my request—but that the office was not going to tell me about the decision. The telephone conversations I had with the executive secretary of the NSC, the assurance I was given after I asked the vice-president to intervene, were all part of a scheme to mislead me. The intent from the beginning was to deny access, despite the directive of Section 3 of the executive order establishing "a Commission on CIA Activities Within the United States:

> Section 3. *Cooperation by and with Executive Departments and Agencies.* The Comission is authorized to request, at the direction of the Chairman, from an executive department or agency, any information and assistance deemed necessary to carry out its functions under this order. Each department or agency shall furnish such information and assistance to the Commission, to the extent permitted by law. . . .

There was one final footnote. The entire chapter on the investigation of assassinations was deleted from our report. This is what Nelson Rockefeller—a close friend of Henry Kissinger's—demanded.

# 23

## The Scuttling of the Findings on Assassination Plots

There is a syndrome in Washington that I call the "U-2 Syndrome." It is propagated by the CIA and the State Department. Most recently it can be applied to the Reagan administration with regard to Iran.

Its adherents believe the president can get into great and serious trouble if he "acknowledges the existence of certain facts"—in other words, if he tells the truth.

Admiral Poindexter carried this one step further in Irangate by adopting the philosophy that you not only do not want the president to acknowledge the existence of certain facts but also that the country is better off if the president does not even know about the facts.

When the Russians learned about the reconnaissance flights of the U-2 spy plane over USSR territory in the late 1950s, they did not publicly complain. According to the CIA, the reason was that by complaining publicly, the Russians would have implicitly acknowledged they did not have the technical capability of shooting down the aircraft. The Russians did not want to admit this, so they kept quiet. Finally, after months of overflights, the Russians did shoot down a U-2 being flown by Gary Powers. It was only then that they made public charges against the United States. According to the CIA rationale, no serious consequences would have occurred—except momentary embarrassment for the United States—if President Eisenhower had denied knowing of the U-2 flight. He should have taken the position that this was merely a caper of the CIA, the CIA believed.

But Eisenhower told the truth. He acknowledged that he knew about the U-2 flights and that they were authorized. According to CIA officials, this put the Russians in an untenable position. They could not very well meet with the person who had violated Soviet territorial airspace rights. Therefore, a summit meeting between Eisenhower and Nikita Khrushchev was canceled.

Time and again the CIA has cited the cancellation of that summit to pressure officials into denying the existence of facts that everyone knows are true.

That's why the Rockefeller Commission Report did not include the proposed chapter 20.

The evidence the staff produced was so compelling that most commissioners, including Ronald Reagan, agreed we had to include a chapter on CIA participation in assassination plots directed against foreign leaders in peacetime.

Rockefeller, though, was initially very much against this, and he did not want to let the press know that the report would include a chapter on assassination plots. As chairman, whenever he was present at the conclusion of a commission meeting, he would handle the press conference. He rarely disclosed anything.

On May 5, 1975, witnesses at the commission hearing included Kissinger, who then was secretary of state as well as national security adviser to President Ford; Secretary of Defense James Schlesinger, who once had headed the CIA; John McCone, the DCI in the Kennedy administration; and Walt Rostow, national security adviser to President Johnson. One reporter asked Rockefeller whether there was any discussion about CIA assassination plots. The vice-president responded:

"Well, as I have said on various occasions, the only relationship to alleged assassination attempts which this commission has is:

Was there any relation to, if such activities were undertaken, were there any violation of domestic statutes."

The next commission meeting was May 12. Rockefeller could not attend, so he asked C. Douglas Dillon to handle the press briefing.

On May 12, Dillon let the cat out of the bag.

Q. "Do you feel that you have got the answers you were looking for on assassination plots. Are you satisfied with the answers that you got?"

DILLON: "I don't know what one means by 'satisfied,' but I think we've found all the evidence that is available and that exists. I think our staff has done a very careful job."

Q. "Did your inquiry into so-called assassination plots bring you then towards Castro?"

DILLON: "That was what the allegation was about—foreign assassination plots—[it] was largely Castro."

Q. "Was that the only allegation?"

DILLON: "Well, no. There were some other allegations consisting possibly of other areas. I think they mentioned the Dominican Republic, Mr. Trujillo as a possibility."

Q. "I take it that the Castro one is the only one in the end that now seems to have some substance worth reporting on?"

DILLON: "Well, we will report on all allegations, including all of them."

That is where matters stood, and as late as May 25 I was working on the final draft of chapter 20 to submit for the commission's review at the May 29 meeting. It was then that Kissinger struck.

The request came to Rockefeller directly through the president. "The State Department"—that meant Kissinger—felt it would be "inappropriate for a presidentially appointed commission" to report that the CIA had been involved in plans to assassinate leaders of foreign countries in peacetime.

In March, Gerald Ford, at a presidential news conference, had made the first public disclosure that the Rockefeller Commission was investigating charges of assassination plots. Now Kissinger was asking through the White House that we not tell what we had discovered. But that decision had to be made by the commission itself.

The final four meetings of the commission were to take place on May 29, 30, 31, and June 2, 1975. On May 29, I brought a proposed draft of chapter 20 for final review by the commission. Rockefeller brought to the commission the request of the White House that chapter 20 be deleted.

Rockefeller made his case. I made mine. I asked the commission to ask the White House to reconsider and not bend to Kissinger. I pointed out that Dillon had already told the press we had the facts. I argued that the real issue was that the United States had engaged in shocking conduct. I argued that it would be far better to bring it out in the open now than to turn it over to Congress.

I was joined by Peter Clapper, our press officer, who thought press reaction would be very bad. The press had already been led to believe that a final report would include a chapter on assassination plans directed against foreign leaders, he noted. But Clapper and I lost to Rockefeller and Kissinger.

There was a problem, though: How would we explain the omission in our report of a section on assassination plans against foreign leaders, particularly when Dillon had told the press that we had the evidence and that "we will report on all allegations" concerning assassination plans?

On June 2, Peter Wallison submitted, on behalf of Rockefeller, proposed language to include in the report and explain why chapter 20 would be omitted:

> After the Commission's inquiry was under way, the President requested it to investigate public allegations that the CIA had been involved in plans to assassinate certain leaders of foreign countries.
>
> The Commission's staff undertook this task, relating to events dating back over a period of many years, but time did not permit a full investigation before this report was due.
>
> The materials in the possession of the Commission which bear on these allegations have been turned over to the President.

I objected. The implication was that the investigation had been undertaken at the request of the president, which was not true. Moreover, the investigation was complete enough for inclusion in our report.

But the president's men wanted to protect the president. As a matter of expedience, they suggested, why not say that since the president had asked us to get into it, he would be justified in asking us to get out of it and to turn the matter over to Congress, which had already established its own investigative committees? There was a basic problem in this explanation: It did not square with the facts. They backed down.

Eventually, we compromised. Thus, the foreword to our June 6, 1975, Rockefeller Commission Report ended with these two paragraphs:

> Allegations that the CIA had been involved in plans to assassinate certain leaders of foreign countries came to the Commission's attention shortly after its inquiry was under way. Although it was unclear whether or not those allegations fell within the scope of the commission's authority, the commission directed that an inquiry be undertaken. The President concurred in this approach.
>
> The Commission's staff began the required inquiry, but time did not permit a full investigation before this report was due. The President therefore requested that the materials in the possession of the Commission which bear on these allegations be turned over to him. This has been done.

I was particularly upset with the decision, because it was wrong. I felt the American people should know what we found. I felt we had shown CIA involvement in plans to assassinate foreign leaders in peacetime. And I felt the president was not being given an opportunity to hear all sides in determining whether it would be in the best interest of the country to have the report include our findings.

I knew the people eventually would find out, because the material we had would be delivered to the Senate Select Committee under the chairmanship of Sen. Frank Church.

It is within this context that I decided to call a press conference on June 18, 1975, as I was about to close our Rockefeller Commission office and return to Des Moines.

# 24

## The Press Conference That Never Was

There were two reasons for holding a press conference. First, I thought it was wrong for the commission not to include chapter 20. Second, I was sure that if I did not release the facts, Congress would spend a lot of time in this area at the expense of other areas that from a public standpoint could be more productive. The publicity benefits from dragging out an investigation into assassination plans against foreign leaders were tremendous. It was a great attraction for Congress.

I asked Peter Clapper to make arrangements for a meeting room—at my expense—at the Mayflower Hotel on June 18. Then I started work on a statement to make before taking questions. Here is what I wrote:

I am speaking today as David Belin, independent citizen from Iowa, and not as Executive Director of the Commission on CIA Activities Within the United States—the Rockefeller Commission. I speak as a citizen in one of the few countries in the world where the actions of a free press combined with the responsiveness of a President such as

Gerald Ford—a man whom I greatly respect and admire—can lead to an independent investigation of the national intelligence agency, and where the head of the investigative staff, after completing his work, can speak directly to the American people, to whom he owes his ultimate responsibility.

There are five reasons why I have called this press conference:

1. First, I believe that one of the basic foundations underlying our heritage of freedom is the public's right to know facts about the conduct of our government where publication of such facts will not adversely affect national security. Our judgment can be no better than our information, and I have an overriding confidence that if the American people get the facts, in the long run we will reach the right decisions.

2. Second, I believe that it is essential that we have an effective national intelligence agency that is under civilian control and that operates within the framework of the laws of our nation. This is just part of the overall need for the American people to get the facts. I also believe it is in the long-range interest of the CIA for me to disclose now the salient facts that I discovered about CIA assassination plans directed against foreign leaders. There are others who share my view for the need for prompt disclosure.

3. Third, I am hopeful that if this information is published now, more attention can be directed toward the nineteen chapters of our report, including the thirty specific recommendations, that we published. This is what constituted the overwhelming majority of the work of the Commission and the staff, and I believe that a substantial portion of our effort has been lost in the publicity about the failure to include a twentieth chapter on CIA assassination plans directed against foreign leaders.

4. Fourth, I speak today because I believe that in many ways our foreign policy over the past thirty years has been too shortsighted and has lacked adequate perspective of overall, long-range consequences. The development of assassination plans in peacetime is one of the most vivid illustrations of the lack of sound long-range judgment exercised by past administrations, both Democratic and Republican.

5. Finally, I speak today because I cannot countenance agents of my country conspiring with representatives of organized crime to commit murder in peacetime. This is totally contrary to the constitutional

and moral principles upon which our country is founded. Rather, it represents adoption of the philosophy of the Communist bloc and other totalitarian societies that the ends justify the means. Those who think they can best fight communism by adopting the standards and tactics of the opposition are doomed to failure. They are actually undermining the ultimate strength of our country, which lies in the full development of our human resources within the framework of the values and standards of our constitution, and not within the framework of the standards and values of totalitarian societies.

In making this public statement directly to the American people, I do not feel at liberty to disclose the specific contents of classified documents I have seen. However, I believe that I can speak about my ultimate conclusions without violating the classification labels which might be put on documents—although I should add that my experience on both the Warren Commission and the CIA Commission confirms my opinion that there is far too much overclassification of documents in government.

This overstress on secrecy can, and has, deprived the American people of facts they need to know in order to form sound decisions on national policy.

With the foregoing as a frame of reference, I will give you a brief, overall summary of what I found in my capacity as Executive Director of the Rockefeller Commission concerning CIA plans to assassinate foreign leaders.

On the basis of our investigation, I determined that the CIA was directly involved in plans to assassinate Premier Fidel Castro of Cuba and that the CIA supplied weapons to Dominicans who assassinated Generalissimo Rafael Trujillo of the Dominican Republic, although there was no direct American participation in that assassination. Both of these matters involved overt acts in the United States outside of the CIA [headquarters] which I believed constituted improper domestic activities of the CIA and were therefore within the jurisdictional boundaries of the President's order establishing the Commission.

Although the evidence of the existence of assassination plans was clear, there was conflicting evidence whether or not the CIA was directed or encouraged by higher authority to make an actual attempt on the life of Premier Castro, or whether this was a matter developed from within the Agency, or whether it was a combination of both. I happen to believe that since there is already conflicting evidence on this question, it is most likely that additional investigation will not remove doubts, particularly since many of the key officials that might have actual knowledge are now dead—including Presidents Eisenhower, Kennedy, and Johnson, and Allen Dulles, who served as Director of Central Intelligence from 1953 until November 1961. Furthermore, either alternative is repugnant to me. On the one hand, if there was no White House direction, we have the CIA operating out of control. On the other hand, the concept of White House direction of plans of this kind is wholly contrary to the principles for which this nation stands.

Although I received what the National Security Council said were copies of all documents in its possession which pertained to either the Castro or Trujillo matters, I do not have first-hand knowledge if the material given me was complete. Also, time did not permit examination of documents that might be available in the Eisenhower, Kennedy or Johnson presidential libraries. Consequently, the investigation is not complete with regard to the question of who, if anyone outside the CIA, authorized or directed the planning of any assassination attempts against foreign leaders. However, with particular reference to the plans directed against Fidel Castro, the investigation was sufficiently complete to show that plans were undertaken by the CIA.

I then summarized the development of the Phase I, Phase II, and Phase III plans and included some background about Robert Kennedy and President Kennedy's knowledge of the development of these plans.

After summarizing our findings about the anti-Castro plots, I turned briefly to Trujillo.

In late 1960 and 1961, the United States, having abandoned its policy of nonintervention in the Dominican Republic, sought to bring about the overthrow of the regime of Generalissimo Rafael Trujillo and the establishment of a moderate successor government. To accomplish this result, several measures were undertaken on the diplomatic level and a special group, which was a predecessor of the 40 Committee, approved a program of covert action as well. At their direction, the CIA encouraged a group of internal dissidents along with several exile organizations. On May 30, 1961, members of the internal dissident group assassinated Trujillo.

There was no direct American participation in the assassination. The idea originated with the Dominicans; they acquired some of the weapons on their own; and they did the detailed planning. They were never subject to American supervision or control.

On the other hand, CIA and State Department officers in the Dominican Republic were in regular contact with the plotters before the assassination, and they were well aware of the group's lethal intentions. The CIA had told the group of practical problems with several earlier assassination plans; it had offered to train a member of the group in the use of explosives to kill Trujillo.

As a gesture of American support, three revolvers and three carbines, along with limited supplies of ammunition, were passed to the plotters about two months before the assassination. One of the carbines was reportedly left at the scene of the crime, although it may not have fired any shots that hit Trujillo.

It appears that high-level State Department and White House officials first learned that guns had been provided to potential assassins some six weeks after the transfer, and about two and a half weeks prior to Trujillo's death. A statement of policy was prepared and approved by the President to the effect that the government must not run the risk of association with political assassination, since the United States as a matter of general policy cannot condone assassination. The preparation of this message, and the required coordination, consumed about two weeks. There is no evidence of any effort during this period to recover the weapons or otherwise interfere with the assassination plans. The policy statement was cabled to the Dominican Republic on May 29, the day before the successful assassination attempt. Both the Consul General and the CIA Station Chief in Ciudad Trujillo promptly protested this change in the policy which they had followed in the belief it had been approved by appropriate authority. Before these cables were received in Washington, Trujillo was dead. . . .

I was not able to find evidence involving any other attempts to assassinate any other foreign leader which had significant overt activities within the United States. However, the nature of the activity and the degree of secrecy and compartmentalization within the Agency are such that it is difficult to find any evidence of this kind unless specific facts are brought to the attention of the investigative body. . . .

Now let me turn to why our Report did not include any specific discussion of the foregoing findings. In the first place, as I have previously stated, our investigation was incomplete concerning whether the CIA was directed or encouraged to undertake the development of these plans, or whether these plans were solely matters developed within the Agency, or whether it was a combination of both. There is no doubt that plans were undertaken. I believe that it is very likely that there will always be doubts concerning how much direction, if any, there was from higher authority. Furthermore, I do not see that a great amount of good can be accomplished by trying to exhaust every possible fact concerning the source of these plans, since there will always be conflicting evidence in the area and since the most important matter to be determined is that actual plans were undertaken.

Nevertheless, the decision was reached that since time did not permit a full investigation of all these matters before the Commission report was due, the materials bearing on the allegations of assassination plans would be turned over to the President. It is my understanding that it was also contemplated that these materials would be turned over by the President to the Senate Select Committee.

A second reason why the commission report did not include a chapter on assassination plans was because of concern that the President or a presidentially appointed commission because of foreign policy considerations should not confirm any CIA involvement in assassination plans. Analogies were drawn to the U-2 incident, where some people felt the open acknowledgment by President Eisenhower of knowledge of U-2 plans had adverse consequences on relationships with foreign governments. The analogy was therefore made to the present situation where it was felt that it would be inappropriate for the President of the United States to confirm the existence of such plans, even though they might have been undertaken during the Administration of a former president.

This is one of the reasons I am speaking today as an independent citizen from Iowa and not as Executive Director of the Rockefeller Commission.

In closing, let me place all of this in perspective. The most important thing to remember about the investigation of the CIA is the fact that such an investigation could happen, and did happen, in the United States of America as a direct outgrowth of the actions of a free press combined with the responsiveness of a President such as Gerald

Ford—and that an independent citizen from Iowa could come to Washington, head the staff undertaking the investigation, and then leave Washington and speak directly to the American people, to whom he owes his ultimate responsibility.

President Ford has firmly announced that assassination is not and should never be a tool of United States policy. I wholeheartedly concur in his statement. It is against the constitutional and moral principles for which this Republic stands for there to be any direct or indirect participation of any agency of the United States Government in any plans involving assassination of any person in peacetime.

My plan was to read the opening paragraphs of my statement, distribute copies at the news conference, allow ten minutes for those present to read the entire statement, and then spend at least an hour responding to questions.

At the same time that I was preparing my statement, several Washington reporters were urging that I "go public." The most persuasive arguments were made by Bill Kovach and Nick Horrock of the Washington bureau of the *New York Times*.

I decided to go ahead. The announcement of the time and place was to be made by Clapper on June 17. The day before, as a courtesy, I submitted my proposed statement to Phil Buchen, counsel to the president, Dick Cheney, assistant to the president, and Ron Nessen, presidential press secretary.

I asked for their opinion. All three said that it was up to me whether I wanted to go ahead with the conference. However, both Buchen and Cheney said that the State Department felt that it was not in the best interests of the country to have the commission include this in its formal report and that even though I was making my statement as an independent citizen, it would still be attributed to the commission because of my role as executive director. On the other hand, Nessen said that he thought that on the whole the commission report should have included a chapter 20 and that he felt that the president might very well benefit from my "going public."

As I pondered the decision, three considerations caused me to decide not to go ahead—which was a major mistake.

First, I was sure that ultimately the public would receive the facts from the Senate Select Committee, so if I did not go ahead, it meant merely a postponement of the time when the public would know the basic facts.

Second, I did not want to overrule the State Department's view that it would not be in the public interest to go ahead, particularly when that decision had been adopted by the president.

Finally, I was concerned that people might misinterpret my motives and believe that I was calling a press conference to gain personal fame. I was sure that this is what Rockefeller would say.

I remained very upset that the CIA in 1964 had deliberately withheld from the Warren Commission evidence that the CIA had been engaged in assassination plots against Fidel Castro. I sought to find a way to respond.

# 25

# Turning the Tables: My Freedom of Information Act Request

**I**n my work on the Rockefeller Commission, I had seen thousands of classified documents in the CIA files relating to the assassination of John F. Kennedy. Some of these items pertained to secret sources and methods the CIA used to collect its information, but most should never have been classified. They contained no state secrets. What's more, with the passage of time, the need for secrecy has diminished.

There was another relevant factor: a doctrine in the law called the "clean hands" doctrine. It says that when a person comes into court seeking equitable relief, that person has to show that he himself is not guilty of improper conduct. If he is guilty of improper conduct, he is held to have "unclean hands" and will be denied relief.

So far as the investigation of the assassination of President Kennedy is concerned, the CIA did not have clean hands. The CIA had been guilty of witholding information from the Warren Commission—information that the CIA had been involved in assassination plots directed against Castro, which was a legitimate area of concern for the Warren Commission.

The CIA also withheld knowledge of the fact that Castro probably was aware of these plans. Existence of the plans was also withheld by the Department of Justice and the FBI. Such information would have been relevant to the investigation of the Warren Commission in light of the allegations of conspiratorial contact between Oswald and agents of the Cuban government. Therefore, I thought it might be interesting if the CIA were to face the problem of losing the protection of secrecy where it operated without clean hands.

For all of these reasons, after completing my service with the Rockefeller Commission, I decided to write William Colby, the DCI, asking that all CIA files involved in the investigation of the assassination of President Kennedy be released. On September 6, 1975, I wrote:

Dear Mr. Colby:

More than ten years has passed since the completion of the investigation of the assassination of President Kennedy by the Warren Commission. Having been intimately involved in this investigation as one of the two Warren Commission counsel concentrating in what we called Area II—the determination of who was the assassin of President Kennedy—I know that beyond a reasonable doubt Lee Harvey Oswald killed both President John F. Kennedy and Dallas Police Office J. D. Tippit on November 22, 1963.

However, as you know, there have been many false allegations about alleged CIA involvement in the assassination of President Kennedy as well as many other false allegations concerning this national tragedy. Since the completion of the Warren Commission investigation in 1964, the CIA has released a number of documents which at one time were classified. Nevertheless, a substantial number of documents have not been released.

Although I understand the concern of the CIA that a release of all of the documents which it made available to the Warren Commission might disclose sources and methods which the CIA believes might not at one time have been in the national interest to disclose, I believe that there is a greater overall national interest in full disclosure of all material that the CIA made available to the Warren Commission.

Ultimately, the strength of our country rests on the confidence that American citizens have in their government. In the aftermath of Vietnam and Watergate, this confidence is relatively low. I would respectfully suggest that a starting point for a rebirth of confidence could be complete disclosure of the facts involving one of the major tragedies of American history—a disclosure which would put to rest many of the false claims by the assassination sensationalists and would also let the American people know the kind of assistance and cooperation that the CIA gave the Warren Commission.

Therefore, I would like to formally request under the Freedom of Information Act and regulations issued thereunder that you make available to me as an independent citizen from Iowa all material and documents which the CIA had in its possession at the time of the Warren Commission investigation which in any manner whatsoever relate to the assassination of President Kennedy and the investigation of that assassination by the Warren Commission.

Would you please advise me of the cost of obtaining access to these documents under your regulations, and I will promptly transmit my check for that amount to the Central Intelligence Agency.

I followed that up with a similar request to Arthur F. Sampson, the administrator of general services of the General Services Administration (GSA), who had jurisdiction over all Warren Commission material and documents in the National Archives. A small portion of Warren Commission documents remain classified. There is no need to continue restricting public access.

To this day, the GSA has not released any documents to me. The CIA has released driblets of material that generally had already been made available to the public through the declassified portion of Warren Commission materials available at the National Archives.

Although I found no credible evidence that the CIA was conspiratorially involved in the assassination of President Kennedy, because the CIA withheld important information from the Warren Commission and because of the birth of a new generation of assassination sensationalists who were gaining a large following on college campuses, I began to reconsider the whole subject of whether the investigation of the Warren Commission should be reopened by Congress.

# 26

---

# Requesting the Reopening of the Warren Commission Investigation

**A**mong the ironies confronting the CIA today is that it has become a victim in this country of techniques of "disinformation" and "black propaganda," techniques the CIA at times uses abroad. The perpetrators in our country have taken advantage of the mood of national distrust about the CIA and the susceptibility of the public to sensationalism in general and charges of conspiracy in particular. They have coupled this with the willingness of much of the media to give broad coverage to allegations of impropriety without following through to determine whether the charges are correct.

Out of this has developed a raft of books seeking to implicate the CIA in all kinds of conspiracies, culminating in claims that the CIA was involved in the assassination of President Kennedy.

Early in our investigation of the CIA, charges were made by entertainer Dick Gregory and others that the CIA participated in the assassination of President Kennedy.

Our charter was to investigate improper domestic activities of the CIA. When allegations were made of CIA conspiratorial involvement in the assassination of Kennedy, we had an obligation to investigate.

Since I had served as assistant counsel with the Warren Commission, I removed myself from the direct responsibility for any investigation pertaining to the assassination. I turned this area over to Senior Counsel Robert B. Olsen.

The vehicle used to gain publicity by assassination sensationalists was the film taken by amateur photographer Abraham Zapruder. One person misinterpreting that film was Robert Grodin. He alleged CIA conspiracy in the assassination, and he sought, and received, an opportunity to testify before the Rockefeller Commission staff. Later he testified before the House Assassinations Committee.

Grodin came to the commission offices with his copy of the film, which was not nearly as clear a copy of the original Zapruder film as was available to the Warren Commission in the initial stage of its investigation. (Ultimately, the Warren Commission obtained the original print.)

Grodin asserted that at frame 413 and at frames 454–78, one could see "assassins" bearing rifles in the area of the grassy knoll.

As the film was run several times, Grodin's comments became more and more ludicrous. Grodin would yell out, "There's the rifle," or, "There's the gunman." Yet no rifle or gunman could be seen. It was as if Grodin were seeing a Rorschach ink blot and interpreting what he saw. Grodin claimed, for instance, that on frames 412, 413, and 414, which have tree foliage in the background, there is a shape that looks like a German army helmet of World War II vintage. However, on frames 411 and 415, the contours of the shadows are entirely different, and there is no resemblance to any German helmet or human head or anything else of that kind.

The Zapruder camera ran at a speed of one-eighteenth of a second per frame. To believe Grodin, you would have to assume that between frame 411 and frame 415, elapsed time of about a quarter of a second, there was a shape of a head with a helmet on it that appeared and then disappeared. Obviously, any human head would not appear or disappear within only one-quarter of a second. This is apart from the fact that anyone wanting to kill the president would surely not be wearing an army-type helmet to call attention to himself in a public area in Dallas.

Grodin then claimed that in frame 413 alone you could see the shape of a rifle. This required the rifle to appear and disappear within one-eighteenth of a second. It required great imagination to see a rifle in frame 413.

Rather than rely on the sheer illogic of Grodin's assertions, Olsen wanted independent, expert photographic analysis. He went to the FBI lab and consulted with one of the top photographic experts in the country, Lyndal Shaneyfelt. On the basis of the extensive photographic work done as a part of the overall Warren Commission investigation, Shaneyfelt determined that Abraham Zapruder was standing on a concrete wall four feet two inches above the ground.

Based on the Zapruder film and other photographic material, Shaneyfelt concluded, with the aid of reports from the FBI lab, that the tree where Grodin claimed there was a rifle at frame 413 and where Grodin claimed there was a human head with a German-type army helmet from frames 412 to 414 was only between six and six and a half feet high. Moreover, that tree was barren of any branches or leaves to a height of about four feet to four and a half feet above the ground, and its foliage was only two feet high and four feet wide, its trunk was only a few inches in diameter, and it was actually located about five feet directly in front of Zapruder's legs. This was the only tree in the immediate vicinity. A human head, with or without a helmet, would have occupied about one-half of the total area of the frame. The nearness of the small ornamental tree had made it appear as a large tree with large foliage in the Zapruder film.

To say the least, an assassin would be unlikely to hide himself in a tree five feet away from Zapruder, a tree only six or six and a half feet high, and one that left his whole person exposed to hundreds of people in the Dealey Plaza vicinity.

Similarly, we were able to determine that frames 454 through

478 of the Zapruder film did not reveal the existence of any human being or an assassin with a rifle or other weapon, as alleged by Grodin. Rather, what Grodin asserted was a rifleman (and at a speed of eighteen frames a second could be seen for only about one and a third seconds) was "clump-type shrubbery" in the background.

Grodin, of course, has given before audiences in colleges across the country, and on television programs, the same kind of commentary he gave Olsen at the Rockefeller Commission offices. He shows the Zapruder film, then flashes on the screen an enlargement of the foliage and points out what he thinks is the shape of a human head, but wholly fails to point out the fact that the tree was only six or six and a half feet tall, just as he wholly fails to point out that it is rather implausible for there to be a rifle in one frame that disappears in the next frame, one-eighth of a second later.

One aspect of Grodin's presentation would seem to pose a valid common-sense objection to the Warren Commission conclusion that no shots struck the president from the front. When you examine the film, you immediately notice that the president's head appears to move violently backward when the fatal shot strikes. Is this not evidence that the fatal shot that struck the president must have come from the front?

This is a logical question that of course I asked when I served with the Warren Commission.

The only way it could be accurately answered was to examine the physical evidence, especially the photographs and X rays taken at the time of the autopsy of Kennedy and the two large ballistically identifiable bullet fragments found in the presidential limousine, which undoubtedly came from the fatal shot.

Olsen wanted permission to gather independent medical experts to review these photographs and X rays to determine whether there was evidence to corroborate the claims of people alleging CIA complicity in the assassination.

He assembled an outstanding group. First, Olsen selected Werner U. Spitz, chief medical examiner of Wayne County, Detroit,

Michigan. He was an expert from a city notorious for having more murders than any other major city in the country. Because a major portion of the evidence involved the X rays, Olsen picked an outstanding radiologist, Fred J. Hodges III, professor of radiology at The Johns Hopkins School of Medicine in Baltimore.

To round out the panel, Olsen picked experts familiar with bullet wounds and reactions to wounds: Lt. Col. Robert R. McMeekin, chief of the division of aerospace pathology of the Armed Forces Institute of Pathology in Washington; Richard Lindenberg, director of neuropathology and legal medicine from the Maryland Department of Mental Health; and Alfred G. Olivier, director of the Department of Biophysics at the Biomedical Laboratories of Edgewood Arsenal at the Aberdeen Proving Grounds in Maryland.*

The panel met at the National Archives in Washington, where the evidence of the assassination is located. I attended that meeting and for the first time saw what had never been seen before by any lawyer serving with the Warren Commission—the actual photographs and X rays taken of the autopsy of Kennedy.

The panel was unanimous in concluding that there was no medical evidence of any bullets striking Kennedy except from the rear.

Meanwhile Grodin and other assassination sensationalists were aggressively promoting on college campuses their false thesis that the Zapruder film proved there was a shot fired from the front. The copies of the film shown were not nearly as clear as the original print, which was owned by Time, Inc. From sources inside the *Time* organization, I learned that the Zapruder film was becoming

---

*Dr. McMeekin is a forensic pathologist who had done extensive studies in the field of accident reconstruction, utilizing computer-assisted analysis of the reactions of human body components to the application of various forces. Dr. Lindenberg is a prominent authority in the field of neuropathology, that is, the pathology of the brain and nervous system. Dr. Spitz is a forensic pathologist who has had extensive experience with gunshot wounds and is an editor of a textbook on forensic pathology. Dr. Hodges is a specialist in radiology and surgery associated with the brain and nervous system. In 1973–74 he served as president of the American Society of Neuroradiology. Dr. Olivier has conducted numerous experiments to study the effects on animals and humans of penetrating wounds from high-velocity bullets. Drs. Spitz, Lindenberg, and Hodges hold faculty positions in the Medical Schools of Wayne State University, the University of Maryland, and The Johns Hopkins University, respectively.

a "hot potato" and they wanted to get rid of it. One would have thought that the most logical thing to do would be to have donated the film to the National Archives, which would not only have made it available for scholars in years to come but would also have given the corporation a tax deduction. However, someone inside the organization—and I do not know who—thought that the best way to get rid of the "hot potato" was to give it back to the Zapruder family, from whom it had been purchased for approximately $150,000. I felt this was fundamentally wrong.

I tracked down the attorney who was handling the matter for *Time*. His name was Kent Smith. We had several conversations in late March and early April, 1975. I pointed out to him why I believed it would be in the public interest to have the Zapruder film and slides donated to the National Archives. I also pointed out why this would be in the interest of the stockholders of the company, since there would be a tax deduction involved.

Nevertheless, Time, Inc., steadfastly refused to honor my request. Then I took a different tack. On April 5, 1975, I wrote Mr. Smith and suggested that if they did not want to donate the film and slides to the National Archives, "then as an alternative I suggest that it [Time, Inc.] consider selling to a nonprofit, charitable foundation the Zapruder film and slides and assigning all of the corporation's rights. . . ." I suggested that this could be done at a price higher than what had been paid to Abraham Zapruder, and that this would be in the public interest. I also called Mr. Smith and told him that I believed that I could find some charitable foundation that would purchase the film and slides and would then in turn make them available for scholars or in the alternative turn them over to the National Archives.

Finally, *Time* told me that they were "too far down the road" with the Zapruder family and they would not honor any of my requests. I subsequently found out from sources inside *Time* magazine that *Time* sold it back to the Zapruder family for a nominal fee—less than $1,000.

The person who had actually first contacted Abraham Zapruder after the assassination was Dan Rather, of CBS, who, after finding

Zapruder, took the film and was able to have the processing of the film expedited. In May 1988, when I related to Dan Rather my Zapruder film—*Time* magazine story, he found it hard to believe that Time, Inc., had given the film back to the Zapruder family instead of donating it to the National Archives.

Abraham Zapruder fooled not only the general public but also the Warren Commission into thinking that the $25,000 he turned over to Officer Tippit's widow represented all proceeds he received from Time, Inc., for his film. Really, this just represented the downpayment. There was another $125,000 or more that came to him.

The public would have been far better served if Time, Inc., had turned the film over to the National Archives. At the very least, it should have been sold to a nonprofit foundation, one willing to pay a higher price and to make the extremely valuable property available to the National Archives. I asked Time, Inc., to consider these alternatives. The corporation refused.

A greater frustration that spring involved public television. As I saw the deception being used by Grodin and his followers, I recalled the equally deceptive Mark Lane and the film he made ten years earlier. That film, though misleading and full of misrepresentations, was effective in reaching millions of people. I thought it should be countered with a film of the vivid firsthand recollections of the key witnesses to the assassination of Kennedy and the murder of Tippit—a film that could be made while the people were still alive.

I called an official of the Public Broadcasting Service (PBS), John Montgomery, who once headed the Iowa Public Broadcasting Network and had moved to Washington to become vice-president of programming of PBS.

I pointed out to him that one major problem confronting the country was lack of confidence in institutions. If the public did not have confidence in the Warren Commission as an institution, the ripple effect could be very broad, I noted.

Montgomery asked me to write a formal letter. On March 18, 1975, I wrote as follows:

Because of the need for an in-depth analysis going to the heart of the truth about the assassination and because of the continued widespread interest in this event, I would suggest that there should be a documentary which would include interviews with key witnesses at the actual scene of events. Actions might be reconstructed on location in Dallas.

I suggested a number of one-hour programs. At least one hour should be devoted to an overview, at least one hour to the Tippit murder, at least two hours to the murder of Kennedy, and at least one hour on the possibility of conspiracy.

I concluded:

> As each year passes by, the life expectancy of the key witnesses will obviously decrease. Although most of these witnesses are still living, some have already died. Therefore, from a historical standpoint, time is of the essence. I would hope that PBS, which has made so many contributions to the people of this country, will consider it important to make a contribution toward the restoration of the credibility in the very government under which there is room for debate in matters of this kind. The ironic aspect of this climate is that the nature of our society fosters dissemination of sensational charges of all kinds but does not foster an objective, in-depth analysis of what the truth really is about a matter of continued widespread public concern.

I called Montgomery several days later. He liked the letter, he said, but he said it had been reviewed and that public television did not believe it was appropriate for it to undertake a documentary of this kind involving a governmental commission such as the Warren Commission.

The false allegations of conspiracy against the CIA, the withholding of evidence from the Warren Commission by the CIA, the sordid chapter of CIA assassination plots directed against Castro, the failure of public television to undertake any independent documentary, the failure of the CIA to respond adequately to my Freedom of Information Act request, the failure to give the original Zapruder film to the National Archives, and the question of credibility and trust and confidence in government, all came together and led me to conclude that the Warren Commission investigation should be reopened. On the twelfth anniversary of the assassination, November 22, 1975, I formally requested

> that Congress should reopen the Warren Commission investigation even though I am confident that a thorough, independent investigation will reach exactly the same conclusion reached by the Warren Commission that beyond a reasonable doubt Lee Harvey Oswald killed both President Kennedy and Officer Tippit. The primary reason for this request is that I believe it would greatly contribute toward a rebirth of confidence and trust in government. . . .

I made specific suggestions and then added an additional request:

> Concurrently with the Congressional investigation, there should be a study undertaken by the National News Council or some other appropriate forum for self-examination by the media to determine the adequacy of the media's continuing coverage of the assassination of President Kennedy in the light of the rebirth of national interest in this area. I have tremendous confidence in the overall ability of the press. At the same time, I have tremendous concern about the fact that the mass media have been exploited to mislead a large segment of the American public into falsely believing that Oswald did not kill President Kennedy and Officer Tippit.
>
> Granted, there is an ever-present problem in the rush to report the news of the day where wide publicity is given to people who make sensational charges. However, in some cases, such as the Warren Commission investigation, most of these charges can be readily disproved by a thorough, objective study and investigation of voluminous materials already available. To the extent that the media fail to do this, they fail in their overall responsibilities to report all of the facts.

Congress did reopen the investigation. Its most important contribution was a thorough investigation of the medical and physical evidence, including the neutron-analysis test on the nearly whole bullet and the bullet fragments from Governor Connally's wounds and the creation of another independent panel of medical experts. They concluded that the bullet that first struck Kennedy entered from the back of his neck, exited from the front, and entered the back of Connally and caused all his wounds. They also concluded Oswald killed Kennedy and Tippit.

However, a majority of the committee was persuaded by its staff at the very last minute to reverse its preliminary draft and erroneously conclude that there was an unseen second gunman who fired a shot that missed everything and that the existence of this unseen second gunman meant that there was a conspiracy. The foundation upon which this second gunman theory rested was so-called acoustic experts who were subsequently proved wrong, but by that time the House Committee had disbanded.

# 27

## The House Assassinations Committee and the Last-Minute Flip-flop

In December 1978, the members of the House Select Committee on Assassinations were reviewing drafts of a report. After nearly two years of work and the expenditure of $5.8 million, they had concluded that Lee Harvey Oswald was the lone gunman who had killed President John Kennedy, wounded Texas governor John Connally, and killed Dallas police officer J. D. Tippit. There was no conspiracy.

It was a report based on an investigation conducted in almost total secrecy, except for a few weeks of public hearings carefully orchestrated by G. Robert Blakey, chief counsel of the committee.

Less than three weeks later, a major flip-flop occurred. The six hundred-plus-page report was rejected, and on December 29, 1978, a majority of the committee approved a nine-page "Summary of Findings and Recommendations" that concluded that although Oswald was the assassin, there was a conspiracy involving an unseen second gunman. This invisible person supposedly fired a single shot from an elevated portion of land known as the grassy knoll, located to the right front of the presidential limousine. According to the committee summary, this shot missed Kennedy and everyone else, and even missed the presidential limousine, barely one hundred feet from the invisible gunman.

How was it that the committee majority reached this erroneous conclusion?

From its inception, the committee was subject to a pro-conspiracy bias. Its first chairman was Cong. Thomas Downing, whose mind was already made up. In January 1976, a few months before the House Select Committee on Assassinations was created, Downing wrote an introduction to a book by assassination sensationalists Robert Grodin and Peter Model entitled *J.F.K.: The Case for Conspiracy.*

In his introduction, Downing referred to his first meeting with Grodin on April 15, 1975, when Downing "viewed, for the first time, his optically enhanced version of the motion picture film of the murder. It convinced me that there was more than one assassin. . . ."

After the committee was organized, it retained a well-known Philadelphia prosecutor, Richard Sprague, as its chief counsel. Downing did not run for reelection in 1976, so in early 1977 he was succeeded by Henry Gonzales of Texas. Gonzales also had fallen prey to the misrepresentations of the sensationalists. He also became embroiled in a disagreement with Sprague, who was demanding a huge budget. Gonzales tried to fire Sprague. The committee refused. Gonzales, in a burst of anger, resigned. The whole probe seemed on the verge of collapse.

Cong. Louis Stokes of Ohio was appointed in early March as the successor chairman. On March 9, 1977, I wrote Congressman Stokes a letter because there had been newspaper comments that in the face of all the initial adversity the House might drop its inquiry into the Kennedy assassination. I also requested that I have an opportunity to appear before the entire committee in an open public hearing where I would be happy to answer any questions put to me. I also said that I thought I might have some constructive suggestions that I might offer to facilitate the investigation and sent copies of my letter to all of the other members of the committee.

Although Congressman Stokes did not respond, I did get a number of replies from members of the committee thanking me for my letter and indicating I would be called as a witness.

The committee soon selected Cornell University law professor Robert Blakey, a person who has been heavily involved in writing and theorizing about the influence of the Mafia in American society, as its chief counsel to replace Richard Sprague.*

Blakey decided to hold everything he could in secret. Not everyone agreed with this approach. Peter C. Stuart, writing in the *Christian Science Monitor*, said:

> Congress, which in recent years has pledged itself publicly to "openness" and backed up its commitment with a series of institutional reforms is finding secrecy a hard habit to break ... the back swing against the trend toward more openness on the part of Congress is led, ironically, by some of its newest committees, its most recently launched investigations and one of its last to be reformed institutions. Congress' most prominent and costly investigations—of the assassinations of John F. Kennedy and Martin Luther King, Jr., and of the alleged South Korean influence-buying scandal—are being conducted largely in secret.
>
> The House of Representatives Assassinations Committee, whose $2.5 million annual budget consumes well over half of the $4 million Congress has invested in major new investigations in the past year and a half, has met in public only rarely.
>
> Since acquiring a new chairman and chief counsel last spring, it also has imposed a gag rule against discussing the probe with outsiders and closed its press office. It is not even required to issue a formal year-end progress report to the House. . . .

In December 1977, Blakey finally telephoned me. He suggested that he did not think the committee was going to investigate the murder of Tippit. I was shocked, and I helped persuade him to change his mind. Fortunately, the Tippit murder was included in the House committee investigation. Unfortunately, Blakey never seemed to find time in his schedule to meet with me.

---

*Professor Blakey is now a professor at the University of Notre Dame Law School.

In July 1978, Michael Ewing of the committee staff called and said they wanted me to come to Washington to give a deposition before members of the staff. I told him I would prefer to testify before members of the committee; in any event, I said, I wanted my testimony to be in an open, public hearing. On August 10, Ewing called and said Blakey turned down the request.

Meanwhile, the committee began an orchestrated set of public hearings and called Robert Grodin to testify on the opening day. When I learned of this, I wrote Blakey and again requested an opportunity to appear before the committee in a public hearing. I said that if the committee refused to do this, I wanted to know whether the committee would let the press be present if I gave a deposition. Blakey said all depositions would be taken in secret. I never appeared.

Several aspects of the investigation of the House committee were well done. The staff independently verified that Oswald killed Tippit. Blakey brought together medical experts who determined that the bullet that passed through Kennedy's neck, struck Connally, and caused all of his wounds. "Neutron-activation analysis" tests were performed on the bullet fragments from Connally's wrist and the nearly whole bullet that fell off his stretcher; these tests corroborated the single-bullet findings of the Warren Commission. And the committee determined that the shots that struck Kennedy came from Oswald's rifle.

After the public hearings, the House staff completed work on the initial draft of the report. Its findings: Oswald was the lone gunman who killed Kennedy and wounded Connally, and Oswald killed Tippit. There was no conspiracy, the committee concluded.

But then everything changed because of a staff theory based on so-called acoustic evidence from a Dictabelt recording of channel 1 of the Dallas Police Department radio system as it transmitted on the afternoon of November 22, 1963. The Dallas Police Department had two radio channels: channel 1 for regular police communications and channel 2 for communications to and from the presidential motorcade. An ordinary listener to the tapes can't hear any gunshots. However, the House Select Committee on Assassinations retained an acoustic expert who asserted that, based on interpretations of oscillating waves on scientific instruments, one could conclude that certain wave patterns meant gunshots. The initial expert retained by the committee asserted there was a fifty-fifty possibility that the recorded sounds indicated a fourth gunshot and that this was just as unique as a fingerprint because it was a composite of the sounds that included the reverberations from the buildings surrounding Dealey Plaza in Dallas.

Since no other evidence indicated the presence of a second gunman, the House committee did not believe that a fifty-fifty possibility was enough to lead it to any conclusions. Accordingly, the draft of the final report had no indication of any conspiracy.

Then, in the middle of December 1987, Blakey brought forward two additional acoustic experts: Mark Weiss and Ernest Aschkenasy. They said they were 95 percent certain that the oscillating waves from the Dictabelt indicated the presence of a second gunman firing a fourth shot from the grassy knoll.

Members of the committee staff said the tape came from a stuck microphone on the motorcycle driven by Dallas police officer H. B. McLain, and they called McLain to Washington to testify at the time of the report from the first acoustic expert. McLain said he had not heard the tape prior to his testimony to determine whether the noises on the tape were what he remembered hearing at the time of the assassination. On the tape there are no noises of the police sirens turning on right after the assassination as the motorcade sped to the hospital. Nor are there any sounds of the motorcycles being revved up as the motorcade accelerated for the high-speed trip to Parkland Memorial Hospital. On the other hand, the tape records chimes, and there were no chimes in the vicinity of Dealey Plaza. It also contains the sound of sirens approaching, approximately two minutes after the supposed recording of the shots, and then the sound of sirens receding, as if the motorcycle with a stuck microphone were at a point along the freeway that the motorcade passed on its way to the hospital.

After McLain heard the tape, he stated, "It just couldn't be me. There was no way my mike was stuck." However, the House committee refused to call McLain back.

The committee staff failed to call key witnesses, and the questioning of the witnesses they did call left much to be desired. McLain was never asked whether he had his motorcycle's siren on all the way to Parkland Memorial Hospital. Certainly the noise of his siren would have been recorded if his microphone had been stuck on. *Los Angeles Times* reporters Jerry Cohen and Mike Goodman did ask McLain the question. They wrote:

> McLain said if he had been asked if he immediately turned on his siren after he heard gunfire, his response would have been yes. He said he kept his siren on all the way to Parkland Hospital and, if his had been the supposed open mike in Dealey Plaza, his siren would have drowned out all other sounds on the Dictabelt.
>
> Asked why McLain was not asked the question, Chief Counsel Blakey said: "I don't know."
>
> McLain also said he was never asked to listen to the recording of both channels 1 and 2 while in Washington. He said that when he listened to both on his return to Dallas, he recognized nothing on channel 1. Conversations and events were familiar to him on channel 2, however, meaning that he was tuned to channel 2 at the time of the assassination.
>
> Asked why McLain did not listen to the recording of both channels before or during his testimony, in the interest of verification, Blakey replied: "He never asked to."

There were other examples of the failure of the staff to bring key witnesses to the attention of the committee, where those witnesses might refute the conspiracy bias of Blakey and his subordinates. Dallas Police captain J. C. Bowles, who originally transcribed the Dallas Police radio tape for the Warren Commission, claimed that the motorcycle with the stuck microphone was not even in Dealey Plaza at the time of the gunfire but was sitting approximately two miles away. When he heard of the conspiracy findings of the House Assassinations Committee, he publicly stated he had informed a committee investigator the previous summer that he "could refute" the committee's acoustic evidence. He was never called to Washington to testify.

On December 29, 1978, the House Select Committee on Assassinations published its "Summary of Findings and Recommendations." The publicity timing was perfect. The release was embargoed "until 12:00 midnight, Saturday, December 30, 1978, or for publication in A.M. editions of newspapers dated December 31, 1978."

The committee wanted to ensure that every Sunday paper in the United States carried a front-page story on the dramatic conclusion it had reached: There was an unseen second gunman standing in an area known as the grassy knoll who, according to the committee, fired a single shot from close range at Kennedy. The claimed shot missed Kennedy and even missed the presidential limousine. Nevertheless, if true, it meant there was a conspiracy in the assassination.

To be sure, the committee concluded, as did the Warren Commission, that it was Lee Harvey Oswald who fired the shots that struck Kennedy and Connally. This was confirmed in the first section of the findings of the House Select Committee on Assassinations:

I. Findings of the Select Committee on Assassinations of President John F. Kennedy in Dallas, Texas, November 22, 1963.

A. Lee Harvey Oswald fired three shots at President Kennedy. The second and third shots he fired struck the President. The third shot killed the President.

1. President Kennedy was struck by two rifle shots fired from behind him.

2. The shots that struck President Kennedy from behind were fired from the sixth-floor window of the southeast corner of the Texas School Book Depository Building.

3. Lee Harvey Oswald owned the rifle that was used to fire the shots from the sixth-floor window of the southeast corner of the Texas School Book Depository Building.

4. Lee Harvey Oswald, shortly before the assassination, had access to and was present on the sixth-floor of the Texas School Book Depository Building.

5. Lee Harvey Oswald's other actions tend to support the conclusion that he assassinated President Kennedy.

But then:

B. Scientific acoustical evidence establishes a high probability that two gunmen fired at President John F. Kennedy. . . .

The chronology underlying the major error of the second-gunman conspiracy theory was summarized in the concluding portion of the dissenting views by Cong. Robert Edgar:

> I believe that Exhibit "A" will clearly demonstrate a rush to conspiratorial conclusions. You will note three sets of black letter findings. The first, in column 1 [which concluded there was no conspiracy], was presented to the committee for its consideration on Monday, December 18, 1978 [the date of the draft was December 13, 1978]. It was on that Monday that we met in executive session to discuss our findings and come to our final conclusions. It was also that Monday when Weiss and Aschkenasy [the 95-percent-sure acoustic experts] interrupted our session to share their final report. Less than two weeks later, on December 29, 1978, we met in public session to review the report finding. . . .
>
> I believe the Members of Congress did not have sufficient time or expertise to ask the tough questions. I believe the committee failed to properly consider how much weight to assign this evidence due to our own limitations of time and familiarity with the science. I believe we rushed to our conclusions and in doing so, overshadowed many important contributions which other aspects of our investigation will have on history. We did a great job up to the last moment, when in our focus on the acoustics, we failed to give proper weight to other findings of the investigation.

Congressman Edgar, of course, was right.

Cong. Harold Sawyer of the House Assassinations Committee also dissented. In addition to the reasons outlined in Edgar's dissent, Sawyer wrote:

> The officer who has been identified by the committee staff as the rider of the motorcycle on which the stuck transmitter was located has testified that he was in fact guarding the correct channel, namely channel 2, and denies that he was equipped with the stuck transmitter.
>
> The same officer, together with other police officials located near the presidential limousine at the time the shots were fired in Dealey Plaza all agree that sirens were activated, and motorcycles and other vehicles were subjected to emergency acceleration within not more than a few seconds following the shots having been fired. No change

in the rhythm or intensity of the motorcycle noise appears anywhere on the relevant Dictabelt. There is no audibile sound even resembling sirens until a full two minutes following the last of what is interpreted by the acoustical experts as the shots.

The committee report tried to find an excuse for there being no sounds of sirens, but it did not say anything about the absence of the noise of the motorcycles revving up.

Sawyer, a trial lawyer, added:

> It would appear to me that there are far too few, if any, established or verifiable facts in this entire acoustical scenario. . . . As a committee, we were presented with the expert acoustical testimony which I have described by three experts who were all in agreement with each other, one of whom had somewhat inexplicably drastically modified his earlier testimony to conform with that of the other two . . . an exercise in simple mathematics.

There is an issue of greater importance than the fact that the committee majority erred in its rush to find an invisible second gunman. That issue concerns the ramifications of a secret congressional investigation coupled with excessive delegation of powers to the committee staff. The committee's erroneous conclusion concerning Jack Ruby is the most vivid example of the pitfalls of this process.

Blakey and his staff succeeded in their efforts behind closed doors to convince a majority of the committee at the last moment that the invisible second gunman corroborated Blakey's theory that Jack Ruby stalked Lee Harvey Oswald from the hours immediately after the assassination until he killed Oswald on the Sunday morning following the assassination.

Meanwhile, Blakey, as soon as the report was put to bed, started writing his book, which was co-authored with Richard W. Billings. The title was *The Plot to Kill the President*, and the publication date was February 24, 1981. The essence of the book, according to the promotional material, was as follows:

> In 1979, the House Select Committee on Assassinations offered new acoustical evidence that four gunshots—including one from a second

gunman from behind the famous "grassy knoll" were involved in the assassination of President John F. Kennedy in Dallas in 1963. . . . Blakey, the Select Committee's Chief Counsel and Staff Director, and Billings . . . analyze the events in Dealey Plaza in the light of the new evidence and conclude Kennedy was murdered in a plot involving organized crime. Sifting information gathered by the Select Committee, they . . . show both Lee Harvey Oswald and his killer, Jack Ruby, had ties with mob figures opposed to J.F.K.'s anti-crime activities. "Organized crime figures had a motive to kill the President; in Oswald, they had the means to kill him," they write. Ruby's "silencing" of Oswald, they say, had "all the earmarks of an organized crime hit." Their disturbing book is a serious indictment of the Warren Commission's efforts and raises new doubts about J.F.K.'s death.

It seemed the perfect end for the investigation of the House Assassinations Committee. Who would defend organized crime? And, more particularly, who would defend Jack Ruby, now that he is dead?

If there had been public hearings on Blakey's theory, the allegations of Ruby's involvement in a conspiracy could never have been sustained because of the overwhelming evidence to the contrary and in particular the testimony of Rabbi Hillel Silverman, who visited Ruby in the Dallas County jail once or twice a week and became extremely close to him.

During the investigation of the Warren Commission, while Ruby was alive, Silverman could not be called to testify about these conversations because the conversations between a rabbi and his congregant are privileged. That prohibition did not necessarily bind the House Select Committee on Assassinations, since Ruby was dead. Yet the committee staff, during the multimillion-dollar two-year investigation, did not even try to take Silverman's testimony. He told me in 1979 that he would have testified had he been called. Blakey's book doesn't mention that Silverman had many intimate conversations with Ruby in the Dallas County jail and that Silverman is certain Ruby was not conspiratorially involved.

I sincerely regret that Professor Blakey and I have been at odds with one another, because a substantial portion of the work that was done by the House Select Committee on Assassinations was worthwhile—particularly the findings of the independent panel of medical experts, who concluded that the same bullet that passed through President Kennedy's neck struck Governor Connally, and the neutron analysis of the bullet fragments. But as pointed out by committee member Robert Edgar, in its rush to reach the false conclusion of a second gunman, all of the good work of the committee was obscured.

# 28

## Proving There Was No Fourth Shot

One marvelous aspect of our free society is the opportunity for citizen participation in government. One citizen who played a little-known—but important—role is Steve Barber of Mansfield, Ohio. He helped prove that the acoustic experts hired by the House Assassinations Committee were just plain wrong.

After the completion of the Report of the House Assassinations Committee, there was much controversy. Accordingly, the National Research Council, under a grant from the National Science Foundation, assembled acoustic experts to determine the reliability of the assertions of the experts retained by the House Assassinations Committee. The committee's experts had alleged a 95 percent probability of a fourth shot fired by a second gunman from the grassy knoll.

The new panel became known as the Committee on Ballistic Acoustics of the National Research Council. It was chaired by Norman F. Ramsey, Higgins Professor of Physics at Harvard University. Included on the committee were other Ph.D.s from the University of California, Massachusetts Institute of Technology,

Princeton University, Columbia University, and several research centers of major American Corporations such as Bell Telephone Laboratories, Xerox, Trisolar Corporation, and IBM, plus an expert from the Firearms National Laboratory Center of the Department of the Treasury.

All possessed impressive scientific capabilities that enabled them to conclude accurately that the acoustic experts who testified before the House Assassinations Committee were wrong.

But there was a second independent basis that also proved the point. That basis was supplied by Steve Barber, a musician, who wrote the committee that he was convinced from his own listening that there were clear instances in which phrases recorded on the channel 2 tape were distinctly audible on the channel 1 tape. It was a common-sense approach and could be readily explained if one were to assume that there were two police motorcycles together and that the motorcycle with a stuck microphone would pick up the sounds that were emanating from the loudspeaker from the other nearby motorcycle, which was tuned to the other police channel.

Indeed, when the experts followed Barber's suggestions, they found that this is exactly what happened. There were a number of instances in which both kinds of cross-talk were clear, and the experts were able to match sections on the two channels. It turned out that the portion of the tape where the House committee's experts claimed oscillating waves indicated gunshots actually contained talk that occurred at least one minute *after* the time of the assassination. (Nowhere on the tape are there any sounds of gunshots.)

On May 14, 1982, the Committee on Ballistic Acoustics of the Commission on Physical Sciences, Mathematics and Resources of the National Research Council issued a ninety-six-page report in which it unanimously concluded there was no basis for a claim of a second gunman firing from the grassy knoll. The committee said:

> The acoustic analyses do not demonstrate that there was a grassy knoll shot, and in particular there is no acoustic basis for the claim of 95% probability of such a shot.
>
> The acoustic impulses attributed to gunshots were recorded about

one minute after the President had been shot and the motorcade had been instructed to go to the hospital.

Therefore, reliable acoustic data do not support a conclusion that there was a second gunman.*

How did the House Committee get led astray in the first place? There are two major factors:

1. Almost all the investigation and hearings of the committee were conducted behind closed doors. The press did not have an opportunity to review and report what was taking place over the twenty-month multimillion-dollar investigation except for some orchestrated public hearings in the fall of 1978.

2. The House Select Committee on Assassinations, like virtually all congressional committees, relied too heavily on its staff. It was the staff that led the committee majority to its erroneous second-gunman conclusion.

Why was the staff so intent on finding a second gunman? This enabled it to kill three birds with one stone. From a financial standpoint, their conclusion justified the expenditure of millions of dollars by the committee. From a psychological standpoint, it enabled the staff, consciously or subconsciously, to justify its own two years of work. From a political standpoint, it took the heat off the committee and its staff, because even though they said the FBI and the CIA were not involved, they did find a conspiracy, and they stated that their alleged second gunman was unknown. This statement left the door open for continued attacks on the CIA and the FBI. In essence, the finding of a second gunman was a sop to the group of assassination sensationalists led by Mark Lane and Robert Grodin, who for years have been proclaiming Oswald's innocence in books, radio and television programs, and lectures on campuses across the country.

There was great deference paid to assassination sensationalists

---

*In a September 13, 1982, letter to me, Professor Ramsey, who chaired the Committee on Ballistic Acoustics, referred to Steve Barber's suggestion as "a critically valuable contribution to our report." Another committee member wrote me and said, "I cannot share your belief that 'the truth will ultimately prevail' in this case, because it seems to be much more fun to believe in exotic hypotheses."

during the entire investigation. Some of these people, such as Grodin, were even paid as consultants by the committee.

In addition, in its findings of conspiracy, the committee and its staff made an important distinction between possible pro-Castro and anti-Castro involvement. With reference to the anti-Castro Cuban groups, the committee's December 29, 1978 "Summary of Findings and Recommendations" states:

> The Committee believes, on the basis of the evidence available to it, that anti-Castro Cuban groups, as groups, were not involved in the assassination of President Kennedy, but the available evidence does not preclude the possibility that individual members may have been involved.

On the other hand, with reference to involvement of the Cuban government or pro-Castro groups, the conclusion of the committee was merely as follows:

"The Committee believes, on the basis of the evidence available to it, that the Cuban government was not involved in the assassination of President Kennedy."

In other words, although Oswald was an avowed Marxist and for years had professed great admiration for Castro both orally and in writing, the committee made no reference to the possibility of pro-Castro groups being involved, nor did it even state that "the available evidence does not preclude the possibility that individual members may have been involved," as it did with anti-Castro groups. This difference is particularly important in light of the determination by the committee that it "is unable to identify the second gunman or the extent of the conspiracy."

If there had been an unknown second gunman, you could not prove that the individual conspirator was *not* a member of an anti-Castro group. But by the same token, how could you prove that he was not a member of a pro-Castro group? Therefore, why did the House committee not also say that "the available evidence does not preclude the possibility that individual members [of pro-Castro] Cuban groups may have been involved?"

In fact, if there was any difference, in light of Oswald's political background it would be more reasonable to preclude the possibility with reference to anti-Castro elements rather than pro-Castro elements. At the very least, this is indicative of either bias or incompetence on the part of the House Assassinations Committee.

At any rate, the erroneous conclusion of the majority of the House Assassinations Committee is a vivid example of the dangers of secret congressional proceedings coupled with excessive reliance on committee staffs. Congressional staffs are like an "unelected hidden legislature," James Reston wrote in the *New York Times*. He said:

> Over the years these staff members have taken on more and more responsibility—so much so that in some cases they not only seem to assist their masters but to replace them. Staff members not only write speeches but conduct hearings, draft legislation, write committee reports, negotiate conference compromises between the Houses, mobilize public opinion and advise lawmakers on how to vote.
>
> In recent years, they have even been conducting investigations at home and abroad, sometimes on their own, without the presence of their chiefs. And with the rise of subcommittees, each with its own staff, the congressional staff bureaucracy has grown even faster than the Civil Service in many of the Executive departments.

The problem has continued to grow since the 1979 Reston column. According to a March 22, 1988, report of the *Wall Street Journal*, "These personal staffs grew to a total of 7,920 for the House and 3,774 for the Senate in 1986."

Those staffers of the House Assassinations Committee now know their experts were wrong, of course. But Professor Blakey continues to lend support to the specious claims of those who allege that the acoustic testimony before the committee proves there was a fourth shot. For instance, Scheim's 1988 book *Contract on America* goes into detail about the acoustic testimony before the House committee and heavily relies on the conclusion that " 'with a probability of 95 percent or better,' the third shot was fired from the grassy knoll." The back cover of the book has at the very top in boldface type, " 'Should be read by anyone seriously interested in knowing what happened to President Kennedy in Dallas.' G. Robert Blakey, Chief Counsel, House Select Committee on Assassinations."

After the summary of the final report of the committee was released, I wrote an article for the *National Review* entitled "The Second-Gunman Syndrome." Blakey read it and wrote a letter to the editor, which was published together with my reply. Blakey then prepared another rebuttal. For space reasons, the *National Review* did not publish this final exchange but allowed the readers to obtain copies if they so desired. William Buckley, Jr., did add an editor's note stating that "we cannot foreswear to give our own conclusion that Belin has the better of the argument, i.e., that John F. Kennedy did, on November 22, 1963, die as a result of the firing of a rifle by Lee Harvey Oswald, who acted, that day in Dallas, alone."

In his rebuttal, Blakey wrote:

> "The Department of Justice has announced [*New York Times*, January 6, 1980] that it is going to verify the acoustics testing done by the House Assassinations Committee. I assume it will be done with competency and integrity. If so, I will abide by its results. If it indicates that there is not a 95% probability that there was a gunshot from the grassy knoll, I will write a letter to the *Review* and withdraw all that I have said. . . ."

The National Science Foundation's study was done by the Committee on Ballistic Acoustics of the National Research Council. It was composed of experts. That report made it clear that not only was there "not a 95% probability that there was a gunshot from the grassy knoll" but that as a matter of fact there is absolutely no probability at all.

The *National Review* is still waiting for Blakey to "write . . . and withdraw all that I have said."

# 29

## Why Did Oswald Kill President Kennedy?

**W**hy did Oswald kill Kennedy? It is a question that was not satisfactorily answered by the Warren Commission. It is a question that was not satisfactorily answered by the House Assassinations Committee. It has not been sufficiently discussed because assassination sensationalists and conspiracy cultists have deceived much of the American public into believing Oswald was not the lone gunman who killed President Kennedy and Officer Tippit. Thus, instead of the debate centering on why Oswald killed Kennedy, it has centered on claims that Oswald did not do anything or at least was not the lone gunman.

Oswald is dead, and no one can prove why he did what he did. But a person can speculate.

First, review just who Lee Harvey Oswald was. From the Tippit murder, we know he had the capacity to kill. From his interrogation, we know he lied about crucial matters. We also know he tried to assassinate someone before he killed Kennedy. On April 10, 1963, not too long after Oswald received his rifle in the mail, he tried to kill Maj. Gen. Edwin A. Walker at Walker's home in

Dallas. Walker had been an active and controversial figure identified with the right wing of the American political scene since his
resignation from the army in 1961. At the time Oswald pulled the
trigger, Walker moved, and the shot narrowly missed.

When Oswald's rifle was found, there was an attempt to link it
to the Walker bullet. FBI experts stated that the bullet was too
mutilated to be ballistically identifiable, although it had characteristics similar to those of bullets fired from Oswald's rifle. An
independent expert retained by the Warren Commission believed
that although he could not say that the bullet absolutely came from
Oswald's rifle, he thought it "probably" did.

In Marina Oswald's testimony, she admitted that on the night
of the Walker shooting, when Oswald did not return by 10:00 or
10:30 P.M., she became concerned, went to his room, and discovered a note written to her in Russian. It said:

1. This is the key to the mailbox which is located in the main
post office in the city on Ervay Street. This is the same street where
the drugstore, in which you always waited is located. You will find
the mailbox in the post office which is located 4 blocks from the
drugstore on that street. I paid for the box last month so don't worry
about it.

2. Send the information as to what has happened to me to the
Embassy and include newspaper clippings (should there be anything
about me in the newspapers). I believe that the Embassy will come
quickly to your assistance on learning everything.

3. I paid the house rent on the 2d so don't worry about it.

4. Recently I also paid for water and gas.

5. The money from work will possibly be coming. The money will
be sent to our post office box. Go to the bank and cash the check.

6. You can either throw out or give my clothing, etc. away. Do not
keep these. However, I prefer that you hold on to my personal papers
(military, civil, etc.)

7. Certain of my documents are in the small blue valise.

8. The address book can be found on my table in the study should
need same.

9. We have friends here. The Red Cross also will help you. (Red
Cross in English.)

10. I left you as much money as I could, $60 on the second of the month. You and the baby [apparently] can live for another 2 months using $10 per week.

11. If I am alive and taken prisoner, the city jail is located at the end of the bridge through which we always passed on going to the city (right in the beginning of the city after crossing the bridge).

Handwriting experts said the note, which had been turned over to the police with some of Oswald's belongings by Mrs. Ruth Paine (with whom Marina Oswald was staying), was written by Lee Harvey Oswald. Marina Oswald subsequently admitted that Oswald told her he had taken a shot at General Walker, did not know whether he had hit Walker, learned on the radio and in the newspapers the next day that he had missed, and was "very sorry that he had not hit him." Although the note referred to the location of the city jail when in fact the location was of the county jail, there was no doubt it referred to the main post office where Oswald rented post-office box 2915. Most important of all, Oswald had taken photographs of General Walker's house, and scientifically it was determined that they were taken with his camera.

We know, too, that Oswald was emotionally unstable; he had tried to commit suicide in Russia. We know his marriage was a troubled one; Marina berated his low earning ability and made fun of his lack of sexual prowess. We know that Oswald had an unhappy childhood. His mother, Marguerite, was first married to Edward Pic, Jr. Two years later she was separated, and eventually they divorced. She married Robert Edward Lee Oswald on July 20, 1933. They lived in New Orleans and had a son named Robert, Jr. It was her second son—she had had a son from her first marriage. In 1939, Marguerite Oswald became pregnant again. In August 1939, Robert Oswald died of a heart attack. Two months later, Lee Harvey Oswald was born.

Marguerite Oswald was not the world's best mother. She tried to put Lee in an orphanage when he was two but was told that he was too young; the orphanage did accept his older brother and half brother. When Oswald was three, he was placed in the orphanage and stayed for over a year, until his mother moved to

Dallas. Marguerite Oswald had an off-again, on-again relationship with an older man named Edwin Ekdahl. She and Ekdahl married when Lee Harvey Oswald was five and a half. A year later, Marguerite Oswald and Ekdahl separated, later reconciled, and eventually divorced. By this time, Oswald was nearly nine.

Throughout Oswald's childhood there were many changes of address in New Orleans and in Dallas, and after the divorce there was another move. Then, in August 1952, Mrs. Oswald and Lee moved to New York City. There were several moves inside New York City. Lee Oswald began experiencing an increasing amount of trouble at school. He attended classes less than half of the time. Truancy proceedings were undertaken on March 12, 1953, when Lee Oswald was thirteen and a half. The attendance officer in charge of Lee's case filed a petition in court alleging that Lee had been "excessively absent from school" between October and January, that he had refused to register at Public School 44 or to attend school there, and that he was "beyond the control of his mother insofar as school attendance is concerned." On the same day, Mrs. Oswald appeared in court alone and informed the judge that Lee refused to appear in court. Evidently impressed by the proceedings, however, Lee did register at Public School 44 on March 23. On April 16, Justice Delany declared him a truant and remanded him to Youth House until May 7 for psychiatric study.

Oswald eventually was released on parole, and he was referred to the Community Service Society for psychiatric treatment. The society did not take the case, though, because it had a full caseload and did not have the time for the intensive treatment Oswald appeared to need.

Oswald's report cards contained notations by teachers that although he received passing grades in most subjects, he was "quick tempered," "constantly losing control," and "getting into battles with others." Early in the following year, Mrs. Oswald and Lee returned to New Orleans, where they moved frequently over several years.

In high school, Oswald became interested in Russia and Marxism. On October 3, 1956, he wrote to the Socialist Party of America:

Dear Sirs;

I am sixteen years of age and would like more information about your youth League, I would like to know if there is a branch in my area, how to join, ect. [*sic*], I am a Marxist, and have been studying socialist principles for well over fifteen months I am very interested in your Y.P.S.L.

Sincerely
/s/ Lee Oswald

Accompanying the letter was an advertisement coupon on which he had checked the box requesting information about the Socialist party.

Shortly before his sixteenth birthday, Oswald dropped out of school. He tried to enlist in the marines, using a false affidavit from his mother that he was seventeen. The attempt failed. He turned seventeen on October 18, 1956, and six days later, on October 24, he enlisted in the marines.

In the marines, he learned to shoot a rifle. Although his practice scores were not very good, on December 21, 1956, when his company fired for record, there was a three-category scale of "Marksman/Sharpshooter/Expert." Oswald qualified in the middle range as a "Sharpshooter."

The most significant aspect of his marine life, apart from having learned to shoot a rifle, was that on August 17, 1959, he asked for a dependency discharge on the false ground that his mother needed his support. Actually, he intended to go to Russia, and he applied for a passport. He was released from active duty on September 11. Oswald booked passage on a freighter scheduled to sail from New Orleans to France on September 18. From France he went to England and from England to Finland; in Finland, he obtained a visa into Russia.

In Russia, Oswald told an official he wanted to become a citizen of the Soviet Union. He sought to renounce his U.S. citizenship. Initially, however, Russia did not accept him, and he was notified that his visa would be expiring and that he had to leave Moscow within two hours. His response was to slash his left wrist in an apparent suicide attempt.

Oswald was finally allowed to stay in Russia. He obtained a job and met Marina, whom he married after a short courtship. For a while he was relatively happy. Soon, though, he became disillusioned with life in Russia. The entry in his diary for January 4–31, 1961, reads, complete with misspellings:

"I am stating to reconsider my disire about staying. The work is drab. The money I get has nowhere to be spent. No nightclubs or bowling allys, no places of recreation acept the trade union dances. I have had enough."

The diary title was "Historic Diary," and it evidenced another of Oswald's character traits: delusions of grandeur.

Oswald asked the U.S. embassy about getting back his passport. He wanted assurances he would not be prosecuted if he returned to the United States. After more than a year, he was able to leave. He returned to the United States in June 1962 with Marina and their young daughter. They first went to Fort Worth and then to Dallas. Lee Oswald and Marina became acquainted with a number of people in the Russian-speaking community in the Dallas–Fort Worth area. That is where they met Ruth Paine, who at the time was living with her husband.

Oswald tried different jobs. His work was not satisfying; his marriage to Marina was not satisfying. But Oswald did find satisfaction in staying involved in politics, and he started to correspond with the Communist Party, U.S.A., and the Socialist Workers' party.

In January 1963 he ordered his revolver. In March he ordered the rifle. Both weapons were shipped on March 20, 1963, mailed to his postal box in Dallas.

After the Walker shooting incident, Oswald decided to move to New Orleans, where an aunt lived. He had a succession of low-paying jobs.

Although Oswald had been disillusioned about life in Russia, he still called himself a Marxist, and he started to take a great interest in Fidel Castro and his Marxist regime in Cuba. After

Oswald and Marina moved to New Orleans, Oswald began to plan a New Orleans branch of the "Fair Play for Cuba Committee." Using an alias, "Lee Osborne," Oswald ordered printed circulars demanding "Hands off Cuba" with application forms and membership cards for the proposed chapter.

Oswald's political activities in New Orleans culminated in two events. On August 16, 1963, he passed out Fair Play for Cuba literature in front of the International Trade Mart. Television newscasts ran pictures of his activities. He then was invited to a local radio station for a debate, and on August 21, Oswald and an anti-Castro Cuban, Carlos Bringuier, engaged in the debate.

During this period, Oswald wrote V. T. Lee, then national director of the Fair Play for Cuba Committee, telling him about his activities, sometimes in exaggerated terms. However, try as he could, Oswald was not able to obtain a national charter for his one-man Fair Play for Cuba Committee. Oswald also wrote to the Communist party and asked whether he should "continue to fight, handicapped as it were, by . . ." his past record and whether he should "compete with anti-progressive forces, above ground or . . . should always remain in the background, i.e., underground." The Communist party replied back, "Often it is advisable for some people to remain in the background, not underground."

September 1963 was a crucial month. Marina Oswald had become pregnant again. Mrs. Paine visited the family in New Orleans in September, and it was decided that Marina would go back to live with her in the Dallas suburb of Irving until after the birth of her second child, which was anticipated in October.

Meanwhile, Oswald suddenly decided to go to Mexico. On September 17, 1963, he obtained from the Mexican consulate general in New Orleans a "tourist card." Marina and their daughter, June, left with Mrs. Paine on September 23. Oswald told Marina that she should not tell anyone that he was planning to go to Mexico. On the afternoon of September 25, he left New Orleans for Houston, and the next day he left for Laredo, Texas, and from there to Mexico.

As soon as Oswald got to Mexico City and registered in a cheap hotel (which cost $1.28 per day), he tried to get to Cuba. He first went to the Cuban embassy to obtain a visa or an in-transit visa to go to Cuba and ostensibly from there to Russia. He could not do so through the Cuban embassy. He then tried to get the co-operation of the Russian embassy, but he was unsuccessful.

His trip a failure, Oswald returned to the United States on October 3, 1963. He expressed to Marina his frustration and disappointment about having been unable to go to Cuba. A few weeks later, he wrote the Russian embassy in Washington expressing his unhappiness and his rationale that it was "a gross breach of regulations" on the part of the Cuban embassy.

So Oswald remained an alienated, troubled man, unstable, unhappy, and unpredictable. Why did he shoot Kennedy? The best answer the Warren Commision could give was:

> Many factors were undoubtedly involved in Oswald's motivation for the assassination, and the Commission does not believe that it can ascribe to him any one motive or group of motives. It is apparent, however, that Oswald was moved by an overriding hostility to his environment. He does not appear to have been able to establish meaningful relationships with other people. He was perpetually discontented with the world around him. Long before the assassination he expressed his hatred for American society and acted in protest against it. Oswald's search for what he conceived to be the perfect society was doomed from the start. He sought for himself a place in history—a role as the "great man" who would be recognized as having been in advance of his times. His commitment to Marxism and communism appears to have been another important factor in his motivation. He also had demonstrated a capacity to act decisively and without regard to the consequences when such action would further his aims of the moment. Out of these and the many other factors which may have molded the character of Lee Harvey Oswald there emerged a man capable of assassinating President Kennedy.

The immediate attacks on the findings of the Warren Commission by those who professed that Oswald was innocent covered up the real question. These sensationalists asserted that Oswald did not kill either President Kennedy or Officer Tippit and that the basic question was who committed these two murders. In fact, the real question was *why* Oswald killed the president. At first, the sensationalists claimed the Dallas police were trying to frame Oswald. Then, when confronted with the testimony of Johnny Calvin Brewer and others, they shifted their claims and said that there must have been a conspiracy and that Oswald was framed as a part of that conspiracy. However, here they were confronted with the murder of Officer Tippit by Oswald.

The next shift was to try to assert that Oswald was framed for this murder by people who tried to plant in the bushes cartridge cases from the pistol with which Oswald was apprehended in the Texas Theatre. They were wrong here also, so their next concentrated effort focused on earlier false claims that President Kennedy was struck from the front.

Finally, when the report of the House Assassinations Committee and the medical and ballistic findings of the Warren Commission were confirmed, there was another shift. The defenders of Oswald sought to make him some sort of a patsy in a CIA conspiracy or an organized-crime conspiracy. There was always the fictitious unseen second gunman. Prove that Oswald wasn't associated with the CIA; prove that he wasn't associated with or duped by organized-crime figures.

There is nothing in the files of the CIA to give even the slightest hint that he was a CIA agent. Moreover, it is relatively obvious that a man of Oswald's background and emotions is not the kind of a person the CIA would entrust with anything.

Nevertheless, although the CIA was in no way directly involved with the assassination of President Kennedy, there may have been an indirect connection between the CIA assassination plots directed against Castro and the assassination of Kennedy by Oswald. Here are the reasons.

On September 8, 1963, there had been a newspaper report of a threat by Castro to retaliate against American leaders if they did not stop their assassination attempts against Cuban officials. This report was featured in the New Orleans papers a week before Oswald applied for his trip to Mexico City. As an avid reader of newspapers and an admirer of Fidel Castro, Oswald very probably saw the article.

Oswald may have wanted revenge against the person who was seeking, according to the newspaper reports about Castro, to assassinate the political leader that Oswald admired most. What better way for recognition in Cuba could there be than to kill the person—Kennedy—who was (allegedly) responsible for attempts to kill Castro?

Is there any objective evidence to support this theory? The strongest factors are the lies of Oswald during his interrogation by the Dallas Police Department about key matters—the ownership of the rifle, the place of purchase of the pistol, the picture of Oswald with the rifle and the revolver, his location at the time of the assassination, and his trip to Mexico. Is it possible that he lied about the trip to Mexico because, directly or indirectly, it had something to do with the fact he assassinated Kennedy?

There was an important piece of physical evidence that indicated Oswald's destination at the time of the Tippit shooting. Because of the events of November 24, when Ruby killed Oswald, there was wide speculation that there was some relationship between the two. The speculation was compounded because the apartment of Jack Ruby was only two-thirds of a mile from the scene of the shooting of Officer Tippit and at the time of the shooting Oswald was headed in the direction of that apartment.

Oswald didn't know Tippit. Oswald didn't know Ruby. And Ruby did not know either Oswald or Tippit. (There was another Tippit on the police force whom Ruby did know.)

However, when Oswald was apprehended, he had a bus transfer. Shortly after the assassination, he boarded a bus, and when the bus stalled in traffic, he left it and hailed a cab. As Oswald left the bus, he asked for a transfer.

Why did he ask for the transfer? Was there some nearby bus-transfer point toward which Oswald was walking when he was stopped by Tippit? There was.

Evidence is circumstantial, but it is likely Oswald was fleeing to Mexico City when he encountered Tippit. While in the marines,

Oswald once told a buddy, Nelson Delgado, that if he were ever trying to escape law enforcement authorities in the United States, he would try to get to Mexico and from there go to Russia via Cuba. "This is the way I would go about it."

From Oswald's rooming house, where he had stopped to pick up his gun, the nearest boarding point for use of the transfer was at Jefferson and Marsalis, and he had almost arrived there when he was stopped by Tippit.

The first southbound bus Oswald could have taken after the assassination left downtown Dallas at 3:15 P.M. and made a flag stop at Lisbon, which was part of the metropolitan area of Dallas. The Lisbon stop could be reached through the bus transfer, and the intersection of Jefferson and Marsalis streets was the only transfer point in the Oak Cliff section of Dallas where Oswald could have used his transfer. Oswald had almost arrived at that transfer point when he was stopped by Tippit, no doubt because Oswald's description matched the description broadcast over the Dallas police radio after the assassination.

So, again, why did Oswald kill Kennedy and Tippit? We can start with what we know:

1. Oswald was the lone gunman who killed Kennedy and Tippit.

2. After the assassination, Oswald went back to his rooming house to get his pistol. Why did he not have his pistol with him on Friday morning? One possibility is that it was not until Thursday, after he went to work, that he decided to visit his wife that night and get his rifle and therefore he did not carry his pistol with him when he went to work Thursday morning. The more likely reason is that he recognized that there was a great possibility that witnesses would see a gunman fire from the Texas School Book Depository, that the building would be sealed off before he could get out, and that there would be a search conducted of people inside the building. If he had had a pistol, he could have been arrested.

Similarly, when Tippit got out of the police car (Oswald closely matched Brennan's description of the gunman broadcast over the police radio), there was the possibility he would approach Oswald and immediately run a quick search for weapons, find the pistol, and detain Oswald. For Oswald, the obvious alternative was to kill the policeman.

3. There is little doubt that Oswald was trying to set the stage to escape. He left the depository. He was headed toward a destination to catch a bus that would take him to Mexico. He left his wedding band with his wife. He left her most of his money. And here we have a crucial question:

*If Oswald was planning to escape to Mexico (or anywhere else), is it not reasonable to assume that he would have taken cash with him unless he was in league with someone who could provide funds to him when he reached his destination?*

If this is the case, then the question becomes, who would that someone be?

Professor Blakey would have you believe that it had something to do with Jack Ruby and organized crime, the centerpiece of the argument being that Ruby shot Oswald to silence him. But such claims do not hold water in light of the testimony of Rabbi Hillel Silverman, the happenstance of Postal Inspector Holmes coming to the Sunday morning interrogation and thereby delaying the transfer of Oswald, the willingness of Jack Ruby to step forward and volunteer to take a polygraph exam against the advice of his own attorneys, the result of that exam, the happenstance of Ruby being downtown to wire funds to an employee at a time that would have been much later than the originally scheduled 10:00 A.M. transfer of Oswald, and common-sense realization that organized crime "hit men" don't murder someone when they are surrounded by police and are sure to be caught, sent to jail, and tried and convicted of murder.

Some cultists say it was not organized crime but rather assert that Oswald was duped by anti-Castro Cubans. Oswald may have been emotionally unstable, but he was a committed Marxist and was nobody's fool. Moreover, there is no evidence to show there were any specific contacts between anti-Castro Cubans and Oswald in the United States, much less in Mexico.

4. Some people assert that the CIA or the FBI was in league

with Oswald in some way. That is hogwash. There is no evidence to link the FBI or the CIA with the assassination of Kennedy.

5. On the other hand, there may have been an indirect relationship between the activities of the CIA in trying to assassinate Castro, the continuing pronouncements of President Kennedy calling for Castro to be dethroned, and the motives of Oswald, who, as evidenced by his "historic" diary, thought of himself as a person of history. At the very least, it is reasonable to believe that had the CIA not tried to assassinate Castro through use of the Mafia —a plan that was infiltrated by Castro agents and that came to the attention of Castro—then Castro would not have given his warning in September 1963 that there might be retaliation—a warning Oswald probably read.

6. To all of this we have to add a most important factor: the lies of Oswald during his interrogation about his trip to Mexico. Why did Oswald try to hide from his interrogators the fact that he had been in Mexico? What was the reason? It was part of the pattern of lies that related to the most crucial aspects of his guilt—his ownership of the rifle, his whereabouts at the moment of the assassination—all key lies. Is it not reasonable to assume that the denial of his trip to Mexico is strong circumstantial evidence pointing to someone in Mexico who was in some way involved, directly or indirectly, with the assassination?

Who might that person be? And would it be someone who could provide the cash to help take care of Oswald's needs after he left most of his cash with his wife on the morning of the assassination?

These questions lead back to the Russian and Cuban embassies that Oswald visited in Mexico City. Oswald probably told people at these embassies about his commitment to Marxist ideals. Could he have boasted about his Fair Play for Cuba activities in such a way that led to a discussion about getting back at Kennedy if the opportunity should arise? Might he have mentioned his attempt to shoot Walker?

On the other hand, when Oswald went to Mexico, the public did not know Kennedy was going to be in Dallas in November. However, with the 1964 election approaching, it was certainly likely that Kennedy would sometime come to Texas to campaign and if he came to Texas, Dallas was going to be one stop. Certainly there was speculation in the newspaper about the possibility of a presidential visit.

Were it not for Oswald's lies about his trip to Mexico, I would state unequivocably that there was no conspiratorial complicity between Oswald and anyone else. I would suggest that the actions of Oswald were those of a loner and that he was not conspiratorially involved with any pro-Castro agents in Mexico.

However, if there is any possibility of conspiracy, the scenario that best fits the facts is that Oswald was influenced as an outgrowth of Castro's knowledge that he was a target of American assassination attempts, which in turn led Castro to call for retaliation, or that Oswald was influenced by the continued pronouncements of Kennedy calling for the overthrow of Castro, or most probably a combination of these two. As soon as these possibilities are considered, one must add the possibility that while in Mexico City, Oswald had a conversation with a Castro agent or sympathizer about getting back at Kennedy and was promised financial and other support if he ever was able to succeed.

Indeed, in 1975, I told John McCone, former CIA director who had been ignorant of the plans, the details of how the CIA had sought to assassinate Castro and of Robert Kennedy's knowledge of these plans. McCone replied that for the first time he could now understand the reactions of Kennedy right after the assassination when the two of them were alone. McCone said he felt there was something troubling Kennedy that he was not disclosing, although they did have a close relationship. McCone said he now feels Kennedy may very well have thought that there was some connection between the assassination plans against Castro and the assassination of President Kennedy. He also added his personal belief that Robert Kennedy had personal feelings of guilt because he was directly or indirectly involved with the anti-Castro planning.

Related to this is the sequence of events that occurred in the summer of 1964 when the Warren Commission was approaching the end of its investigation. On June 11, 1964, Earl Warren wrote

Robert Kennedy asking about the possibility of "any additional information relating to the assassination of President John F. Kennedy which has not been sent to the Commission" as well as "any information suggesting that the assassination of President Kennedy was caused by a domestic or foreign conspiracy."

Robert Kennedy did not respond until August 4, when he wrote that "all information relating in any way to the assassination of President John F. Kennedy in the possession of the Department of Justice" had been referred to the Warren Commission. Kennedy further said:

> I would like to state definitely that I know of no credible evidence to support the allegations that the assassination of President Kennedy was caused by a domestic or foreign conspiracy. I have no suggestions to make at this time regarding any additional investigation which should be undertaken by the Commission prior to the publication of its report. . . .

Why did it take Kennedy so long to reply? Perhaps it was the traumatic task of having to write a letter of that kind about the death of his brother. Or perhaps there was another reason: Perhaps Robert Kennedy could not decide whether to tell the Warren Commission about the assassination plots against Castro. He eventually decided to withhold the information.

Thus you have three scenarios: (1) Oswald was not influenced by Castro's call for retaliation or Kennedy's calls for dethroning Castro; (2) Oswald was influenced by either Castro's calls for retaliation or Kennedy's calls for overthrowing Castro, or both, but he was not involved in any conspiratorial way with Castro agents in Mexico City; (3) Oswald was not only influenced by Kennedy's calls for dethroning Castro and Castro's calls for retaliation; he was also influenced as a result of contact with Castro agents while he was in Mexico City. In this last scenario, there would have been at least indirect conspiracy, and there would be direct conspiracy if Oswald was headed to Mexico to get not only the recognition and praise he craved but also promised financial help. No one, of course, will ever know. However, I believe that when Oswald shot Kennedy, he felt he was acting on behalf of the man he idolized, the man whose first name was adapted by Oswald to form his alias of A. J. Hidell—Fidel Castro.

I also believe there is a substantial possibility that Oswald was influenced by the extreme anti-Castro rhetoric of the Kennedys and perhaps by Castro's call for retaliation.

But was there any Cuban conspiracy growing out of Oswald's trip to Mexico? There is no evidence to prove this, although it is possible.

# 30

## The Warren Commission and CIA Investigations in Perspective

In perspective, I've come to the realization that if there is a dominant reason the Warren Commission Report has not been accepted as the truth by a majority of Americans, it is because all our investigative work was undertaken in secret. The public was denied not only the benefit of reports on the developments unearthed as the investigation proceeded but also the testimony of the witnesses.

No doubt it was far easier to work inside the commission without the presence of the press. Yet if there had been public hearings when, for example, Howard Leslie Brennan told what he saw as the gunman took aim to fire his last shot; if the press could have reported what Amos Euins saw in the southeast-corner window of the sixth floor of the depository and what Harold Norman, James Jarman, Jr., and Bonnie Ray Williams heard from the floor below; if the eyewitnesses to the Tippit murder, if Johnny Calvin Brewer, who trailed Oswald into the Texas Theatre, and if all of the other witnesses had testified in public, Mark Lane and his fellow purveyors of falsity would never have had a chance.

The problem was compounded by the decision to withhold the

X-ray and autopsy photographs of President Kennedy from the exhibits to the Warren Commission Report. John McCloy, the member of the Warren Commission who had the greatest and broadest trial and corporate legal experience, later wrote to me:

> I agree wholeheartedly with your criticism of the Commission itself for failure to demand the original X-rays and photographs. I agreed to having the Chief Justice's viewing them alone if he would do so and I understand he was to do this. The argument against their being viewed by the Commission as part of the record was that the X-rays and photographs of the President's body did not in themselves carry as much weight as the interpretation of them by the experts. This together with what I thought to be the over-sensitivity of the Chief Justice to the attitude of the family, resulted in a good bit of just criticism of the Commission which in my judgment could have been avoided. The criticism of the Commission may be unimportant, but it was the duty of the Commission to provide to the country and the world the fullest confidence in the Commission's conclusion as a result of a penetrating and objective, no-holds-barred, investigation.

Then, McCloy turned to what has been one of the most disturbing aspects of the post-assassination debate: The response of the media and the universities. In McCloy's words:

> I never cease to be amazed at the willingness of so much of the public to accept the statements of the charlatans and the sensationalists rather than the facts and record. The media and the reviewers were really fatuous, if not worse, but what really astounded me was the doctrinaire approach which so many of our colleges and universities took toward the Commission's conclusions. Led in many cases by members of the faculty who should have known and acted better, they applauded and accepted with open arms the people like Mark Lane whom they invited to their campuses to lecture as courageous independent investigators. I visited at a number of universities as in those days I was a rather frequent visitor to them for reasons totally unconnected with my position on the Commission. It was actually thought "liberal" to be convinced that President Kennedy had been shot as a

result of a conspiracy by a group of Texas millionaires or chauvinists and that it was quite "illiberal" to think that he has been assassinated solely by a little "punk" who perhaps had some personal communistic leanings.

A further problem was bias of the staff of the House Assassinations Committee. In its investigation into the CIA plots directed against Castro, for instance, the committee never called as witnesses the two men directly involved in the CIA AM/LASH operation; instead, the committee relied on the testimony of a man not directly involved. The committee members did not know it, but this witness significantly changed his testimony from what he had told the Senate Select Committee on Intelligence in 1975.

A former high CIA official said the staff called the unreliable secondhand witness because his new testimony "served a purpose of the staff and might be inconsistent with that of persons actually knowledgeable."

It was this kind of bias that led the staff to its erroneous second-gunman conclusion. It was this kind of bias that led Robert Blakey to use Jack Ruby as his fall guy. It was this kind of bias that led to the differentiation in treatment of the possibility of pro-Castro Cubans as individuals possibly being involved in a conspiracy, if there would have been one.

Related to all of this is another serious problem—the practicalities of news reporting. Television screens and front pages shout charges, but thoughtful responses bolstered by facts get less notice. Much television and radio news consists of thirty-second or sixty-second capsules. America's judgment is no better than its information. When the press investigates, it makes a difference. Watergate is proof of that. But when the press doesn't investigate or is hampered in its investigations, deception abounds. The success of the assassination sensationalists in creating mistrust of the Warren Commission is proof of that.

Every American should be concerned about the ramifications of how tens of millions of Americans have been so readily deceived by a relatively small group of assassination sensationalists and how that might be indicative of other small groups being able to deceive the great majority of the American public on crucial national issues, including those involving war and peace.

An important aspect of this concern is the demoralizing impact that all of the attacks on the Warren Commission have had on citizen confidence in their government, particularly in the aftermath of Vietnam, the revelations of Watergate, the improper activities of the CIA, and the more recent revelations of the Iranian arms scandals.

The assassination itself was a shocking event that shattered the trust and confidence of many. And when you compound this with the sensationalist attacks of the Mark Lanes, the Robert Sam Ansons, the George O'Tooles, the Robert Grodins, the David Liftons, and the Henry Hurts of the world, it takes a tremendous toll. After all, if the citizenry cannot believe the findings of an independent commission chaired by the chief justice of the United States appointed to find out the truth about who killed their President, whom can it trust?

Fifty years hence, historians will agree the Warren Commission was right. They will have access to the transcripts of the interrogations, and they will know what the witnesses said, and their analysis will undercut all claims of the assassination sensationalists. Each and every attempt by the latter to try to prove Oswald's innocence can be refuted. The truth has a long fuse, and ultimately it prevails.

A word, finally, on the CIA. "Pearl Harbor" is still probably the term most suggestive of the need for effective intelligence to prevent national disasters. Having spent many months investigating the highest echelons of our chief investigating agency, the CIA, I am convinced it is necessary for the safety and welfare of the people that this agency be altogether effective.

What disturbs me most is to observe how easy it is for the CIA to yield to pressures from the executive branch, from the White House. I have seen how the CIA itself adopts the methods of the "opposition," namely, that the ends justify the means. It then circumvents statutory authority as well as the statutory procedures of checks and balances. A CIA out of public control is a dangerous matter.

In the 1970s the agency was bombarded, perhaps excessively so, by people who were too one-sided and did not recognize the importance of maintaining an effective CIA. In the 1980s, the pendulum may have swung too far the other way. Moreover, the 1987 revelations about the arms sales to Iran and improper diversion of profits to the Nicaraguan Contras and the involvement of top officials in the NSC and the head of the CIA indicate how quickly Americans can forget what happened as recently as ten years ago.

For Americans to control the CIA rather than have the CIA control Americans, first we must understand it and understand what its role must be. That is another reason I undertook this book. You must know the past to cope with the present and plan for the future.

I have heard our top military leaders admit that the ultimate difference in military success is the moral commitment of the fighting man.

In the matter of weaponry, we can talk about being "second to none." This permits parity—it just says that no one else can be ahead.

But the one thing we cannot permit is being "second to none" in moral standards. If that is all we are, this nation is doomed to failure, for it cannot survive on the basis of our being no worse than the Communists—or to use a CIA term, "the opposition."

Yet time and time again our national leadership in general as well as the CIA in particular have lacked the sensitivity and vision to understand the importance of morality in government. Illegal mail openings, unlawful spying on American citizens, and assassination plots in peacetime are specific examples. For all of these, the rationale is basically the same: national security, the rationale of self-preservation, the rationale of the opposition that the ends justify the means. The unlawful diversion of profits from the sales of arms to Iran is the most recent example of this rationale.

Ironically, the extensive use of improper means in the long run detracts from national security, and this is what those who profess to be most concerned about the spread of communism all too often forget.

We must not forget. Our constitutional standards, our moral standards, must be maintained. For above all, if America is to survive the challenge, we must not grant the opposition moral parity!

# Epilogue

Nearly twenty-five years have passed since the hour of two murders on November 22, 1963. I had more firsthand, direct contact with the key witnesses to these two murders and with the physical evidence than anyone else in the world. I had this contact in 1964, right after the events took place, when the recollections of the witnesses were most accurate. It was clear beyond a reasonable doubt that Lee Harvey Oswald was the lone gunman who killed President Kennedy.

Yet a majority of Americans believe otherwise. Why should I care whether they are right or wrong? After all, President Kennedy, Officer Tippit, and Oswald are long dead.

Why should I be concerned if there are people who purvey distortions and deceive the American public, like the Mark Lanes of the 1960s, the Robert Sam Ansons and George O'Tooles of the 1970s, and the David Liftons and Henry Hurts of the 1980s—and who knows who else in the 1990s?

I care.

I care about our country. I care because I believe that to continue to enjoy freedom and democracy, we must recognize how crucial it is to have citizen participation.

I believe I made a difference in the way I went about my work as counsel to the Warren Commission. I believe I made a difference in my work as executive director of the Rockefeller Commission. I hope this book will make a difference.

If the American public can be so readily deceived on such "black and white" issues as who killed Officer Tippit and who killed President Kennedy, then they can also be deceived by a small cadre of people about issues that can be far more directly related to the survival of a country—those of war and peace.

People might say, "It can't happen here," but it did happen here. The truth has been obscured, and very successfully, by people who in total numbers can be measured only in the hundreds.

Let me turn to the CIA. The central issue in the Rockefeller Commission investigation was the potential conflict between the need for intelligence for national security purposes and the need to protect constitutional rights of citizens, including the right of privacy. Privacy is not a precious luxury of a free society; it is a fundamental attribute of a free people.

Beyond the issue of constitutional rights was another crucial issue: the preservation of trust between the citizens and their government. Trust is the mortar that holds the structure of our government together. If trust erodes, our democracy can crumble. In the Iran-Contra fiasco in the 1980s, the worst aspect was not the stupidity of the act itself but, rather, the subsequent coverup, which tremendously damaged the trust and confidence of citizens in the president and in the entire government.

I am terribly concerned that our nation be secure from foreign military threats in general and from foreign intelligence operations in particular, and therefore I am a strong supporter of the CIA. But I am equally terribly concerned about the other side of the ledger, where the CIA has eroded citizen trust and has thereby done great harm to our nation's well-being.

The continued deterioration of trust and confidence in our governmental institutions is just as great a threat to our free society as are the intercontinental ballistic missiles behind the Iron Curtain. My concern for citizen trust in government as well as my concern for the truth are central reasons why I have written this book.

Finally, I have written this book because America is a wonderful country.

How many other countries are there in the world in which a citizen from the heartland—away from the centers of governmental or financial power—can come to the capital of the country and investigate the assassination of a head of state with no holds barred and with just one standard: the reporting of the truth?

How many countries are there in the world in which a free press can call to account before the people of the country the activities of the secret intelligence agency of that country and in turn pressure the chief of state to appoint an independent commission to investigate those activities? How many countries are there in the world in which such an independent commission would pick a citizen with no ties to government, wholly independent, to head the investigation of a secret intelligence agency and present a report that all of its citizenry can read?

This is the essence of our freedom. This is the perspective in which we must place the criticism that we level day in and day out against our government and its leaders.

Throughout my work I have never lost sight of the fact that it was the free society in which we live that enabled me to come to Washington and investigate the assassination of a president and to later come back to Washington and investigate and discover all of the improper activities about which I have written in this book.

Life is a very precious gift. So is freedom. Neither should be taken for granted.

# Appendix

*Anatomy of the Cover-up Technique of Assassination Sensationalists*

David Scheim's book *Contract on America*, subtitled "The Mafia Murder of President John F. Kennedy" (published in 1988), is a typical example of how assassination sensationalists mislead the public. Scheim cleverly builds his house of cards by omitting critical evidence, taking out of context statements made by key witnesses, relying on erroneous conclusions by alleged experts, and at the same time making false accusations that the Warren Commission was some kind of a "cover-up."

Scheim's thesis is that the Mafia was responsible for the death of Kennedy, and the key figure was Jack Ruby. Central to this thesis is Scheim's claim that the timing of Ruby's murder of Oswald (which took place on Sunday, November 24, 1963, at approximately 11:21 A.M.) was so precise that it was, in Scheim's words, "Murder on Cue."

In order to reach this conclusion, Scheim first has to overcome the testimony of Postal Inspector Holmes, which independently disproves Scheim's claims. On November 24, Holmes was on his way to church with his wife. At the last minute, he had his wife drop him off at the Dallas police station, where he entered the interrogation room and participated in the interrogation of Lee Harvey Oswald, thereby extending it by more than a half hour. Meanwhile, Jack Ruby went downtown to the Western Union office (located near the police station) to send a money order to one of his employees. The money-order stamp read "11:17

A.M." From there, Ruby walked down the ramp into the Dallas police-station basement and mingled with reporters awaiting Oswald's transfer to the county jail, which had been scheduled to take place at 10:00 A.M. Less than five minutes after Ruby left the Western Union office, he shot Oswald. Had Holmes continued on to church with his wife that morning, the length of interrogation would have been shortened by more than half an hour, and Jack Ruby would never have had the opportunity to kill Oswald.

Scheim, like virtually all of his predecessors, overcomes the inconsistency of his arguments by failing to disclose to his audience the existence of Postal Inspector Holmes and the happenstance of the transfer of Oswald being delayed because Holmes at the last minute decided not to go to church.

With the Holmes testimony out of the way, David Scheim then builds his case for conspiracy by extracting two sentences from Jack Ruby's testimony and quoting them in the preface to his book and again in part III, which he subtitles "Murder on Cue":

> "Who else could have timed it [the Oswald shooting] so perfectly by seconds. If it were timed that way, then someone in the police department is guilty of giving the information as to when Lee Harvey Oswald was coming down."

If one simply takes these two sentences and at the same time ignores the Holmes testimony, one might conclude that what Ruby meant was that someone in the police department gave him some secret information about exactly when Lee Harvey Oswald was "coming down." As a matter of fact, the press was told that Oswald would be transferred around ten o'clock that morning. The police did not try to keep it a secret.

But even if the police had not conveyed the information that Oswald was to be transferred at 10:00 A.M. and even if Postal Inspector Holmes had not extended the interrogation so that Oswald was not actually transferred until after 11:00 A.M., the context of the two sentences extracted by Scheim clearly shows that in no way did Ruby mean he was part of any conspiracy. Here is the entire sequence of this portion of Ruby's interrogation by Warren Commission general counsel Lee Rankin. (The names Ray Hall and Sorrels refer to persons who interrogated Ruby after he shot Oswald. The italicized portion is the extract by Scheim):

Mr. Rankin: "I think, Mr. Ruby, it would be quite helpful to the Commission if you could tell, as you recall it, just what you said to Mr. Sorrels and the others after the shooting of Lee Harvey Oswald. Can you recall that. . .?"

Mr. Ruby: "I spent an hour with Mr. Hall, Ray Hall. And I was very much, *I was very much broken up emotionally, and I constantly repeated that I didn't want Mrs. Kennedy to come back to trial,* and those were my words, constantly repeated to Mr. Hall. . . ."

Mr. Rankin: "There was a conversation with Mr. Sorrels in which you told him about the matter. Do you remember that?"

Mr. Ruby: "The only thing I ever recall I said to Mr. Ray Hall and Sorrels was, I said, 'Being of Jewish faith, I wanted to show my love for my President and his lovely wife.'

"After I said whatever I said, then a statement came out that someone introduced Mr. Sorrels to me and I said, 'What are you, a newsman?' Or something to that effect. Which is really—what I am trying to say is, the way it sounded is like I was looking for publicity and inquiring if you are a newsman, I wanted to see you.

"But I am certain—I don't recall definitely, but I know in my right mind, because I know my motive for doing it, and certainly to gain publicity to take a chance of being mortally wounded, as I said before, and *who else could have timed it so perfectly by seconds.*

"*If it were timed that way, then someone in the police department is guilty of giving the information as to when Lee Harvey Oswald was coming down.*

"I never made a statement. I never inquired from the television man what time is Lee Harvey Oswald coming down. Because really, a man in his right mind would never ask that question. I never made the statement 'I wanted to get three more off. Someone had to do it. You wouldn't do it.' I never made those statements.

"I never called the man by any obscene name, because as I stated earlier, there was no malice in me. He was insignificant, to my feelings for my love for Mrs. Kennedy and our beloved President. He was nothing comparable to them, so I can't explain it.

"I never used any words—as a matter of fact, there were questions at the hearing with Roy Pryor and a few others—I may have used one word 'a little weasel' or something, but I didn't use it, I don't remember, because Roy said it. If he said I did, I may have said it.

"I never made the statement to anyone that I intended to get him. I never used the obscene words that were stated.

"Anything I said was with emotional feeling of I didn't want Mrs. Kennedy to come back to trial."

Like other assassination sensationalists and conspiracy buffs who use similar techniques to try to show that Jack Ruby was conspiratorially involved, Scheim also ignores the testimony of other crucial witnesses, such as Rabbi Hillel Silverman. Perhaps most important of all, these people ignore the common sense fact that so-called Mafia hit men do not murder someone in a situation where they are 100 percent sure of being apprehended for murder.

The third technique used is to build a foundation on erroneous evidence and buttress the false claims by citing other so-called experts whose conclusions are wrong. Scheim does this in part V, which he subtitles "A Mafia Contract," where, in the opening portion of this section of his book, he builds a foundation on the erroneous acoustic evidence given at the very end of the investigation of the House Assassinations Committee. He claims this proves conspiracy, and he cites as his principal authority none other than Professor G. Robert Blakey. Scheim writes:

An objective investigation of the JFK assassination, which the Warren Commission obsequiously skirted, was finally carried out in the late 1970s by the House Select Committee on Assassinations. In 1979, after a two-year probe, the Committee reported that President Kennedy "was probably assassinated as a result of a conspiracy"; this conclusion was shared by 75 percent of assassination experts and 80 percent of the American public polled in the early 1980s. The Committee also found that the Mafia had the "motive, means and opportunity" to kill him, while its chief counsel, G. Robert Blakey, asserted his firm opinion that the Mob murdered President Kennedy.

The evidence presented earlier certainly points to this conclusion. As established by acoustical and eyewitness evidence, a second gunman fired at President Kennedy from the grassy knoll. Three assassination suspects, Ferrie, Oswald and Brading, had ties to organized crime. Key Mob figures, including New Orleans Mafia boss Carlos Marcello, discussed plots to murder John and Robert Kennedy. And Jack Ruby, a Dallas Mobster, murdered Oswald as part of a carefully orchestrated conspiracy.

In turn, G. Robert Blakey joins with Scheim by lending his name (on the jacket) to promote Scheim's book. One wonders how Professor Blakey can continue to support Scheim's views.

By the time Blakey endorsed Scheim's book, he knew very well that the Committee on Ballistic Acoustics of the National Research Council had completely demolished the purported acoustic evidence that there was a second gunman firing a fourth shot from the grassy knoll. He also knew that, as first suggested by Steve Barber, the acoustic impulses on the tape that the House Assassinations Committee experts attributed to gunshots in fact were recorded about one minute after the president had been shot and the motorcade was on its way to the hospital.

Blakey also knew (assuming he read Scheim's book in advance before recommending it to others) that central to the thesis of Scheim's book was his claim of a second gunman. As a matter of fact, chapter 2 is entitled "Crossfire In Dealey Plaza." Here is how Scheim introduces the chapter:

> In contrast to the testimony of the witnesses who heard and observed shots fired from the [Texas School Book] Depository, the Commission's investigation has disclosed no credible evidence that any shots were fired from anywhere else.

The Warren Commission, in its 1964 report:

> Scientific acoustical evidence establishes a high probability that two gunmen fired at President John F. Kennedy.
>
> —The House Select Committee on Assassinations, in its 1979 report.

Later in the chapter, Scheim goes into extensive detail and quotes the House Assassination Committee experts' testimony that "with a probability of 95% or better" there was an additional shot fired from the grassy knoll.

I have been surprised that Professor Blakey, in the face of the findings of the Committee on Ballistic Acoustics of the National Research Council, has not followed through on his written commitment to the *National Review* to withdraw everything that he has said (if the Committee on Ballistic Acoustics did not affirm the 95 percent probability findings of the House Assassinations Committee experts). But I have been shocked that Professor Blakey has not only failed to admit he was wrong, but he has affirmatively contributed to the continued deception of the American people by lending his name and whatever credibility he has to support the marketing of what I believe to be a fallacious book that misleads the American people.

Ironically, in the face of all this deception, Scheim makes the false accusation that the Warren Commission was nothing more than a "Blue Ribbon" cover-up, a charge that in essence slanders the good name of Chief Justice Earl Warren as well as the other members of the commission and the commission staff. Since the publication of the *Warren Commission Report*, in each decade assassination sensationalists have come forward to make this charge. The common denominator of all of their claims is the omission of critical testimony (such as that of Johnny Calvin Brewer, Rabbi Hillel Silverman, and Postal Inspector Holmes) coupled with quoting testimony out of context, as vividly shown by the two-sentence extract of Ruby's testimony on which Scheim builds his claims of a Mafia contract to kill President Kennedy.

These techniques were used in the 1960s by people such as Mark Lane, in the 1970s by people such as Robert Sam Anson, in the 1980s by people such as David Scheim, and no doubt they will be again used in the 1990s and beyond.

# Notes

## 1. *The Trip to Texas*

The primary sources for this chapter—as in the rest of the book—arise from my work as counsel to the Warren Commission (the President's Commission on the Assassination of President Kennedy) and the Rockefeller Commission (the Commission on CIA Activities Within the United States). They include personal interviews, personal notes taken during the course of my work with these two commissions, the Warren Commission Report, and the twenty-six supplementary volumes of exhibits and hearings before the Warren Commission that were published by the Warren Commission.

## 2. *The Assassination*

All of the quoted material in this chapter is derived from testimony before the Warren Commission.

## 3. *Appointment to the Warren Commission*

Comments about Earl Warren in the chapter are from personal conversations with the chief justice. All quotations from witnesses are from testimony before the Warren Commission. Reference to one of the early better-selling books refers to *Inquest* by Edward J. Epstein.

## 4. *Tippit's Murder—The Rosetta Stone*

All quoted materials of witnesses are from testimony before the Warren Commission.

## 5. *The Real Cover-up About Oswald's Arrest*

*They've Killed the President!* was published by Bantam Books in 1975. Quoted material of witnesses to the Tippit murder is from hearings before the Warren Commission. *Accessories After the Fact*, by Sylvia Meagher, was published in 1967 by Bobbs-Merrill Co., Inc. *Best Evidence*, by David Lipton, was published by Macmillan in 1981. *Assassination Tapes*, by George O'Toole, was published by Penthouse Press, Ltd., in 1975. *Contract on America*, by David Scheim, was published by Shapolsky Publishers in 1988. The source material for ballistic testimony is in the Warren Commission Report and in testimony of the expert witnesses published by the Warren Commission.

## 6. *Jack Ruby and the Murder of Oswald*

References to Rabbi Hillel Silverman are from testimony before the Warren Commission and personal interviews. Quoted material from Jack Ruby is from testimony before the Warren Commission. The polygraph examination results are from the Warren Commission Report and testimony before the Warren Commission.

## 7. *Mistakes Inside the Warren Commission*

Comments concerning Earl Warren are from personal discussions with him and with President Gerald Ford and John J. McCloy, former members of the Warren Commission. *Marina and Lee*, by Priscilla Johnson McMillan, was published by Harper & Row in 1977.

## 8. *Trying to Prove Conspiracy*

The source material concerning the Zapruder film is from the Warren Commission Report, testimony by expert witnesses before the Warren Commission and House Assassinations Committee, and from personal notes.

## 9. *Leaving the Scene of the Crime*

The source material for this chapter is testimony before the Warren Commission and exhibits.

## 10. *What Might Have Been*

All of the source material for this chapter is testimony before the Warren Commission.

### 11. *The Obvious Conclusion*

*Reasonable Doubt*, by Henry Hurt, was published by Holt, Rinehart in 1986. The source material for comments by Seymour Hersh is personal discussions with Seymour Hersh.

### 12. *The Paradox of the Birth of the CIA*

The source material for this chapter is from personal notes taken in the course of my work as executive director of the Rockefeller Commission and from the Rockefeller Commission Report.

### 13. *The CIA Investigation Begins*

The source material for this chapter, other than quoted material from newspapers, is from personal notes made in the course of my work as executive director of the Rockefeller Commission and from copies of correspondence that I retained.

### 15. *"The Family Jewels"*

The source material for this chapter is personal notes that I made during the course of my work as executive director of the Rockefeller Commission.

### 16. *The Battle to Investigate Assassination Plots*

The source material for this chapter is personal notes that I made during the course of my work as executive director of the Rockefeller Commission.

### 17. *CIA Plans to Assassinate Castro—Phase I*

The source material for this chapter is personal notes made during the course of my work as executive director of the Rockefeller Commission. The quoted material from former CIA official Sheffield Edwards is from an audiocassette tape that I made of the interview.

### 18. *Executive Action Capabilities and the Phase II Plans*

The source material for this chapter is personal notes made during the course of my work as executive director of the Rockefeller Commission. The quoted material from former CIA official William Harvey is from an audiocassette tape I made of the interview.

### 19. *The Amnesia Syndrome—McNamara, Bundy, and Taylor*

The source material for this chapter is primarily personal notes that I made during the course of my work as executive director of the Rockefeller Commission.

## 20. *The Phase III Plans*

The source material for this chapter is primarily personal notes made during the course of my work as executive director of the Rockefeller Commission.

## 21. *The CIA's Spying on American Citizens*

The primary source material for this chapter is personal notes made during the course of my work as executive director of the Rockefeller Commission and the Rockefeller Commission Report, which was transmitted to President Ford on June 6, 1975.

## 22. *Kissinger and Belin—The NSC Stonewall*

The primary source material for this chapter is personal notes made during the course of my work as executive director of the Rockefeller Commission. The quotation by Henry Kissinger is from "America and the World: Principle and Pragmatism," *Time* magazine, 27 December 1976, pp. 41, 43). The correspondence from me to Mrs. Jeanne W. Davis of the NSC is from copies of correspondence that I retained.

## 23. *The Scuttling of the Findings on Assassination Plots*

The primary source material for this chapter is personal notes made during the course of my work as executive director of the Rockefeller Commission, and the Rockefeller Commission Report.

## 24. *The Press Conference That Never Was*

The source material for this chapter is personal notes and the actual formal press conference statement that I prepared.

## 25. *Turning the Tables: My Freedom of Information Act Request*

The source material for this chapter is copies of correspondence sent to the CIA and the General Services Administration.

## 26. *Requesting the Reopening of the Warren Commission Investigation*

The source material for this chapter is copies of correspondence that I retained and personal notes that I made during the course of my work as executive director of the Rockefeller Commission, personal correspondence with *Time* magazine and PBS, and copies of the formal statement I made on November 22, 1975, formally requesting that Congress reopen the Warren Commission investigation.

## 27. The House Assassinations Committee and the Last-Minute Flip-flop

The source material for this chapter is copies of correspondence with members of the House Assassinations Committee and with its chief of staff, Robert Blakey, personal notes made during the course of the investigation of the House Assassinations Committee, personal interviews with Congressman Edgar and Congressman Sawyer, members of the committee, a review of the preliminary draft of the final report in which it was concluded that there was no conspiracy, copies of the Report of the House Assassinations Committee, including copies of dissenting opinions, and House Assassinations Committee press releases. The book *The Plot to Kill the President* was written by Professor Blakey and co-author Richard Billings and was published by Quadrangle/The New York Times Book Company.

## 28. Proving There Was No Fourth Shot

The source materials on this chapter include the complete "Report of the Committee on Ballistic Acoustics of the Commission on Physical Sciences, Mathematics and Resources of the National Research Council" and personal correspondence with members of that committee. The commentary by James Reston was in the January 12, 1979, issue of the *New York Times. Contract on America* by David Scheim was published in 1988 by Shapolsky Publishers. "The Second Gunman Syndrome" was published in the April 27, 1979, issue of *National Review.*

## 29. Why Did Oswald Kill President Kennedy?

The source material for this chapter includes the Warren Commission Report, testimony of witnesses and exhibits that were published in the twenty-six supplementary Warren Commission Report volumes, the September 8, 1963, *New Orleans Times Picayune*, and personal notes made during the course of my work with the Warren Commission and the Rockefeller Commission.

## 30. The Warren Commission and CIA Investigations in Perspective

The source material for this chapter is personal notes made during the course of my work as counsel to the Warren Commission and executive director of the Rockefeller Commission, personal correspondence with John J. McCloy, and personal interviews with former CIA and Defense Department officials.

# Index

# About the Author

**D**avid W. Belin is a senior partner of the Des Moines, Iowa, law firm of Belin Harris Helmick Tesdell Lamson McCormick. His work has primarily been in the areas of corporate matters and litigation, including constitutional cases. In addition to his work as counsel to the Warren Commission and as executive director of the Rockefeller Commission, Belin has a broad spectrum of public service and has been particularly active in support of education and the arts. Since 1984, he has served on the President's Committee on the Arts and the Humanities. He has also received from the National Conference of Christians and Jews the Brotherhood Award "for distinguished leadership in the field of human relations and community service."

Belin worked his way through the University of Michigan, where in six years he earned undergraduate, master in business administration, and Juris Doctor degrees—all with high distinction. From the University of Michigan Law School, he received the Henry M. Bates Memorial Award made "to each of the two most outstanding seniors in the Law School." He is a member of many honorary societies, including Phi Beta Kappa and Order of the Coif.